TO FREE A DOLPHIN

RICHARD O'BARRY
with Keith Coulbourn

RENAISSANCE BOOKS
Los Angeles

Library of Congress Catalog Card Number: 00-105819
ISBN: 1-58063-102-9

10 9 8 7 6 5 4 3 2 1

Design by Amanda Tan

Published by Renaissance Books
Distributed by St. Martin's Press
Manufactured in the United States of America
First edition

I dedicate this book to these dolphins that I most recently got to know:

Iris and Ivo (Belgium); Bogie, Bacall, Molly, Lady, Sugar, and Lolita (United States); Luther, Buck, Jake, Ikaka, and Modock (United States, U.S. Navy); Lilly, Fiodra, Mark, Max, Bob, and Gals (Israel); Menique and Belin (Cuba); Tana and Neptuno (Peru); Rocky, Missy, and Silver (Turks and Caicos Islands); Duke (Canada); Flipper (Brazil); Chispa, Geko, Chicky, Chalders, Bacchus, Fritzie, Alpha, and Angel (Switzerland); Cheryl (Argentina); Stephania, Dano, and Kika (Colombia)

Contents

Acknowledgments

Among those I wish to thank specially are Lincoln O'Barry, Helene Hesselager O'Barry, Fred Neil, Debora and Mary Mosley, Barbara Connelly, Noelle DeLaquis, Sigi Luber, Keith Coulbourn, Caren Ward, Kathleen Brooks, Shaney Frey, Vanessa and Jack Martini, Capt. Ron Canning and Capt. Gary Elston, Jay Temple, Meher Baba, Andrew Dickson, Richard Dickson, Mark Berman, Robi Damelin, Benny Schlesenger, Axel Knigge, Judith Anderson, Marco Antonio Ciampi, Dr. Jose Truda Palaza, Dr. Marco Antonio Carnaro, Dr. Mario Rollo, Gabriela Dienhart, Richie Havens, Susan and Jerry Jeff Walker, Dr. Cyril Hue, Korina Gutsche, Robert S. Steinberg, Dr. Alan Cohen, Dr. John C. Lilly, Diana Thater, and Rafael E. Viera.

The list could go on and on, but most of the time I work with people through organizations set up on behalf of animals and the environment. Here's a list—in no particular order—of the organizations I have worked with the last few years, groups without which I would never have been able to do what I do. Some are mentioned in the pages that follow, but all of them are equally important to me:

Dolphin Watch, The Swiss Working Group for Marine Mammal Protection (ASMS) and Tierschutz Bund (Switzerland), Kyd Moses (Germany), SOS Grand Bleu (France), Delphus, Planete Vie, Cetus, and GAIA (Belgium), Coalition Against the U.S. Exporting Dolphins, The Ark Trust, Center for Defense Information, South Carolina Association for Marine Mammal Protection, Re-Earth (Bahamas), Midwest Whale Protection, Reseau Cetaces (France), Progressive Animal Welfare Society, Committee for Clean Air & Clean Water, In Defense of Animals, ORCA Lab (Canada), Culture and Animals Foundation, Planetary Coral Reef Foundation, Bellerieve Foundation (Switzerland), Australians for Animals (Australia), Wildwatch (Australia), People for the Ethical Treatment of Animals (PETA), International Dolphin Project, Friends of Animals, The Fund for Animals, Ground Zero, International Society for Animal Rights,

Cetacean Society International, Performing Animals Welfare Society, Animal Rights Foundation of Florida, Friends of the Dolphins (Canada), Let the Animals Live (Israel), Noah (Israel), Fondation Brigitte Bardot (France), Marine Mammal Fund, World Society for Protection of Animals (England), Marine Biology Department of the Florida Keys Community College, Institute of Hydrobiology (Peoples Republic of China), Najing Normal University (Peoples Republic of China), Dolphin Connection (Texas), NOAH (Norway), TALIS (France), Monde de Gaia (France), Friends of the Earth (Hong Kong), Dolphin Project Arion (Germany), Cruzada Por La Vida (Peru), The Born Free Foundation (England), Animal Adoption Foundation (Germany), Earth First, Chicago Animal Rights Coalition, No Jails for Whales, American Society for the Prevention of Cruelty to Animals (ASPCA), Lifeforce Foundation (Canada), Animal Protection Institute, Project Jonah (Australia), Citizens for Marine Mammal Protection, Dolphin Public Education Committee (Germany), Earth Care (Bahamas), International Cetacean Education and Research Centre (Australia), Reef Care (Curaçao, Dutch Caribbean), Accion Ambiental (Aruba, Dutch Caribbean), National Geographic Society, Pieterburen Seal Hospital (Holland), Network for Ohio Animal Action, Animal and Environmental Defense Association, Dallas for Dolphins, Institute of Marine Mammal Studies (Brazil), Orange County Community College Marine Biology Department, Asociacion Para La Defensa de los Derechos del Animal (Argentina), and M.E.E.R. La Gomera (Germany).

1

PAYBACK (FEBRUARY 1999)

As I was walkin' down the street,
Whistlin' the blues to the tappin' of my feet,
Some old crank called the cops on the beat . . .
And that's the bag I'm in.

> —Fred Neil, "That's the Bag I'm In"

WE HAD ALL GATHERED, my old adversaries and I, in the two-story federal district courthouse on lovely tree-shaded Simonton Street of old Key West. For almost thirty years I had been tweaking the federal government's nose about its incestuous ties to the billion-dollar captive-dolphin industry, daring them to call me on it, almost begging them to debate. I had dedicated my life to exposing them in their colossal perfidy, just as they had dedicated their lives, it seemed, to ignoring me.

Until now.

Now that I had freed a pair of dolphins—just moments before an army of federal, state, and local law-enforcement officers swept down upon us by land, sea, and air to confiscate them—now it was payback time, and they came down on me with all their bureaucratic wrath. When translated from the garble of governmentese, the charge was transporting and releasing two dolphins without permits.

Charged with me was Lloyd A. Good III, director of Sugarloaf Dolphin Sanctuary, where all this had happened, barely seventeen miles east by northeast on US 1 from Key West. Lloyd, whom I had come to think of as a surprising mixture of brilliance and buffoonery, was a burly young man with long blond hair and a beard. He was also the eldest son of the man who owned most of Lower Sugarloaf Key.

I was among the first to arrive at the courthouse that morning. I had been living in Paris, helping put together the first European halfway house for captive dolphins. I'd flown in the day before with a single suit of clothes, the clothes I had been wearing in Paris. This included brown boat shoes, a dolphin tie, khaki pants, and a brown tweed coat. Tweed in Key West? It was the dead of winter but compared with Paris, Key West was balmy, and as I dressed that morning, I smiled. Though tweed was comfortable in Paris, I wondered idly how many people had ever worn tweed so near the tropics. Surely, I thought, no one with any choice. But I would wear it anyway, not merely because I had no choice, but as a reminder that my heart now lay with my love in Paris.

I was waiting in the parking lot when Lloyd, my codefendant, arrived. When he climbed out of his pickup, I couldn't believe my eyes. He was wearing the very same thing as I—brown boat shoes, khaki pants, and a brown tweed coat. I looked from him to myself again just to make sure. Yes! And I almost laughed. We looked like a couple of German tourists. I walked over to him. "Lloyd," I said, "look at what we're wearing. This is all I've got."

It all came rushing back, that endless time at Sugarloaf, a twilight zone of hoping, planning, desperate struggles, and bizarre behaviors. What memories! As we walked into the courtroom, I was having one of those *ding* moments, when everything suddenly becomes blindingly clear, and I could now see that I had to get out of there as quickly as possible.

Legally, we were dead. The United States Department of Commerce had three brilliant lawyers, two men and one woman, who had been preparing for this encounter for the past two years. They had a gallery of twenty witnesses ready to testify. Lloyd and I, defending ourselves, could barely talk to each other. In fact, the last time I had spoken to him on the phone, I had hung up on him. Lloyd and I couldn't even agree about how to free captive dolphins, a debate that was at the center of the storm at Sugarloaf. I had freed a dozen dolphins; Lloyd had freed none. His experience with dolphins consisted of training Sugar, the family pet of about thirty years.

Before the trial got under way I had given this some heavy thought and believed that our only sensible course was to throw ourselves on the mercy of the court, to plead ignorance and nolo contendere (no contest), pay our fine, and get on with our lives.

This was a civil case, not criminal, and we faced a total fine of $60,000, though prosecutors would urge the judge to increase it. I couldn't personally pay even a portion of that, but in a flamboyant gesture I informed Lloyd and his mother, Miriam, that I would pay whatever fine was assessed against both of us if we could simply end the trial. Supporters of mine in Europe—a hot German rock 'n' roll band, Kyd Moses, in particular—had pledged to raise whatever I needed by doing benefit performances. "I'll pay the whole thing," I said, "if we can just nolo contendere out of this thing."

Lloyd's mother, a tall and lovely woman, saw the wisdom of my proposition, but Lloyd was of another mind.

So I was in the middle of a trial with a codefendant I couldn't see eye-to-eye with, both of us representing ourselves not before a jury of our peers, whose opinion we might expect to sway, but before a judge: Judge Peter A. Fitzpatrick. I couldn't tell a thing simply by looking at him, so I studied his body language. He seemed systematic, patient, a good listener. *Perfect*, I thought.

Lloyd and I had been charged as if we had done everything together, but in fact we had been opposed at key moments, and my defense strategy was to separate myself from him. Early on I sensed the breath of doom and urged the court to accept my plea so that I could get out of there and start paying my fine. In a private session with the judge, opposing counsel, and Lloyd, I explained that justice seemed to depend directly on how much money one had, and I had no money. "Tell me what the fine is and I'll arrange to pay it."

The judge, who functions as a referee, said that if both sides struck a deal, that would be okay with him. He would still, however, need evidence to be presented in order to assess penalties. The government lawyers would have agreed with my attempted plea, but because Lloyd refused, the trial was on, a methodical march of witnesses who told their own bureaucratic version of the tragicomic events at Sugarloaf.

Could this contorted view of things become the official version of what had happened? Was this to be my legacy? What about our plan to free the dolphins? Our devotion to them? The heartache, magic, and dreams of glory? In their spin of what happened at Sugarloaf, federal witnesses were skipping the parts that I believed really mattered. I gazed out the second-story courtroom window at the dark green of the mahoganies lining the parking lot of the courthouse; from below I heard the muted street sounds of horns honking, a distant siren. Then suddenly it all came back, the very moment this nightmare began.

And how different things were then, a mere seven years ago. Seven years? It seemed like seven lifetimes.

2

THE LONG ROAD BACK (SUMMER 1992)

You want my advice? Get a life.
—Bubba Jones

MY OWN CAR, A twenty-year-old BMW, would break down on the one-hundred-mile trip to Melbourne, Florida, so I rented one—a new, gleaming white Lincoln Town Car—got in and slammed the door. What a sound! No, I didn't pay for it. I can't afford such things. I use frequent flyer miles for rental cars because I fly a lot. I don't pay for flying either. I'm a dolphin troubleshooter, and people who want my services pay my expenses. When people discover a captive dolphin in trouble, they call me for help, and off I go. It sounds crazy, I know, but that's what I do, and it's not that I chose to do it. For a long time, I tried not to do it. I had my own life. But they wouldn't go away, these problems, and because I was a big part in getting them started, I couldn't say no. I trained the original television star Flipper, you see, and a lot of the trouble captive dolphins are in now is because of me.

I had been in the captivity industry for ten years. I captured marine mammals for the Miami Seaquarium—including Carolina Snowball, the rare albino dolphin still proudly mounted in the

Seaquarium. Then I became a trainer there and met Ricou Browning, a film director who was preparing dolphins for the role of Flipper and needed someone to help him train them. Though the character of Flipper in the movies and TV series was a male, the role was played by five female dolphins. I had to know not only what Flipper the amazing TV dolphin would do in whatever circumstances the writers conjured up, but also what the actual dolphin playing Flipper *could* do. Sometimes it worked the other way, my discovering something new the dolphins could do and the writers working it into a script. The dolphins had no idea they were playing a role of course. I was tricking them into doing what I wanted them to by giving and withholding their food.

A dolphin that is not hungry will not do tricks. If I wanted them to do a flip, they would get no fish until they flipped. Same for tail-walking, jumping through hoops, scooting up on the deck with a big smile and wagging their tail-flukes. All this was nonsense to them, but they did it anyway because it was the only way they would be fed. And to me it seemed perfectly okay while I was doing it.

During those years, I was too busy cleverly doing the job to think about what I was doing. But when the TV series finally shut down and I had time to be with myself, I realized that this whole thing about dolphins jumping through hoops was terribly bizarre. I knew it was somehow wrong, but I wasn't clear about why—it was only a feeling. I made a pilgrimage to India to see Avatar Meher Baba, whom I thought might help me understand the feelings I was experiencing. I didn't expect a miracle and I didn't get a miracle, but when I got back, a friend of mine called and said that Kathy, my favorite dolphin, was dying in a tank at Miami Seaquarium. I hopped on my bicycle and peddled furiously across the causeway to the Seaquarium, where I found her floating in a tank, barely hanging on to life.

At first I couldn't believe it was Kathy. She played Flipper most of the time because she was so smart, so beautiful, and so loyal. And now—to see her in this condition was heartbreaking. Her skin was black. She was blistered, her eyes lifeless. I jumped in the water with her. She swam into my arms. I hugged her to me and she died. I tried to save her, I desperately tried to undo what I felt I had done to her. But I was too late. She died of a broken heart.

You cannot undo the things you do; you can only make amends. After Kathy's death, I formed the Dolphin Project, dedicated to the freedom of captive dolphins, and, to my surprise, I began getting calls about dolphins in trouble all over the world.

Rarely does anyone call me first when they see a dolphin in trouble and want to help. They call one of the high-profile organizations—Greenpeace, the World Wildlife Fund, or the Humane Society of the United States— organizations that sound like they're into helping animals. They do help some animals, I'm sure, but in my opinion they're mainly set up for memberships, dues, and goals of the highest abstraction. They aren't usually the ones in the trenches, doing the hands-on work involved in rescuing animals. If someone who discovers a dolphin in trouble is serious about helping, they keep trying and eventually someone refers them to me. Then, if I'm not already committed, I hit the dolphin trail again.

These giant nonprofit corporations used to refer people to me routinely. But no more. Having tried and failed to get them involved in my work, I've become one of their severest critics. Helping animals is not their main goal, I tell people. They're mainly into marketing themselves and collecting money.

So what can people do who really want to help animals? All over the world, local organizations have sprung up to handle problems of animal abuse. These are the people I work with most of the time. These grassroots organizations can handle problems related to most animals, but with dolphins they need an expert. And that's where I come in.

There's no way to know in advance what can or should be done for a desperate captive dolphin. Each case is different. I check out the dolphin personally, its health and history. Sometimes the dolphin is a candidate for freedom, sometimes not. Whatever the dolphin needs, I help organize a campaign to make it happen. First I get the message out. Without public support, we can do nothing. Once we get the media's attention, these campaigns tend to take on a life of their own.

And what do I get out of it? I get expenses, including travel, which is how I pick up so many frequent flyer miles. Also, sometimes, an invitation to speak.

o   o   o

The trip to Melbourne was like that, a speaking engagement. I speak to groups whenever I can because I'm always trying to get other people involved in the dolphin and whale captivity issue. Meantime, it's an opportunity to sell books and T-shirts. Because of my nonprofit status, I don't sell these things as such. I arrange the T-shirts and books on a table, and announce that for a $20 donation they can have one or the other. If all goes well, I make enough to pay my rent and a month's phone bill.

In my white rental Lincoln, I drove by the cottage where I lived in Coconut Grove, the original Miami, and loaded two boxes of books and a couple dozen T-shirts. Then I took off for Melbourne, 150 miles up the coast. I was wearing blue jeans and a T-shirt driving up, but in my bag were my power clothes—a double-breasted dark-blue suit and a maroon tie with gray dolphins and whales. I would wear that at the talk because this group included engineers and scientists from nearby Cape Canaveral and I wanted them to take me seriously.

When I first began making appearances on behalf of dolphins, I gave no thought to what I wore. What mattered, I thought, was the message, a message about dolphins so important that I could have appeared in a clown costume and it would be okay. I showed up at news conferences, TV talk shows, debates, and book signings in whatever I happened to be wearing at the time. I should have known better. As a stuntman and character actor in dozens of feature films and TV shows, I always dressed the part. But I had the impression that there was a big difference between real life and make-believe, that you didn't need to dress the part if you were living it.

And I was dead wrong. I realized this after an appearance on the *Today Show* with Jane Pauley, during which, via satellite, I debated someone from a swim-with-the-dolphins program in the Florida Keys. I was wearing jeans and a T-shirt with Top Siders and no socks. I looked like I had been working on a boat—in fact, I probably had been. I won the debate. No doubt of that.

But when I got home, flushed with victory, my wife, Martha, brought me down to earth. She was good at that. A cool, analytic Virgo, she shook her head and said, "No, Ric. You didn't win. You lost because of how you looked."

I couldn't believe what she was saying. "How I looked? Are you kidding? What does that matter? What does it even mean? Didn't you listen to what I said? How can you say that I lost?" I went on and on, my arms flailing around. I hate to lose. I don't take criticism well, either. Martha was a beautiful woman, tall and thin. When I was wrong about something, she had a way of looking straight at me without blinking, which she was doing now. We were married nineteen years, then got divorced. It was not about the clothes. It was something else, a triangle, Martha and I and the dolphins. No, it was me. I blew it. I didn't have my priorities lined up. Anyway, we went our separate ways. We're still friends. We get together now and then. But it's over.

And since then I've been at least trying to look the part I'm playing. But what is that exactly? How is a dolphin activist supposed to look? I've dressed up and I've dressed down, I've tried a dozen things, including the power suit I packed for the talk in Melbourne. It depends on the venue. The outfit I like best is a jean jacket with "Dolphin Project" embroidered in blue on the back. I feel most comfortable dressed like that—most of the time. Whatever else I wear at a public function where there will be questions from the crowd, I usually wear sneakers, because of the vegans. I learned the hard way about the vegans—a group of strict vegetarians who delight in attending animal welfare meetings, their eyes cocked for leather shoes or belts. They're experts at exposing a certain hypocrisy. If you're willing to wear leather shoes, they argue, you might as well kill animals yourself and eat them. So I wear the sneakers and a web belt, and up front I tell the crowd that I'm a vegetarian or at least I'm trying to be one, but also I'm only human and sometimes make mistakes.

o   o   o

The talk at Melbourne was the first I'd given in a while. I had been invited up by someone on the phone, Joe Roberts, who said he had heard of me and wanted me to speak to his group, the Down Under Dive Club.

He said he expected at least one hundred people, standing room only, so we arranged that I would drive up and give the talk at the Palm Bay Yacht Club, which faces the Indian River Lagoon. I would show a video and answer questions. I wouldn't receive any payment, but he would provide the audio and visual equipment I'd need for the talk and a complimentary hotel room for my stay. I could sell books, T-shirts, anything I wanted.

My presentation would be simple. First I would show "Back to the Sea," National Geographic's twenty-three-minute video about Joe and Rosie, two dolphins who were returned to the sea after seven years of scientific experiments. These were two of a dozen captive dolphins I had been involved in successfully returning to the sea again. I have a whole box of videos like this, which I use like a calling card. When people see the videos they know exactly who I am and what I do.

◦   ◦   ◦

Though I've dedicated my life, like a comic-book hero, to helping free captive dolphins, I live with the realization that only by luck have I myself survived as long as I have without a regular paycheck. I don't know how, but I've been doing this since April 22, 1970—the first Earth Day.

Dolphins were released before then of course. When dolphins got old and cantankerous and their owners got tired of feeding them twenty pounds of expensive fish a day, the dolphins were treated like gold fish that get flushed down the toilet. When I worked as a trainer at the Seaquarium in Miami, about six of us put them in a sling, hauled them over to the seawall and dropped them into Biscayne Bay. We called it a "dump and run." Did we wonder what happened to the dolphins next? Some of us did, sure. I did. At least, it crossed my mind. But I dumped them anyway along with everybody else because that's how things were done. I believed in life as I found it because it was good to me.

Later on, as the trainer of Flipper in the original TV series of the 1960s, I had a great job, lots of money, a new Porsche, and girls galore, beautiful girls who flocked around me because of the dolphins. I was young and single, life was filled with music, and I believed in happy endings because that's the only kind I knew.

Then suddenly it was over. The television series ended, and for the first time in my life I came face to face with myself. I was just another guy in a wet suit following orders—like the captive dolphins. And I knew exactly how the dolphins felt. If you think dolphins are happy jumping through hoops because they're always smiling, think again. Dolphins always smile because that's the way their faces are. I know lots of people who train dolphins and swim with them all the time and don't have a clue about them. Even though they're part of the fish-for-tricks scheme, they still seem to think that the dolphin is jumping through hoops and tail-dancing because it's having fun.

The trainer is using a psychological method called "operant conditioning." To the trainer it means rewarding behavior he wants repeated. In broad terms, it's manipulation, which we're all involved in most of the time. It's the carrot in front of the donkey, the salesman's friendly smile, or the sexy TV commercial. To a dolphin, it's a fish. Many of us can see ourselves in the dolphin doing tricks, except that the captive dolphin never understands the game he's in. And even if he did, he could never get out of it.

Training a dolphin is not like training a dog. Dogs are not just tame, they're domesticated. They've lost their wild identity. They're still dogs, but also they're part of our world and they want to be accepted. You can get them to do things with a pat on the head. But dolphins, for all their trust and friendly curiosity, are still wild animals. When I see a captive dolphin perform, I see a hungry dolphin desperately doing what he must in order to live. I also see people cheering and children clapping their hands and laughing about it.

Does it seem that I'm straining at a gnat, making such a big thing about a relatively few captive dolphins when so many more have been slaughtered by drift nets, tuna fishermen, and scientists? Around the world, about a thousand dolphins are held in captivity, while millions have been killed in purse seine tuna nets and drift nets. Tens of thousands of others have been "sacrificed" in the name of scientific research, some marine mammals merely to find out what they've been eating.

Mary Mosley of Tarpon Springs, Florida, plows through government records with the Freedom of Information Act like a baleen whale through plankton, and she says that of every hundred marine mammals taken with official permission, only one was put in a dolphin show for so-called educational purposes. The others were "lethal takes," killed to fill the requirements of a scientific grant.

Sad as it is, that's not the really big picture. If that were all there was to it, I would have walked away from it by now. But when you look at the really big picture, the slaughter of dolphins and other marine mammals is no more horrible than captive dolphins performing tricks because it's not just dolphins we're talking about, it's also people. Especially children. Whether it's one dolphin being forced to jump through a hoop or a thousand, the effect is devastatingly the same because the millions of people every year who watch and cheer this spectacle of dominance are in some way also cheering every other form of environmental ravishment. If the dolphin is a reference point in our relationship with nature, then when we teach people that it's okay to abuse dolphins, we're teaching them that it's also okay to abuse the rest of nature. It may sound grandiose, but I'm fighting not only for individual captive dolphins and dolphins in general but also for people, for the mind and sensibilities of future generations toward the world itself.

Anything less and I don't know that I could keep doing it.

3

THE MOUSE THAT CRINGED

If liberty means anything at all,
it means the right to tell people
what they do not want to hear.
—George Orwell

JOE ROBERTS MET ME at the hotel with a big smile, walked me up
to my room, and proudly showed me newspaper clippings announc-
ing my lecture, the result of his promotional efforts. Joe had a dark
tan and was balding, with short-cropped graying hair around the
side. I looked at the tear sheets and flyers he had laid out for me,
picked up one, and read a few lines. "This is excellent," I said. I shot
him an admiring look.

I got into my power suit and we drove over to the yacht club,
where he had set things up: about a hundred chairs facing a large
TV and VCR on a table, promotional leaflets in every chair. At the
entrance to the hall was a long table for my stuff. It was perfect. This
guy, I said to myself, is a pro.

On the long table at the entrance, I laid out my demonstration
items, the skull and lower jawbone of a dolphin I found some years
ago on a beach in Baja, California, several vertebrae, and some
conical teeth of a dolphin. Later I would go over each of these items,
the skull, for instance, to show not only how large the dolphin's

brain is—larger than our own—but also how dolphins pick up sounds in the water and conduct them along their jaw bones to the brain.

Mary Mosley arrived. She and her daughter, Debora, had driven in from their home in Tarpon Springs on Florida's West Coast to receive a plaque for their work on behalf of captive dolphins, especially for Sunset Sam, a dolphin held captive for years in a gloomy tank in Clearwater, Florida. Liberating him had been the special project of Mary Mosley and the garden club in which she was an officer.

As Joe Roberts had promised, the place was jammed. He got the show going in a folksy way, the same style he used in contacting me by phone the first time. I remember thinking that I would be fortunate to get this guy to run a branch of the Dolphin Project in this area. He introduced me, beaming warmly. The room fell silent. This was an air-conditioned hall, all the windows closed, but I could hear a car backing up outside. I looked at them, face by face. Then I said softly, "The first thing you should know is that there's nothing really special about me."

Some cheered, some clapped. They all smiled. This was a good group—mostly guys but also some women. I returned some of the praise Joe had lavished on me, reminding the audience that events like this did not happen by accident, that it took a lot of hard work and organizational skill, and they were fortunate to have someone like Joe Roberts to help them focus their attention on the sea and its many problems.

I had been told that many in the audience had a scientific background. They worked at nearby Kennedy Space Center on Cape Canaveral. We were in Sea World's backyard, about fifty miles southeast of Orlando. The Sea World in Orlando was one of four, the others located in Texas, California, and Ohio. Anheuser-Busch, the biggest advertiser in the world, owns them all and has used its dolphins and killer whales like a logo for its beer. All this commercialism of marine mammals got started less than a hundred miles away at Marineland of Florida, originally Marine Studio of St. Augustine, in 1938. When that facility proved profitable, Marineland of the Pacific in Palos Verdes, California, was built in 1950. Five years later came the Miami Seaquarium, where I first became involved with dolphins.

The Miami facility is still functioning, but barely. Some of its pools have deteriorated to the point, I think, of being dangerous.

My message to groups like this is about freeing captive dolphins. That's my mission, along with exposing the bungled government system that controls them: the National Marine Fisheries Service (NMFS) and its promiscuous permitting process.

o   o   o

But first I deliver a word about dolphins in general for anyone who might wonder what the fascination is all about. This is tough, the toughest part for me, my own summing-up of dolphins, because they have been so large a part of my life for so long that whatever I might say would only scratch the surface. I begin with the obvious, that though the dolphins live in the sea and a few rivers around the world, they're not fish, but mammals. On the other hand, if you order "dolphin" in a restaurant, you don't get the mammal, you get the game fish, *Coryphaena hippurus.*

Unlike fish, dolphins (the mammal) breathe air and suckle their young, and they have a number of vestigial anatomical features found only in mammals. We've always known that whales and fish are different in the way they propel themselves through the water, fish by back-and-forth (horizontal) movements of their tails, dolphins and other whales by moving their flukes or tail-flukes up and down (vertically). By a curious twist of happenstance this has figured into part of the recurring evolution-creation debate. Evolutionists say that life began in the sea and spread to the land, then around fifty million years ago, a few types of land creatures *returned* to the sea, and because their new world in the water was so completely different, over time they adapted. One of those creatures, the enterprising, wolflike *Mesonyx,* became the whale.

Creationists disagree. They say that God created animals the way they are, and that's it. Nothing changes. If whales had changed the way evolutionists claim, they say, where's the proof? They mean fossil evidence. Bones.

Well, for a long time, paleontologists didn't know what to say. But they kept digging and, sure enough, in Pakistan recently they found the bones of an early whale—with legs! Not just vestiges of legs, *real* legs. This fossil is called *Ambulocetus natans,* which means "the swimming-walking whale." He crawled on land and must have moved through the water by lunging forward, kicking with his legs like a frog or as we do in the breast stroke. In paleontological circles, this is "the smoking gun." The up-and-down movement of the whale's flukes is almost certainly a behavioral remnant of the way animals run on land, their spines flexing vertically.

For as far back as our records go, human beings have been fascinated by dolphins, making dolphins the subject of sea tales and myth, affection, and veneration. Some of the stories are obviously fanciful, that dolphins draw the chariots of gods across the sky, for instance, or quaint, that they communicate with extraterrestrials. Other stories might be on the fringe, like whether they have healing powers and can read our minds. Generally I stay out of fringe debates, but of one mystical power, whether it be the dolphins' or something in us, I have little doubt, that when people and dolphins interact, it brings out the best in people—as well as the worst.

The taxonomic scene is that all whales *(Cetacea)* are divided into thirteen families, which are composed of about seventy-six species. Four of those thirteen families are baleen whales *(Mysticeti),* those that swim through the ocean sifting out plankton (like small crustaceans and krill) to eat. All the other families are *Odontoceti,* which means they have teeth. They use these teeth not for chewing, incidentally, but for grasping. One of those families, the *Delphinidae,* is composed of thirty-one species, including the killer whale (Orca), common dolphin, spinner dolphin, and the bottlenose dolphin *(Tursiops truncatus),* the one like Flipper.

Bottlenose dolphins, because of their adaptability and the ease of training them, make up almost all of the dolphins in captivity. Sociable and very intelligent, they live in temperate and tropical waters worldwide, weigh from 300 to 600 pounds, and grow to more than eight feet in length. They live in groups called "pods," made up of anywhere from several individuals to several hundred—males usually hanging out with males, females with females—and swim thirty or forty miles a day, sometimes as much as 100, hunting schools of fish. They're quite fast over short distances, cutting through the water at up to thirty-five miles an hour, and they obviously enjoy riding the bow wave of boats. Their only enemies are sharks, killer whales—and man.

Until recent years, most people in this country referred to dolphins as "porpoises." Many people still think that they're the same animal. They're not. Porpoises, like dolphins, are toothed whales, but they're in another family entirely. All six species of porpoise are in the *Phocenidae* family. Porpoises are smaller and chunkier than dolphins, they have a smaller "melon," which in us is our forehead, and smaller dorsal fins, including some with no dorsal fin at all. They don't whistle like dolphins, and their teeth are different too. Dolphins' teeth are conical (like an ice cream cone); porpoises have spade-shaped teeth.

From a physiological viewpoint, dolphins and other whales are special not only because as mammals they live in the sea, but because they live in a world of sound. They're sonic creatures, like bats. This was realized only a few decades ago, so not much is known about it. Most research has been conducted with bottlenose dolphins because of their availability, and now, it seems, according to reports (by David and Melba Caldwell, Arthur McBride and Winthrop Kellogg, John Lilly, Kenneth S. Norris, and a host of others), that not all whales use sound the same way. They all use sound for communication, but only the bottlenose and perhaps a dozen other toothed whales use high-frequency sound waves to search out their environs, the way we use sonar. The bottlenose dolphin produces relatively pure whistles and a wide variety of other sounds, like clicks or a click-train that sound like the creaking of a rusty hinge, and other sounds sometimes described as blats, yaps, yelps, and even barks. None of their sounds, however, are like the sound produced for Flipper by the late Mel Blanc.

In the *Flipper* movies and TV series, I trained Flipper to swim up to the side of the boat and open his mouth, then remain "on station" quietly throughout the scene. Back in Hollywood, voice-over artist Mel Blanc would dub in his own version of dolphin sounds, a high-pitched chatter. Most people probably thought Flipper was making the sounds with his mouth because his mouth was open. But dolphins don't make sounds with their mouths. They don't even have vocal cords. The dolphin's airborne sounds come from their blowhole, their underwater sounds from inside their heads. They compress the air in the air sacs in their heads, then release it gradually, producing sounds the same way air escaping from a balloon does.

People with unimpaired hearing can detect sounds from between 20 vibrations a second (20 Hz, which is pronounced "20 Hertz") and 20,000. By comparison, the notes on a piano range from a low of 27 to 4,200 Hz. The sounds humans produce are much more limited, running from about 300 to 3,000 Hz. The dolphin, by comparison, can hear sounds between 100 and 150,000 Hz, and can produce them between about 1,000 and 80,000 Hz. Anything beyond what we can hear is called "ultrasound." That's 20,000 Hz and above.

When the dolphin wants to search out the sea around him, he produces these vibrations inside his head and beams them out through the lens-shaped waxy substance of his melon (the "forehead"). The sound shoots through the water, strikes whatever is there, then bounces back as an echo. This is picked up by the dolphin's lower jawbone and transmitted to the brain, where we think the dolphin produces an acoustical "picture," a map of some kind, or something like our radar screens. (We can't know exactly what goes on in a dolphin's brain for the same reason we can't know what goes on in another human's brain.) The dolphin's eyesight is good, but his sonar is even better. You can blindfold a dolphin and he can catch fish as well as ever. Indeed, some researchers have suggested that the dolphin's sonar may be so powerful that it can stun his target fish, making it easier for him to catch them.

When people discover that dolphins have brains larger than ours, they wonder about the dolphin's intelligence, whether they are geniuses or have mystical powers. But how would you test that? To measure anything, you need a common scale. And there's the rub. Surely you wouldn't try to measure dolphin intelligence with an IQ test meant for people. Unless the test involves swimming swiftly, diving, and catching a fish in your mouth at night, what would it mean? To test dolphins, you should test them in *their* world, and in *their* world they're as smart as we are in ours. Maybe more so, because they're smarter in our world than we are in theirs.

But what is their emotional life like? This is especially important to me because people assume that if an animal is always smiling, he must be happy. If they knew what I know about how captive dolphins feel, I'm sure they would help me set them free.

Early on I thought the scientific community would help. When I looked into what scientists are actually doing, however, I realized that for all of their good intentions, those who study animals have a serious language problem. They don't use everyday language, they say, because of its everyday baggage. Languages originated in dark, superstitious times after all, and though they do quite well in ordering a muffin and things like that, they simply cannot describe what happens when, for instance, a lab mouse cringes in fear. Plain old English would have us say that a mouse cringing in fear is frightened. But modern scientists have not proved that animals actually have fear—or any other emotion. So scientists can say only that the mouse "exhibits fear behavior." Fear is a subjective emotion, they say, and we don't know what's going on inside the mouse.

Well, I'll tell you what's going on inside of a cringing mouse, it's the same thing that's going on inside a cringing scientist who's afraid to use the word "fear." No scientist dares to be the first to acknowledge that his jargonized language based on "behaviorism" is a charade. The language he uses is factual, yes, as far as it goes, but in avoiding unwarranted assumptions it leaves out the heart of things. When you say that the mouse "exhibited fear behavior," you've danced around it. What is it to exhibit fear behavior if not to cringe in fear? And what else makes us cringe if not fear? Or do they think the mouse might be faking it?

What they really fear is committing the scientific sin of anthropomorphism, ascribing human characteristics to animals. But in avoiding anthropomorphism, they're falling into the equal and opposite fallacy of anthropocentrism, which assumes that human beings are the be-all and end-all of life itself, that this whole planet and the vast panoply of creation beyond exists for our sake only.

o   o   o

The Down Under Dive Club of Melbourne watched the video of Joe and Rosie, two dolphins that had been subjects in a human-dolphin communication experiment for years under the direction of the venerable sage of dolphinology, Dr. John C. Lilly. Dr. Lilly's study of dolphins goes back to the early 1960s when the Cold War was raging, when the Soviet Union and the United States were racing to claim space itself, and when President John F. Kennedy pledged to put a man on the moon before the end of the decade. Dr. Lilly, a neurosurgeon, received a grant from NASA to help answer what was a nagging question in those days. Before the first moon landing, nobody knew what—or who—we might encounter in space. The question was what we ought to say to an extraterrestrial if we should meet one. More generally, how could we communicate with them at all?

Dr. Lilly proposed doing research on animals with large brains here on earth. Originally he wanted to use elephants. But because of the cost and problems involved in handling such large animals, he decided to study dolphins, also noted for their large brains. His method was to subject dolphins to surgical analysis and electro-stimulus probes. Later he branched out to all sorts of experiments, including LSD, which was popular then (the late Timothy Leary often visited down the block from Dr. Lilly and from me, too, in Coconut Grove).

For years Lilly and others worked on this project, concluding that communication with nonhuman species is more complicated than we thought. When no extraterrestrials showed up in space to communicate with us, Dr. Lilly, who was now experimenting with various drugs on himself, continued trying to communicate with dolphins more or less on his own. Two of those dolphins were Joe and Rosie. And when those experiments ended, they were acquired by Oceanic Research and Communication Alliance (ORCA), led by Virginia Coyle and Jim Hickman, two pioneers of captive dolphin releases. Their privately financed mission was to demonstrate how captive dolphins can and should be returned to the wild. After a year's preparation, the two dolphins were released off one of Georgia's barrier islands in 1987. I was privileged to be a member of that group, in charge of the actual rehab and release of the dolphins.

What I was leading up to with the group in Melbourne was about Bogie and Bacall, two dolphins captured for illegal purposes in the Indian River Lagoon. The room of the yacht club we were in faced that very lagoon. Pointing out the window, I declared, "Those dolphins were captured out there." Everybody turned and looked. It was growing dark but we could still see the water. The capture was illegal, I explained, because the law says dolphins may be captured only for *public* display, not *private*. And Bogie and Bacall were taken to a private club, the Ocean Reef Club (ORC) of Key Largo, where they had been prisoners ever since.

My talks are very casual and I encourage people to ask questions throughout. One member of the dive club, an older fellow with an amused expression, held up his hand. I stopped and he said, "If Bogie and Bacall have been together all this time, have they started a family yet?"

"Not likely," I said. "Dolphins are highly sexual creatures, especially in captivity where there's not much else to do, but these particular dolphins are both females. Those names were given to them as a result of a contest. The movie *Key Largo*, based on a Hemingway novel, was filmed in part not far from the Ocean Reef Club in the early fifties. It starred Humphrey Bogart and Lauren Bacall. And it was cute, I suppose, to name the dolphins that, even though they were both females. The interesting part is that dolphins actually have their own names. I don't know what Bogie and Bacall's real names are," I said. "I never worked with those two dolphins. But each dolphin has a signature whistle, a sound peculiar to themselves. That's their real name. They make the sound from time to time, especially when they arrive on a scene or leave it. It says, 'I'm *so-and-so!*' You can see it quite distinctly on a spectrograph, and it means, if nothing else, that dolphins definitely don't have an identity crisis."

From another part of the room, another question: "If this is illegal, holding these dolphins at a private club, how can it happen?"

In any public appearance there's a moment where everything else has been but prologue, and this was that moment.

"It happens," I said, "because the system doesn't work." I glanced around. The room was silent. "And this is why sometimes we are forced to go *beyond* the system, if you know what I mean."

In a group like this, there's always someone from the other side, someone from the captivity industry with "tough" questions. I've heard them all and I've got the answers, but sometimes all they want is to bog down the meeting. What's "wrong" with capturing animals? they might ask. I'm not a moral philosopher, but I do know dolphins, and I know that it's wrong to capture them and put them in a tiny tank where they must do tricks for our amusement in order to be fed. Dolphins are wild animals, they belong in nature where they can swim anywhere they want to.

The captivity industry doesn't get it. At my meetings, they show up and suggest it's okay to capture animals because that's what we've always done. That's who we are, they say. Doesn't the Bible give us dominion over dolphins? Do you think dolphins are human or equal to humans? Are you saying that they have rights? Should they have rights? Why are you anthropomorphizing them? And what about scientific research? Are you saying that we should stop doing research on dolphins? Isn't overpopulation a problem? Isn't it better for them when we "thin the herd"? If they're so smart, why are we able to capture them? What should our policy be about dolphins born in captivity? Doesn't it cost a lot of money to free a captive dolphin? Should we be doing that when children are dying of hunger in Bangladesh? Shouldn't we be putting people first? Come on, O'Barry, why aren't you answering *these* questions?

And I do answer them. They're serious questions, sometimes posed by noted dolphin researchers, but to answer them properly, you need room for the proper context.

That evening in Melbourne I wanted to focus on action. "How many of you," I asked, "would like to help bring Bogie and Bacall back home again?" Hands went up all over the place. I glanced at Joe Roberts. Both of his hands were up and waving. He had a big smile on his face, his eyes were glistening. Yes, I thought, Joe could handle a branch of the Dolphin Project very nicely. He's enthusiastic. He's organized. He picks things up quickly. He also has a light touch, dancing along the surface of things. Yes, Joe Roberts was good. Very smooth, and maybe too good to be true.

Somebody always asks about Greenpeace and why I don't just leave this job for them to do. "Greenpeace," I tell them, "is not into saving captive dolphins. Greenpeace takes in $150 million a year, but they cannot point to a single captive dolphin that they have helped free." When I mentioned this huge sum of money, Joe Roberts's jaw went slack. A young woman, tanned and very serious, wanted to know what could be done, and I said that if any pair of dolphins could be easily returned to their natural state, it was Bogie and Bacall. Getting the dolphins shouldn't be a problem. We probably merely need to point out that they're being held illegally. Getting permission to release them should not take long either. Three months, I said, maybe less.

I based my estimate on the time needed by Virginia Coyle and Jim Hickman, who were in charge of ORCA and the release of Joe and Rosie. They had worked day and night, camping out at offices in Washington, D.C., refusing to be discouraged by a bureaucratic process that seemed designed to wear you out.

o   o   o

I accepted donations for a bunch of T-shirts and books—enough to keep me and the Dolphin Project going another month or two—and after the talk, Joe Roberts and I and a couple of the others got in my rental car and drove over to Flippers, a yuppie restaurant facing the ocean.

Almost from the moment we sat down, Joe Roberts expressed an interest in the Dolphin Project, its membership, fees, newsletter publishing, and meetings.

"Wait a minute," I said, holding up my hands. "Hold on. You've got this wrong. I'm not running a club. No. I've had it with groups. They're too slow. I'm not Batman, not even close, but can you imagine him with a board of directors?" The others laughed. "I'm into direct action, not direct mail."

Joe Roberts smiled, showing his teeth, and nodded. He appreciated the talent involved in making good bumper-sticker slogans. After twenty-five years of working with animal welfare groups, I had gotten pretty good at turning a phrase myself, phrases that would become TV soundbites, phrases that would fit on a bumper sticker. For instance, "Import Vodka, Not Dolphins" (Tel Aviv campaign), "Flipper Volta Para Casa" ("Flipper Come Home," in Brazil), "Thanks, But No Tanks" and several symbols, including these, which are important in third-world countries:

"Direct action?" Joe Roberts asked. "Against the law?"

"Sometimes, yes, because sometimes the law is wrong." I glanced around to check out reactions. "Does that shock anybody?" One of the young fellows across the table shuffled in his chair uneasily. And that's good. One *should* be uneasy about talk of deliberately breaking a law. I spoke slowly, but not in a condescending way. "Please don't understand me too quickly. I'm not saying don't follow a law because it's a law. We've got to have laws. I'm also not saying we can make up our own laws, that laws are relative or anything like that. Most laws are good, and we need them. But a few laws are bad."

I glanced around the table. "We're responsible for what we do even if we are following the law," I said. "It was Thomas Paine—or was it Hale? Anyway, somebody said it's not our *right* to challenge bad laws, it's our *duty*. And isn't that what Martin Luther King Jr. did?"

I felt a pair of eyes burning on me. I turned. Joe Roberts was staring right into my face. I looked at him. "Yes?"

He had a half-smile working. "Let me ask you this, and you correct me if I'm wrong," he said, his eyes dancing around the table. "But you're talking direct action now, right?"

This guy, I thought, definitely had talent. He led me perfectly into a story about how I deal with "bad" laws: the time a couple of years back that a team of professional dolphin hunters captured six young dolphins in the Abacos, a group of islands in the Bahamas, for a swim-with-the-dolphins program. These programs, where you pay $80 to $100 an hour to swim with the dolphins, are very popular tourist attractions. Now the Abacos are different from the rest of the Bahamas. The original white settlers of the Abacos were Loyalists during the American Revolution, loyal to England. When the war went the other way, they fled, left their homes, and settled in these beautiful islands of the Bahamas. Their descendants today are a special breed of gritty, hard-working people with a lot of old-fashioned ideas, including an abhorrence of humiliating the weak and helpless. You might think such a people would be strong enough to prevent a dolphin-swim program from opening in their midst, that they could simply vote it down. In the old days when the Bahamas was still a British Crown colony, they could have done that. But the Bahamas seems to me to be ruled by money now. And the people who wanted the dolphin-swim program had a lot of it.

"Now the question is," I said to Joe and the others at the table, "do we follow the law when that law itself is so obviously bought and paid for? I don't think so. And neither did the people of Great Abaco. But their problem was that if they had taken direct action, they might well have been destroyed by the people with money."

"And that's where you came in?" Joe suggested.

"Exactly," I said. "They didn't pay me anything, except for expenses. They provided a very fast speedboat and three volunteers, two women and a man. Don't ask me their names. We didn't exchange names. The plan was that if I got caught they could leave me behind. This was my responsibility, not theirs. And the less I knew about them, the better.

"Then one bright sunny day we headed over. The pen was very simple, about 350 feet of heavy-gauge chain-link fencing stretched in a rectangle along about thirty green-heart telephone poles from one part of the beach to the other. This cut off the dolphins. They were being guarded by a huge, black Bahamian man in a straw hat, who was fishing on the pier. Late that afternoon we drove by slowly in our speedboat, playing loud music, waving and laughing. He waved back. We anchored off a nearby wreck, a good fishing hole, and 'partied.' We were all in swim suits, so the women, dedicated environmentalists, went up to the bow of the boat, spread out large towels, anointed themselves with oil and began soaking up the sun. The man with me, a bulging bodybuilder like Sylvester Stallone, broke out a couple of fishing rods and we pretended to fish. The water was blue and green with iridescent moments of turquoise, the colors flashing as if in crystal, a postcard kind of day with a deep-blue sky and white puffs floating drowsily in

air that was drunk on its own wild smells. Way off over the Atlantic somewhere was a row of billowing thunderheads, moving like giants slowly on
the horizon. The sun took forever going down. Inch by inch, a stunning sunset faded and the night closed in. A partial moon would rise later, and I noticed
that the guard had grown used to us and kept on fishing.

"As night closed in, it was dark, but you could still see fairly well in the
starlight and phosphorescence of the water. I strapped on my scuba gear and
slipped silently over the side of the boat away from the beach, a bolt cutter
in my hands. I swam underwater over to the bottom of the fence—it was only
eight or ten feet deep—and began cutting the fence up toward the surface.
I wondered what the dolphins must think of all this strange racket under
water. Without making a sound, I rose to the surface and peeked at the guard,
a dim figure in the darkness. He hadn't moved all day. I swam fifteen or twenty
feet over to the next pole and down to the bottom, where I cut the fence there.
When I had cut a good-sized hole in the fence under water, I swam back to
the boat and waited for the dolphins to escape. But they wouldn't leave. 'I
knew this would happen,' I told the others.

"'You knew?' said 'Sly.'

"'Well, I was pretty sure, yeah. They hate to go through holes like that
in a fence. It's scary to them.'

"'So what'll we do now?' Sly asked.

"'Nothing we can do. We'll have to wait till the guard is gone.'

"We took turns, Sly and I, swimming underwater over to the fence to
see if the dolphins had found the hole and escaped. But the young dolphins
refused to come out. We waited till around midnight. The guard gathered
his fishing gear and trudged away, across the beach to the row of sea grapes.
Was he waiting at the edge of the beach? Waiting for us to do something?
We sat in the boat without moving for maybe half an hour more, then, while
my nameless companions watched, I swam without fins over to the fence,
climbed up on top and, to my astonishment, it fell down! It was nailed with
large galvanized staples but my weight alone was enough to push it down.
We wouldn't have to cut it down after all. By then Sly had joined me, and
the two of us climbed the fence and walked on top of it, jumping wildly

around on the fence together, forcing it to roll back down. We laughed because it was so easy, because it was such a crazy scene, jumping up and down on the fence in the silvery light of a gibbous moon, and we could hear the music from the boat. We simply walked around the top of the fence, squashing it flat to the bottom of the bay. Suddenly I felt the water swirl on both sides of me. The dolphins! Six frightened dolphins shot past me. 'There they go!' I yelled. *'Free!'*"

o   o   o

Back at the table in the restaurant, one of the guys said, "Must have been quite a shock the next morning."

"To them? Yes, and an expensive shock, too. That was $120,000 worth of dolphins—gone."

"Twenty thousand dollars apiece?"

"Yes," I said, "but it was also a message from us—and from the people of the Abacos. We were saying, 'No! We don't want that kind of thing here.' And it worked. They still don't have anything like that."

The serious young man who had seemed troubled about breaking the law was sitting across from Joe and me. He put his hands together and then moved them slowly to his lips, waiting to say something. I stopped, and he asked if they ever discovered who did it.

"I'm sure they know by now," I said. "I've told this story before. It explains what I do—what I have to do sometimes."

"Playing devil's advocate," the serious young man said, "I notice you were not especially eager to confront the Bahamian authorities and have your say."

"The civil disobedience thing?"

"Yes."

"I'm dedicated," I said, "but not crazy. There are no civil liberties in Fox Hill Prison. I've been that route. I've been in jail on protests—I can't count the times—and I avoid it when I can. It's not as romantic as it seems."

We went on talking into the night. I told Joe that if he wanted to open a branch of the Dolphin Project here to help free Bogie and Bacall,

I would help him. "Here's a slogan we can get going with: Welcome Home, Bogie & Bacall!"

"That's good," he said, nodding. "Simple, short, direct. I love it!"

I thought he was buttering me up. But so what?

o   o   o

I returned home to Coconut Grove. For the next few weeks, Joe and I were on the phone every day, mostly talking but also faxing, exchanging stuff of interest in the media. In my field, information is everything. Networking. Get enough people talking about the same thing, and suddenly you've got a plan, a campaign. I've been in dozens of them. If I find something of interest, I put it on the fax and out it goes, sometimes to specific people who would be interested, sometimes to twenty of them all at once. And I know that each of them knows twenty others. We're in a loop, hundreds of activists around the globe, all of us busy faxing and talking and keeping one another up to date. News is going back and forth all the time, especially stories in newspapers or on TV, news of a victory here or a setback there, the plight of a particular dolphin, a new law affecting demonstrations, or anything that happens to one of us. We're a sounding board for one another and in an informal way we keep one another in line, quite aware that our communications may not be private. My phone bills are enormous, averaging $1,000 a month. Can I afford it? Not always. When I can't pay it, I'm disconnected. And then I might as well be dead. So I do whatever I must to pay the bill, realizing all the time how fragile all this is and how without luck, a contribution, or a timely miracle, all this—including me—could dry up and blow away.

Joe spent most of his time working deals on the phone. He lived alone in a small apartment, and I imagined him propped up on his cot, the phone cradled between his shoulder and ear. Pretty soon, he was talking like a seasoned dolphin activist.

Though Joe and I talked mostly about Bogie and Bacall, we understood the project to include Molly and Lady, two other captive dolphins who were with them at ORC. But as Joe Roberts and I both knew, the key to writing slogans is, like wit, brevity, and so we pitched it on Bogie and Bacall.

I based the plan we were making on the successful one by ORCA that freed Joe and Rosie. In that plan, Virginia Coyle and Jim Hickman handled the money and the office, which included getting the permit. My job was handling the dolphins. One day Joe Roberts drove down to my office, which is in my home, and I tossed him a copy of the Joe and Rosie protocol. It's about an inch thick. "This is what I've been talking about," I said. "You should get familiar with it. And the main thing," I told him, "is the permit and other governmental paperwork. Let me tell you something straight out. You can waste a lot of money on a thing like this. You've got to know what you're doing. I want to do a rehab and release as cheaply as possible. This whole thing is a demonstration to show that it's cheaper to return dolphins to the sea, where they can live out their lives in a natural way, than to warehouse them, put them in a tank where it ends up costing hundreds of thousands of dollars each sometimes, and the dolphin would rather be dead."

Joe Roberts was nodding his head. "I hear you," he said. "How much exactly are we talking about?"

I had thought a lot about this. The Joe and Rosie release had cost about $120,000. That's a huge sum, but they were the first captive dolphins ever to be released with government approval and we wrote the book on how to get it through the bureaucracy. Some people say it's frivolous to spend money like that on the rehab and release of captive dolphins when human beings are dying of hunger. But hunger is not the only problem in the world. Hungry people already have their advocates; captive dolphins have only a few of us. In the old days, before the enactment of so many micro-managing governmental regulations, I freed a pair of dolphins—Florida and Liberty—for $600. And that $600 was the cost of flying them from Miami to the waters off Eleuthera in the Bahamas. They had originally been captured in Biscayne Bay off Miami, home of the Miami Seaquarium. It is usually preferable to return dolphins to the area they were captured in, but we could not release Florida and Liberty in Biscayne Bay, because captures were still going on there.

Joe eyed me closely. "How much did you say?"

"To set Bogie and Bacall free? Less than $25,000."

"You can get $25,000?"

"I think so, yes."

If Joe Roberts was half as good as he seemed to be, he would serve the project well. He could run an office, he was good on the phone, he knew people where the dolphins were to be released, and he was a master at dealing with the press. I was also desperate for someone to help free Bogie and Bacall, Molly and Lady. I had several campaigns going on during this time and was in and out of the country a lot. I needed someone in the area to keep an eye on things.

Joe decided not to have a branch of the Dolphin Project; he wanted his own organization, which he called Dolphin Alliance. To me he was still just a guy in a small room with a phone, but now he had a fax, business cards, letterhead with a number of dolphin people listed on it including me and Mary Mosley, and a computer that would produce his newsletter and later leave its mark in a Web site on the Internet. I lent him the Dolphin Project Bus and he drove it proudly around Melbourne, making the TV news. Friends of mine in the area supplied me with newspaper stories by environmental reporter Billy Cox and TV news clips about the campaign.

Joe Roberts became a local overnight celebrity because of the interviews. In my opinion he was using information he heard from me and acting a lot like me. Imitation may be the sincerest form of flattery, but I was not flattered. I had spent much of my life doing this, now this guy, using my stuff, was doing it just as well as I did. He was spreading the word, yes, but why, I wondered, didn't he spread his own word? It seemed to me that he was becoming a one-man "Invasion of the Body Snatchers."

4

A GOOD PLAN IS HARD TO FIND

Don't count your boobies until they are hatched.
—James Thurber

IN SETTING OUT ON a campaign to free captive dolphins, dolphins held illegally in my own backyard where lots of people know me and feel the way I do about it, I thought it would be a piece of cake. Returning Bogie and Bacall to their native waters off Melbourne had all the ingredients of a textbook campaign. Joe Roberts, my new assistant, brought a lot to the table. He had moxie, a friend in the media, and, best of all, he was already in Melbourne. On the other side, the Ocean Reef Club (ORC) was not in the captivity business. Surely it would comply with the law once it was pointed out. A letter might do, a letter pointing out that these dolphins were being held against their will for the private amusement of the people at ORC.

On second thought, Joe Roberts and I decided that a letter might be too formal, that it would be simpler, more courteous if we talked to them in person. "I'll call," I said. "They're right down the road from me. I'll call Mr. Lindner, Carl Lindner Jr. himself, tell him who we are and what the situation is. I'm sure he'll do the right thing."

I called several times and never got through to Mr. Lindner, who owned the club, but finally his right-hand man, George Bradley, spoke to me. He said that it would not be necessary for me to come all the way down to Key Largo, that he was coming into Miami the next day and would drop by for a chat. At the appointed hour he arrived at the gate and rang the bell, and I buzzed him in.

I was living in the guest cottage at Casablanca, the seven-acre Henry Field estate in Coconut Grove on Biscayne Bay. Dr. Field, who died awhile back, was the Field of Chicago's Field Museum. He was an anthropologist and an old friend of mine and John Lilly's. His widow, Julie Allen Field, lived alone now in their Moorish mansion with an Afghan and a Greyhound. She let me live in the guest cottage, which was shaded by some of the largest banyan trees in this part of the world, 120 feet tall if they were an inch.

George Bradley, a man in his late forties, drove up in his big black Mercedes and parked next to my bus. I came out on the porch and greeted him. "Come on in," I said, holding the door open for him.

"What's that?" he said, gesturing to the bus.

"Some call it the bus from hell," I said with a smile. It was a twenty-year-old school bus donated to the Dolphin Project a couple of years earlier by Richard Isley, a member of Sea Shepherd Society in San Diego. I was delighted to get the bus and drove it up to San Francisco where George Sumner, a marine artist, and I covered it with paintings of whales and dolphins. Then Lincoln, my son, and a few of his pals drove it to South Florida where we used it in demonstrations against what I called dolphin "abusement parks" and where it figured more than once in rowdy crowd behavior.

George Bradley and I shook hands and I introduced him to Lincoln and Yoko the dog, who went outside to play catch with a coconut. I was in short pants and a T-shirt, Bradley was in a silver-gray power suit—much more powerful than the one I owned. If regardless of economic ups and downs, a good suit always costs the same as an ounce of gold, George Bradley's would have cost *three* ounces. His shoes and attaché case looked like some kind of reptilian hide and I wondered if he knew how I felt about things like that. As a matter of fact, I don't like it. And though I'm not a fanatic, I might have been and his wearing such things seemed to me a bit careless. Or was it confrontational? Either way, it meant that he had no time for a song and dance, so I got to the point, that ORC had no right to the dolphins and we wanted them so that we could prepare them for life in the wild again and set them free. I offered to show him the law on this but he waved it off. I told him that this did not have to be good guy against bad guy, that it could be win-win for both of us if we did it right. "If we play this smart," I said, "Ocean Reef can come out smelling like a rose."

He said nothing, just nodded with a little smile, taking it all in. We were in my office—the whole front room was glass enclosed and looked out in three directions across the fabulous grounds of Casablanca. When I took a phone call, he wandered around looking at things on the wall: photos, paintings, mementos, awards. The phone was ringing off the hook, people calling me from all over the world. Lincoln came in to answer it a couple of times, and the fax was churning out stuff like a printing press, pages spilling onto the floor. I moved over to my glass-topped desk—this was the formal stage of our meeting—and I said that we didn't want to fight about it, that a lot of this was of a legal nature, it would cost a lot of money and end up hurting a lot of people. "But we *will* fight if we must," I said. "And you ought to know that once we start, we never quit."

Then I put in the video about Joe and Rosie, and while he watched it, I went out and joined Lincoln playing "fetch the coconut" with Yoko.

When the video was over, I went back in. He was ready to leave. I said, "You know, Mr. Bradley, the Ocean Reef Club is going to get lots of publicity about this in the next year. Whether it's good publicity or bad depends on how we handle things now."

We exchanged pleasantries, I repeated my wish that we might do this amicably. I was so elated when he left, I called Joe Roberts on the phone. "It's in the bag," I said.

o   o   o

When you step back and look at what was happening, it must seem strange, a simple citizen like myself, someone no more endowed with authority than anyone else, playing watchdog over governmental affairs. I'm as aware of this as anyone else, and I have a problem explaining it, not so much *what* I do as *why* it's necessary. In the case of Bogie and Bacall, the law is quite clear. The Marine Mammal Protection Act of 1972, Permits Public Display Section at 104(c)(2), states:

A permit may be issued for public display purposes only.

And that ought to be the end of it. Yet these dolphins were being held against their will at ORC—a private club! And we were practically begging the people of ORC to let us have them. They should have been begging us to take them off their hands.

I am against anyone owning dolphins for *any* purpose. First of all, it's an oxymoron, owning a wild animal. People who make their living in the captivity industry and who control how laws are written assure us that it's educational, that they want to show the public what a dolphin is. But if they wanted to show the public what a dolphin is, why would they show a *captive* dolphin? The pathetic captive creatures that do tricks at dolphin shows in order to be fed are in no way like they are in nature. To see a dolphin as it really is, you must go into *their* world.

The government itself knows little about dolphins, so it relies on "experts" for advice. But these experts are the same people who make their living by keeping captive dolphins. Am I the only one who sees a problem with this? That we're letting the foxes guard the chickens?

The problem may have begun quite innocently at the highest level. The U.S. Department of Commerce is in charge of commerce in general, including marine fish. To control fish specifically, the Department of Commerce has the National Marine Fisheries Service (NMFS). This is made up largely of people in the fishing industry who make the rules for catching fish and maintaining a profitable supply. They're like the board of directors of a large business, setting and enforcing policy supported by the majority of the stockholders.

Marine mammals are also in NMFS's custody. NMFS controls catching marine mammals, importing and exporting them, and doing scientific research on them. Their interest in marine mammals is basically limited to how they affect marine fish—and fishermen. When the U.S. Congress passed the Marine Mammal Protection Act (MMPA) in 1972, it also established the Marine Mammal Commission (MMC), which makes recommendations to NMFS about marine mammals. This commission is made up of veterinarians, dolphin trainers, representatives of tuna interests, business people, scientists, and various other members of the captivity industry.

Notice something missing here?

Nobody represents the captive dolphins.

But wait a minute, you might say. Aren't veterinarians looking out for captive dolphins? It might seem so, that there's a doctor-patient relationship between veterinarians and the animals they tend. But the relationship is not between marine mammal and vet, it's between the vet and the *owner* of the animal. Big difference.

My name was once submitted as a candidate for membership in the MMC to provide a voice for the captive dolphins. In 1988 Professor Dennis Kelly, marine mammal biologist of Orange Coast College in Southern California, recommended me to President George Bush as a member of the board, citing my work with TV star Flipper, and pioneering the effort to free captive dolphins, including Joe and Rosie in the National Geographic documentary. For whatever reason, they chose to ignore it.

I've lived in the shadow of this bureaucratic tangle most of my life and I've asked myself a million times how it happened. For all their life-and-death recommendations over capturing and sacrificing marine mammals, none of these government agencies—NMFS, MMC, and APHIS (the Animal and Plant Health Inspection Service, a division of the Department of Agriculture)—none of them is in charge of *releasing* them. Government officials give the impression that they have authority over releasing captive dolphins. But in fact, no law, no regulation, no directive gives them authority over that. If this were changed by the stroke of a pen, it still wouldn't happen. They would need a set of rules telling how it should be done. And they don't have a clue. In fact, the experts they rely on say it can't be done.

o   o   o

As our campaign for the release of Bogie and Bacall was warming up, a funny thing happened. Three of the dolphins escaped: Bacall, Molly, and Lady. Bogie hung back. Apparently there was a hole in ORC's fence. How did it get there? Some people accused me of making it, which I denied. However it happened, a four-foot lemon shark got in and scared the dolphins out. Rick Trout was the trainer of the dolphins, along with his girlfriend, Lynne Stringer, and Mary Lycan. They directed three dolphin shows a day at the private club.

Trout was short and muscular, full of energy. He bounced around like a club fighter ready to rumble. Or to talk. He could talk your ears off. Especially on the phone. With his soft, whispering, seductive voice, Trout could almost put you in a trance. Exactly how he did this, I'm not sure, but it involved his dramatic and conspiratorial style. Most of the time he was grinning or right on the verge of it, as if he was sharing a private joke with you. I never knew what to expect next from Trout. One day he was with the captivity industry, the next with animal welfare.

A long-time trainer and a member of the International Marine Animal Trainers Association (IMATA), Trout worked for about three years for Seaco, the civilian firm that trained sea lions and dolphins for the Navy in San Diego. After he left, he charged in the Summer 1990 *Dolphins in Peril* newsletter that his former fellow employees at Seaco mistreated dolphins at the base. Trainers kicked the dolphins, he said, and threw things at them. The Navy's "dolphins of war" program was first criticized in the 1970s by Dr. Michael Greenwood, so Trout was following a well-worn path. Then when the Navy planned to guard nuclear subs with dolphins in the icy waters of Bangor, Washington, Trout opposed that too. In my opinion, credit for squelching that bad idea should go to PAWS (Progressive Animal Welfare Society), which organized a coalition of animal welfare organizations (including the Dolphin Project) that filed and won a Federal lawsuit against using warm-water dolphins in such cold water. Though Trout made a few headlines with his dramatic anti-captivity charges, he continued to work on the captivity side, getting a job at ORC training Bogie and Bacall, Lady and Molly.

When the dolphins of ORC escaped, the Miami news media went into a feeding frenzy. Nobody knew where the dolphins had gone until a friend of mine spotted them about twenty-five miles north—in a lagoon off the eighteenth fairway of the Key Biscayne Golf Course—and called me. I knew Trout was looking for them. I called him and told him I was going to try to lead them to freedom. "You want to help?" I asked. "Sure," he said. I told him where they were. We met there and began working together on the side of the dolphins—or so I thought.

About three hundred yards north of the golf course on the bay side was a marina, and the dolphins began doing their dolphin act there three times a day (10:00, 2:00, and 4:00). Translation: they were hungry. By then, of course, lots of people knew where they were and flocked around to watch the show, cheering, throwing them mullet, and laughing like they were at a circus.

I got in front of the people and yelled at them: "No! No! Don't feed the dolphins! Don't feed the dolphins! We're trying to *free* them!" I waved my arms. "Don't feed them—please!"

No effect. I ran to my car and got my banner, came back and unfurled it high above my head—it read "Freedom!" in big red letters. It was a strange scene: The dolphins, especially Molly, leaping around in the marina and doing tricks; the crowd joyous to see this apparent dedication to show business; me running up and down, waving the banner, and yelling like a mad man.

But before we could do anything more, two women and a man from the National Marine Fisheries Service arrived and took charge. The woman I took to be in charge had a pistol on her belt. I had never seen an armed NMFS officer before. Marine police arrived in their speedboats and I explained that we—Trout and I, Lynne and Lincoln—were trying to lead the dolphins back home. All we need, I said, is a little more time. "We have as much right to these dolphins as anyone else," I said. I drew the woman in charge off to one side. "Look," I said, "you want the real story about what's going on here?" She was frowning, avoiding my eyes. I took that as a yes. Then I told her that the dolphins had been held illegally at Ocean Reef Club, that in effect they were prisoners being held against their will. She turned away. But I got in front of her and kept talking.

"You should realize," I said, "that ORC is a private club, which means that dolphins are not permitted there. That's the law. The law says that dolphins may not be held in any facility that is not public." She looked away, annoyed. I wondered if she had heard anything I said. "Now the dolphins have escaped," I continued. "Does that tell you something? For four days they've been free. *Free at last!* Know what that means? I'll tell you what it tells me. It means that they can make it in the wild." The moment I said that, I wished I hadn't. Some people automatically think that "the wild" is a bad place. "Please," I said, "please don't take this the wrong way, but when we call it 'the wild,' to them, of course, it's *home.*" When she frowned, several heavy ridges formed between her eyebrows and I knew that I had lost her, that I was not helping my cause, and that I should shut up.

One of the inhabitants of Key Biscayne, a dolphin advocate, had lent us his cellular phone. Trout was using it to call everyone he knew and tell them what was happening. Trout and Joe Roberts are equally addicted to telephones. And I wondered in an idle moment what would happen if there were only one phone left on earth. One of them would surely have it, and probably try to call the other. I don't pretend to be immune to this addiction. I use the phone a lot myself. I borrowed the one Trout had and called Joe Roberts to make sure he understood what was going on here, that if we were able to free these dolphins, which were swimming free even as we spoke, then our Welcome Home Project for Bogie and Bacall wouldn't be necessary.

Shortly after the NMFS officers showed up, a capture boat hired by NMFS appeared. The *Dolphin Doll,* a large, powerful open boat with about ten burly men on board, moved slowly into the marina. None of them smiled. Piled high in the back of the boat was a net. And tagging behind that, a second open boat. Everything at the marina got very still. We looked at the vessels as they circled slowly. And though nobody said a word, we knew that the party was over.

Their capture technique is simple. When they locate the dolphins, they drive them to shallow water, one man gets in the skiff, which has an outboard motor and is attached to the end of the hundred-yard net. At a signal, he puts his skiff in reverse to hold his spot in the water. The capture boat speeds ahead of the dolphins and cuts across their course, spilling out the net as it goes, then it circles around to the skiff and the net is drawn tight. Some of the guys in the capture boat go over the side, grab the dolphins and wrestle them into a sling, then into the skiff. Dolphins are kicking and screaming, frenziedly beating the water to a froth with their flukes. And yes, some dolphins get hung up in the net and die of suffocation.

o   o   o

It should have been easy to capture these three dolphins because they had settled in a small lagoon off the marina, a lagoon like the one they lived in at ORC. The dolphin catchers merely needed to stretch the net across the mouth of the lagoon, then close in on them. But the dolphin catchers stalled till the dark of night, I suppose so the media couldn't see them. That made it more difficult for them to capture the dolphins, and more dangerous to the dolphins. But clearly they underestimated what they were up against. They didn't know about Molly, that she was the alpha-female dolphin, the leader of this pod, and very "net wise."

I didn't know Molly at that time, but later I worked with her a lot and, like everybody else, fell completely under her spell. It's hard to say what made Molly so special. Despite several disfiguring scars received during her long show business career, she was a beautiful dolphin. You couldn't keep your eyes off her. And clever? She had adapted to captivity in an almost eerie way. Those of us who work with dolphins, whether training or un-training them, are supposed to treat them all alike. No favorites. But the dolphins are playing another game. They're doing everything they can to attract our attention. They're jumping out of the water, turning flips, walking on their tails, racing back and forth, eyeing us, smiling, and—I can think of no better way to describe it—they're *flirting* with us! And suddenly you realize that they're in charge. Or Molly is. Molly the charismatic dolphin charmed us into her game, and we loved it. We never talked about it. It would have been embarrassing even to mention. But I noticed that each of us gave Molly a little something more than the other dolphins, an extra live fish that she especially liked, a closer medical inspection, more meaningful eye contact, and bigger smiles. Indeed we couldn't keep from falling in love with Molly just a little more deeply than with the others, and I for one would have done almost anything in my power to gain her respect. For the same reason, I suspect, that the other dolphins followed her.

This is the story I've been able to piece together about Molly. She was captured when she was about three years old. She was swimming with her family pod off the West Coast of Florida one day in 1968, when Captain Frank O'Conner, a dolphin trainer, happened by with a net. He captured her because a wealthy man living in Key Largo wanted a "pet porpoise" for his girlfriend. Captain O'Conner transported Molly to a canal behind the man's home, the girlfriend lost interest, and Molly, neglected, fell ill.

Hearing of this, O'Conner took Molly back to his dolphin pens, nursed her back to health, and taught her dozens of tricks. She was now in show business. Then, when Capt. O'Conner took off for Lebanon, he turned her over to Rusty Nielsen and Ocean Experience, Inc., who put her in a traveling dolphin show at Playland Park, Rye, New York.

That summer she was shipped in a small truck to Brunswick, Georgia, where she was used to promote a shopping complex. Originally she was scheduled to perform with Susie, the only surviving dolphin of the five who played the role of Flipper in the TV series. But Susie, who had just been flown in from France, was ill and couldn't perform, so Molly carried on alone. While Molly and Susie were being loaded aboard a plane to fly back to Key Largo, Molly received a serious cut on the left side of her body, a huge, ugly scar she still bears.

When Captain O'Conner returned in 1974, he discovered that Molly and another dolphin, Ginger, had been flown to Puerto Rico, where they had performed until one afternoon the pool sprang a leak, the water ran out, and the two dolphins were left high and dry on the bottom. Rusty Nielsen shipped them back to Key Largo, where Dolphin Plus is now, and during the rush to get her back, Molly received serious stretcher burns to her pectoral fins.

For several years until 1977, Molly and Ginger did five or six shows a day in a small portable metal tank, the same one they had used in New York and Georgia. Ginger, small and always sickly, died after a long, painful illness, her stomach clogged with indigestible Spanish mackerel jawbones. Steve McCulloch, dolphin trainer, acquired Molly in 1977 and a year later transported her to Lancaster, Pennsylvania, where that summer she gave hundreds of performances. After that, Molly was transported in a van to a small, run-down aquarium in Hull, Massachusetts, where she met Lady and Sprite, two other captive dolphins.

McCulloch built some small pens at Key Largo and the next year transported the three dolphins to the Theater of the Sea on Islamorada. Lady and Sprite were shipped around the country for shows while Molly did shows at Islamorada. Late in 1980, McCulloch and Rusty Nielsen began training the three dolphins to look for sunken treasure with Mel Fisher, famous for his find of the *Atosha* off the Dry Tortugas. Molly was also trained to carry cameras and strobe lights to get shots of the Loch Ness Monster in Scotland, where the water is fresh and freezing cold. That venture would almost certainly have been fatal, but fortunately for Molly, Ocean Experience ran out of money and the project was aborted.

Molly and Sprite were shipped to the same depressing Massachussetts aquarium that Sprite had spent so many miserable years in, and the next day Sprite was dead. The cause of death was suicide. When she saw that she was to be put in the same tiny show pool she had always hated, she couldn't stand another day of it. Yes, dolphins can and do commit suicide. They hold their breath until they die. It's deliberate. They can do this because each breath a dolphin takes is a conscious effort. Even when asleep, part of their brain is conscious and in control of breathing. Most other mammals, including human beings, breathe automatically. If we are trapped under water, we lose consciousness, automatically breathe water into our lungs and drown. But if the dolphin is trapped under water, he loses consciousness—and suffocates! Necropsy shows that such dolphins have no water in their lungs. Millions of dolphins are said to drown in tuna nets, but many of these actually suffocate. I have seen it happen. Indeed Kathy, the dolphin I loved the most and who usually played the role of Flipper, died in my arms that way.

Shortly after Sprite's death, Molly was taken to Virginia Key off Miami for work in a TV film production, *Key Tortuga,* the story of a dolphin who found sunken treasure. Then she was transported to South Dakota, where she worked indoors with Lady. In 1982 Ocean Experience needed money and sold Molly and Lady to Jim Tiebor of Florida Dolphin Show, Munich, Germany. According to *The Rose-Tinted Menagerie* (Heretic Books), Tiebor was a trafficker of dolphins in Europe. Many dolphins had already died in his facilities. This surely would have been a death sentence for Molly. But instead, Ocean Experience went belly up, and they dumped Molly at ORC where she and Lady did three shows a day. They were joined in 1988 by Bogie and Bacall, who had been captured to replace Molly and Lady when they died. But the indomitable Molly lived on. And so did Lady—for a while.

o   o   o

Molly and Lady were "pre-Act" dolphins, captured before the Marine Mammal Protection Act of 1972. That means no permit was required for their release. It also meant that ORC didn't have to give them up, and we had no legal claim to them. And they knew it. When the Florida Marine Patrol came to control the crowd, when NMFS arrived with badges and pistols on their belts to take charge of the dolphins, and when the capture team rolled in, this was obviously one of those moments in life for using the ultimate weapon. And it was there in the form of a shining piece of logic, that these dolphins were now free and nobody, not even the NMFS itself, can capture a free dolphin without a capture permit.

What irony, I thought, turning their own rules against them. But the veterinarian in charge quickly got to work on that. He was the vet of record at ORC and practically all the facilities for captive dolphins in lower Florida, including the Navy in Key West. I had seen him often on the TV news, kneeling beside a stranded dolphin or manatee, looking up gravely into the camera, letting it be known that he was the animal's last hope. However, it seemed to me that his real job was damage control for the owners, making statements and issuing sound bites to fend off animal welfare groups who wanted to shut down the show.

Before the capture permit arrived, Trout and I tried one last time to lead the dolphins away from the lagoon by feeding them from the stern of our small boat. Marine Police and ORC officials stood by and watched, glowering, but we explained that we were trying to get them back to ORC, that leading them like this was less stressful than capturing them in a net. The latter part was true. But ORC faces the ocean, and once we got them out of the bay, we intended to let them go free. When we got the three dolphins about half a mile away, it was as if they hit a barrier. They stopped dead in the water and Molly led them back.

It was a hot July day, not a breeze stirring, the sun beating down about 90 degrees. The dolphins had turned back to the lagoon once again and, without a word, Trout and I went over the side of the skiff and into the water to cool off. Trout had his snorkeling gear and was checking out the bottom, but at one point we were treading water with just our heads sticking up. "You know," I told him, "I really appreciate your help with the dolphins. No matter how it comes out, this is a big step for you." He was grinning. I continued, "I know what it means because I went through the same thing myself. I know what it feels like to put everything on the line . . . your job as a trainer at Ocean Reef . . . maybe your whole future as a trainer. It's a big decision. And it's possible—did you ever think of this, Trout?—it's possible that you might never train another dolphin again?" I gave him a friendly nod, saying, "That's a long time, never. It says something about your character, I think, and I like what it says."

o   o   o

News reports of dolphins on the loose are to some people like raw meat to a shark. Amid the mass of onlookers, I had seen Russ Rector working the crowd of reporters, trying to get them to interview him about dolphins. Trout and I were heading back to the dock and I told him: "Don't encourage that guy. He's a publicity hound. And he's no help at all."

Rector had been involved with the Dolphin Project in shutting down Ocean World, a dolphin park at Ft. Lauderdale. My guess is that when he saw his name in the paper, his face on TV, and the adoring looks of people he didn't even know, he was hooked. A former announcer at Ocean World, Rector opened a nonprofit organization, Dolphin Freedom Foundation, and began wearing dolphin trinkets.

When the campaign against Ocean World was going full blast and TV reporters interviewed me about it, I took them out in a boat a few miles to the Gulf Stream in the Atlantic, and with cameras rolling, I pointed back to land and said, "They call that Ocean World, the place we're trying to shut down. But that's not Ocean World." I would stare into the camera a moment, then sweep my arms around the sea in all directions. Then while the cameras panned the scene, I would say, "*This* is Ocean World." It was very effective. A day or two later, I turned on the TV, and there was Rector, saying the very same thing I said, and gesturing the same way, too.

I want all the help I can get in trying to free captive dolphins, and you can say that Rector was trying to help. But I don't think he was helping. Or maybe I saw something in him I didn't want myself to become. Or maybe it was just bad chemistry. Anyway, when I saw him at the dock trying to aim his video camera at the escaped dolphins, I sidled up to him and said, "Get lost."

A hundred people had gathered to watch the great dolphin capture. CNN was there, which meant that it would be shown all over the world, and so were all the local news media. It was growing dark, a dangerous time to try to net dolphins, and several patrolmen ordered me off the dock. "No way," I said. "I have rights." I grabbed a handrail. One officer grabbed me around the waist and two others grabbed my ankles. "What about reading me my rights?" I yelled. One of them yanked my legs up, and down I went with a crash, my hat flying off. A moment later I was trussed up with my hands cuffed behind me. "At least give me my hat," I said. One of them plunked my hat on my head at a rakish angle and they trundled me off to the Dade County Jail while TV cameras recorded it all. The charge was "trespassing"—on a public dock. That night I spent sleeplessly rolled up in a blanket on the floor. The next day the charge was dropped.

While I was in jail, the capture team persuaded Trout to help them. They strung the net across the lagoon, but this was nothing to Molly. She simply leaped over it, and the others followed. The dolphin catchers, which now included the Dolphin Research Center (DRC), corralled them back into the lagoon and stretched a cable about five feet above the water from one side of the lagoon to the other. It's like the rod of a shower curtain, the net like the curtain itself hanging down into the water to the bottom. But Molly jumped that, too. Down came the net, they herded Molly back into the lagoon and the cable was re-strung *ten* feet above the water. That was too high even for Molly.

Trout was under the impression that his helping with the capture meant that he was back in ORC's good graces, but he was fired anyway. A scene shown on TV news the next day captured Trout's anguished reaction. What made him newsworthy is that the ORC official who delivered the news made the mistake of being on a dock with Trout at the time. Trout bumped the club official into the water with his shoulder. So Trout was jailed too.

5

BATTERING THE GATES OF ORC

Can't we all just get along?
—Rodney King

THOUGH ALL THE DOLPHINS were back in captivity at ORC, I thought we had a gentleman's agreement, George Bradley and I, that both sides would win if we got together and quietly worked out the details of transferring the four dolphins over to us, the Dolphin Project and Dolphin Alliance. We wouldn't need to take the dolphins anywhere. We could do what we had to do at ORC. As I explained to George Bradley, we could work together, preparing the dolphins for life in the wild again. It would be truly educational, and the people of ORC would be a part of it. I thought it was a done deal. I waited for some response from ORC.

A week went by, nothing happened. I called Mr. Lindner, who was not available, then I tried to speak to George Bradley, who was also unavailable. I called a number of times, and each time they said he had just left or he was in a meeting and could not be disturbed. I left messages, asking that he give me a call. I wrote to them both on Dolphin Project letterhead, polite, formal reminders of our pleasant meeting and assurances of our continued interest in the dolphins.

But I received no answer. Gradually I realized that they were stonewalling, as if they thought by ignoring us, we would go away.

Talk about misjudging one's opponent. I was not about to go away. Not that I enjoy campaigning; I don't. The rough and tumble of a campaign is exhilarating, but I've done all that. I'm tired of it. I do it now because the alternative, apathy and guilt, is unacceptable.

And so our campaign at ORC began, like the hordes gathering at the city gates. My weapons of choice in a campaign like this are reason and debate. I enjoy the free exchange of ideas, the crashing of false idols, and truth rising in all its glory. In my first few campaigns, it was like that. In those days I enjoyed a tremendous advantage. Having been part of the captivity industry, I could see both sides; the opposition could not. To them we were a complete mystery, at best a bunch of fanatics. Motive to them is always a function of money, and they would ask themselves what we were getting out of it. Who would pay us to do this? And why? They simply don't understand the passion we live in day and night, that we believe in what we're doing, that we've given ourselves to this, to these dolphins, to their beauty and freedom as if it were God and country and everything else worth dying for.

o   o   o

Knowing what the other side would say in debates and how I would respond, I saw these encounters not as happening so much as unfolding. It was as if we were following a script. And for me this was not a debate, not even a game, but ritual, ritual that might at any moment break into chanting—and sometimes did. Most of the people who attend and follow debates like this have already made up their minds. They hardly ever change. They hang on each word, knowing them almost by heart, listening not for information but to make sure that they are properly represented. Probably only a small percentage of the people at these debates are trying to make up their minds which side to join. Though our main effort is aimed at keeping our own people in line, we try to sign up the new people, too, and strategically, I think, the drift of history is on our side. Freedom is on a roll. And right now, the other side's arguments sound puny:

MYTH: We own the dolphins.

TRUTH: Wrong! You can capture and cage a wild animal, but you can never *own* them.

MYTH: Millions of people come to dolphin shows every year, so there must be something right about it.

TRUTH: Talk about non-sequiturs! Millions of people go to bullfights every year, too, but that doesn't make them right.

MYTH: If we weren't showing dolphins doing tricks, inner-city kids would never see a dolphin.

TRUTH: So what? The very same kids will never see a snow leopard.

MYTH: If dolphins were not on display, people would not care about them or protect them.

TRUTH: Nonsense! Humpback whales are protected by people who have never seen them in captivity.

MYTH: What's wrong with keeping a few dolphins in captivity? There are millions of them out there.

TRUTH: It's abusive, that's what's wrong. There are millions of women and children out there, too, but that doesn't mean it's okay to abuse a few of them.

MYTH: The Bible says using dolphins is okay.

TRUTH: Alas, like an arrow through the heart, yes, unfortunately the Bible does say this. The Bible is the source of almost all our problems with the captivity industry. The Bible quotes God putting Man in charge of earth: " . . . Be fruitful, and multiply, and replenish the earth, and subdue it: and have dominion over the fish of the sea, and over the fowl of the air, and over every living thing that moveth upon the earth." —Gen. 1:28

What does it mean to have "dominion" over something? It doesn't come from Latin, but we know it through its Latin translation, and in Latin the word "dominus" means "lord and master." It's related to other words like "domain," "dominate," "domineer," and "don," also "danger" and "dungeon".

So this is where the problem begins. But that's not the worst of it. In the seventeenth century Rene Descartes, who probably influenced modern thought more than anyone else, argued that since animals do not themselves have souls, they are machines, and, as such, feel nothing.

As breathtakingly silly as that sounds, many people with a religious background truly believe that they are the "chosen species" and, as such, it's perfectly okay to do whatever they want to with animals. We have souls, they say, and animals don't. Or if you want a distinction that you can actually measure, we're more *intelligent*, they say, than other animals. They mean *human* intelligence, of course. But so what? As Mary Midgley said in *The Beast and Man* (1980): "If the talk is of elephants, we can do justice to the miracle of the trunk without pretending that nobody else has a nose."

I've debated with these True Believers till I'm blue in the face, and the best argument—the only one they understand, I think—is action. That's why I do what I do.

o   o   o

When Mary Mosley wrote official letters of complaint to both the NMFS and ORC pointing out the obvious violation of law at ORC, NMFS should have sent a representative to ORC, checked out the complaint and required the club to comply with the law. In other words, ORC should have been ordered to open their gates to the public or to send their dolphins to a public display facility, but NMFS did nothing. Unofficially, however, one member of NMFS, a closet dolphin advocate, appeared at the gates of ORC, showed her badge and asked to see the dolphins. They didn't even let her in.

Mary Mosley, an old pro at these campaigns, showed Joe Roberts some of the tricks to generating publicity from practically nothing. And he schmoozed the state legislature and more than a dozen city and county officials into passing nonbinding legislation banning dolphin captures in their territory. "Nonbinding" legislation is like a resolution. It's merely an expression of feeling. But it made the local press, with Billy Cox, environmental writer of *Florida Today,* writing stories with big headlines each time it happened. They might as well have banned the capture of polar bears, because dolphins hadn't been captured in that lagoon for years. And local or state officials have nothing to do with controling the capture of dolphins, anyway; it's a federal matter.

Nobody bothered to mention that the plan for returning Bogie and Bacall to their home waters was fatally flawed from the beginning, that it would never work—or it shouldn't—because the Indian River Lagoon was polluted and had been for years. Joe Roberts and Billy Cox must have known about this. It seemed to me that anyone who lived around the lagoon would have noticed this. But no one said one word about it to me.

o   o   o

The months dragged on and we battered the gates of ORC to free the dolphins. During this time I was in and out of campaigns all over the place: Indiana, Kentucky, Ohio, Minnesota, Iowa, Oklahoma, Hawaii, Georgia, Missouri, Nevada, and California. Foreign countries too: Israel, Switzerland, Germany, Belgium, Italy, Holland, Brazil, and Argentina.

In Las Vegas, Nevada, for instance, about a hundred of us picketed Steve Wynn's Mirage Hotel and Gambling Casino in an attempt to forestall his dolphin-swim program. This was like old-home week for me. About a year earlier, I had worked several months for Steve Wynn, trying to turn his facility into a halfway house for dolphins en route to freedom. I told Steve when I signed on that this was my objective, and he okayed it. When that didn't work, he offered me a cushy job there. If ever I was tempted to sell out to the other side, it would have been then. It would have been the end of my financial problems. It would have saved my marriage too—at least for a while. I liked Steve personally. At one point he talked to me about my living in a special underwater habitat with the dolphins. It could be educational, he said. And that was true. Millions of people go through there every year and I could have been one of the acts. I considered it, and several people including my wife, Martha, urged me to accept. But in the end, I couldn't. I would have been Steve's "token environmentalist." And I knew that never again could I stand to be with captive dolphins.

When our group protested—perhaps too much—in Las Vegas, eleven of us were arrested and thrown in jail. I've been in jails all over the country.

It's part of what I do. And though we made our point, they went on with their dolphin-swim program anyway.

During all these campaigns, I kept tabs with Joe Roberts about the Welcome Home Project for Bogie and Bacall. Though it may seem strange that we had to work so hard and so long to free the dolphins at ORC when they were so blatantly being held illegally, we were up against some very big people. ORC, which began in the 1940s as a fishing camp, was more than a private club, it was like a small city for the very rich. The owner of the club, Mr. Lindner, was one of the wealthiest and most influential men in the country. His family owns Chiquita Banana. President George Bush was in and out of ORC throughout his term of office, and before him, Richard Nixon and Ronald Reagan. You probably saw President Bush on TV news, flashing his boyish grin and waving from a powerful open speedboat that whipped across the flats en route to a fishing spot, several similar boats of the Secret Service streaking after him at a discreet distance. Well, Bush was visiting Lindner and fishing just off his front stoop.

Over the years I've done a few favors for fellow activists, people who have devoted themselves to the welfare of animals as I have. They're in organizations like People for the Ethical Treatment of Animals (PETA), Friends of Animals, Fund for Animals, In Defense of Animals (IDA), Animal Rights Foundation of Florida (ARFF), Dolphin Rescue Brigade, Coalition Against the Export of U.S. Dolphins (CAUSED), and Performing Animal Welfare Society (PAWS). A few of us began working on behalf of various animals before it became popular or profitable, and when any of my fellow activists are campaigning and call on me, I do what I can to help. Usually they want me to give interviews, speak to groups, march with banners and signs, or maybe get arrested again to make a point. I want to help them because I know that one day I will need their help in a campaign of my own.

That day came in our campaign with ORC when I told them we needed them to write letters to ORC, MMC, and NMFS, demanding that the law be followed. Like any other public movement, people interested in animal welfare are large in number and quite varied in intensity and style, lily-white legal on one side, a dark rumbling underbelly on the other. I'm lily white in some campaigns, rumbling darkly in others. You can never tell what might happen in a campaign because nobody has complete control. Or complete knowledge. Things tend to take on a life of their own.

If this campaign were to follow standard tracks, we would first attempt to reason with the other side, sit down with them in pleasant surroundings and go over the situation together, listing the type of things we might possibly do. This assumes that they know at least what's in their own best interest, a safe assumption in this case since we were dealing with people who had already demonstrated that they knew what their best interests were. We were sure that when they felt the widespread urging from a sometimes hot-headed group of citizens insisting that they simply follow the law—is *that* too much to ask?—we would get their attention.

Planning a campaign like this, you allow for the escalation from negotiations to demonstrations, first a few of our hard-core volunteers marching with signs in a peaceful way. This attracts the media, which seems to think it happened spontaneously. After that, we organize bands and banners and really *huge* demonstrations, mostly people who have free time on their hands— mothers and children concerned about the environment, and retirees— swarms of people that we have no control over, who walk the picket lines and shout whatever might come to mind at everyone going in and out. If there is no response to this, we unleash our looser elements, the people that life has not been kind to and who are attracted to demonstrations against any authority. We know already that we will win because our cause is just, but I'm given to understand that we also have a few anomic souls in our midst who have no sense of propriety whatsoever and who will resort to whatever it takes as a form of self-expression.

o   o   o

Before cranking up what would surely become a long and expensive campaign, I tried once more to make contact with the officials of ORC. And what do you know? Miraculously, I got through. George Bradley answered the phone and I told him we could possibly avoid the impending ugliness if we could talk with Mr. Lindner for just half an hour, long enough to show him a video. Though that was still quite impossible, George Bradley invited me and Joe Roberts to a meeting there.

Joe Roberts drove down to Coconut Grove and I met him. We were both wearing coats and ties. I got in his little Japanese car (my car was in the shop) and we set off on the one-hour drive down to ORC, using the Card Sound toll road. I asked Joe if he had been thinking about the release permit, reminding him that dealing with Washington bureaucrats involves lots of paperwork. He said there was nothing more to do until we got the dolphins. He knew that I depended on him to get the permit, that I had plenty of things to do myself. And since that was our tenuous relationship, we rode on mostly in silence through the Everglades to Key Largo.

Again I wondered if Joe Roberts was the right guy for the job. I really didn't know him from Joe Schmoe. I closed my eyes, trying to relax. I was tight as a drum. I kept thinking that we had to break through at this meeting or we would be involved in a vulgar display of righteous indignation that could drag on for months. We needed to talk, Joe and I, to plan things. In this last-ditch effort to break through, what were we going to say? What strategy should we use? But I couldn't bring myself to speak, so we rode on in silence, on and on. We went through the toll bridge. We were almost there. Then he said, "Anything new on the money?"

"Don't worry about the money," I said. "When we get the dolphins, the money will come."

I don't remember our planning it, but somehow our strategy fell into place. It was simple: Good Cop/Bad Cop. Joe the Schmoozer was obviously the Good Cop, I the Ticking Bomb, the Bad.

We met them in their conference room, George Bradley and several lawyers. We shook hands all around, sat down, and Joe Roberts did the smooth talk for our side, I did the glowering. To them I was the 500-pound gorilla, because about a month earlier (July 8, 1992) I had lambasted NMFS and APHIS at a hearing before Democratic Congressman Charlie Rose's subcommittee of the Committee on Agriculture. This was a review of the USDA's enforcement of the Animal Welfare Act, especially of animals used in entertainment, and I think I was the first to yell and scream about how

NMFS and MMC were controlled by the people in the industry they were supposed to be controlling. "What the industry is doing," I had said, "is educating people to accept this abuse as normal and natural. That's the heart of the problem. Teaching a child not to step on a caterpillar is as important to the child as it is to the caterpillar." I included an attachment made up by the Fund for Animals and Mary Mosley, which cited specific rule violations systematically ignored by government agencies. I was attacked at the hearing by representatives of the International Marine Animal Trainers Association, who said I didn't know what I was talking about.

At the same hearing, Michael Blake, who wrote *Dances with Wolves*, submitted comments. Though I didn't see him at the hearing, I had been with him a month earlier. He called me and flew me in to Reno, Nevada, to help him demonstrate against an auction of mustangs by the Bureau of Land Management (BLM). When I arrived, we got in his van and he drove out in the desert to show me several hundred horses in a corral there. They would be sold to the highest bidder, Michael said, and that's almost invariably a slaughter house.

Here's one of his comments, which I couldn't have said better myself: "Animals by the thousands are condemned to lifetimes of imprisonment solely for the *amusement* of human beings."

Back at ORC, Joe Roberts was approaching the rich and powerful people assembled, urging them to do the right thing by Bogie and Bacall. I broke through, waving my hands like a conductor. Everybody stopped. I fixed my eyes in a stare at a point halfway down the table and said with a voice like the edge of a knife: "You can tell Mr. Lindner that we are going to boycott his damned bananas all across the nation unless he gives up the dolphins." The meeting broke up quickly after that.

On our trip back to town, Joe Roberts and I hardly spoke. What was there to say? We hadn't planned the threat of boycott, but there it was and the campaign was on. Full blast. Joe Roberts went back home and appeared at schools around the Melbourne area, inducing children to write hundreds of letters pleading for the release of the captive dolphins. I parked my Dolphin Project bus next to the security post at ORC's entrance and left it there to remind them that we would not go away. And I've heard that at least two other activists waged their own campaign that paralleled ours in everything but method, an underground campaign of dirty tricks.

Besides all this, there must have been another force involved because suddenly ORC teenagers sided with us against their powerful parents and put bumper stickers on cars at the club. "Free Bogie & Bacall from Ocean Reef Club," they said. Messages to free Bogie and Bacall were spray painted on signs. Some miscreant on our side got ORC's fax numbers and filled their faxes with messages to free the dolphins. Phone calls and electronic mail were sent to officials, and a lieutenant of dirty tricks in our camp, someone who shall remain nameless, confessed to me that he put dog doo in the mailbox of an ORC veterinarian. When he boasted of what he had done, I was appalled. Shaking my head slowly, I said, "No, man. That's over the line."

We continued to negotiate, most of the meetings by conference phone, both sides seemingly convinced that the other would see the light if only they would listen. But the light we saw was that they were merely trying to find out what we were going to do next. We had threatened to bring a law-suit against ORC and NMFS. In fact, we were still shopping around for a pro-bono lawyer. They argued that if we loved the dolphins we would not take them away.

We pointed out that they had it backward. "If you loved them," we said, "you would set them free."

We believed that the people at ORC were devilishly clever, ruthless in the pursuit of winning and not to be trusted. Yet *we* were winning all the battles. Our message about freeing captive dolphins was getting out and theirs, whatever it might have been, was not. I should have realized that we were winning the publicity battle because of their hatred of publicity. Day after day we got the stories in the newspaper and on TV, day after day they went on ignoring us. I fancy myself as knowing something about passive resistance. I've done it enough. The trick of passive resistance is getting beat up in public so much you suddenly get the public's sympathy. It's a form of victimology, or winning by losing. Could ORC be doing this? I didn't think so. They had to have something else up their sleeve—but what?

o   o   o

We didn't have long to wait. Though the campaign for Bogie and Bacall, Molly and Lady dragged on into the summer and though we were certain of ultimate victory, we discovered that it was also being waged on quite another level. Dr. Bossart, the veterinarian, announced that Bogie had hepatitis. This is a disease of the liver that has the same cause in dolphins as it does in people: a dirty environment. Because Bogie might spread the disease to other dolphins, she could not be moved. And because the dolphins should be kept together anyway, we wouldn't have moved them even if we'd had custody.

We were surprised, but we shouldn't have been. When you look at the billion-dollar captive dolphin and killer whale amusement industry, you might be surprised where the power actually lies. It's not the owners or the trainers, nor the scientists who experiment and write books for one another. It's not the spectators, who pay more than a billion dollars a year to be amused. Neither is it the promoters nor the animal welfare activists who hold up signs trying to make them all feel guilty.

No, the key person in the captive dolphin industry is the veterinarian. He alone can say whether a dolphin is sick or not, may be moved or sold or captured or anything else. And remember, his client is the owner, not the dolphin. I have never met a marine mammal vet whose eye was not fixed on the balance sheet. His power comes from being the only one who can legitimately claim to know what is going on biologically and whose name, therefore, must appear on any official paper relating to a dolphin. With this arcana, the veterinarian holds the entire empire together.

Was Dr. Bossart's report about Bogie right? How could we ever know? Not by hiring another vet to double check. They always stick together. We were stymied. Then suddenly a little newspaper report jumped out at us. ORC had allowed some of its citizens to live aboard their boats and they had been cited for dumping human waste directly into the water near the dolphins' pen. Was Dr. Bossart aware of this? And if so, was he doing anything about it?

We talked about this endlessly. We faxed back and forth across the nation and into foreign countries about the filthy water at ORC, about the inbred system of laws and regulations aimed at keeping dolphins in captivity. And the best argument we came up with was that if Bogie had contracted hepatitis in the filth of ORC's dolphin pens, why didn't the vet do something about it? What about preventive medicine?

But rational arguments mean nothing in a situation like this. We needed something that would fit a bumper sticker. We intensified our campaign. I kept my big, blue dolphin bus at the entrance to ORC, knowing that every time anyone went in or out, there it was, crying "Freedom!" We were committed now to a war of attrition, wearing them down with our dedication.

o   o   o

We never knew what was going on behind the mask at ORC. Then one day out of the blue they called another meeting and we felt perhaps they wanted out. Joe Roberts and I met at the parking lot of ORC, put on our coats and ties as we walked to the main administration building, but the meeting fell into a song and dance that was going nowhere. For six months or more I had heard all this. And finally I stood up and glared at them. I smacked the table with the flat of my hand. "No!" I said. "The bottom line is that Bogie and Bacall *are* going home. Home to the sea! If you hear nothing else from me, now hear this: We will *never* quit. *Never!*" I glared around at them. "That means we'll keep the letters coming from little school children all over the state. Forever! We'll tell the world about this cold-hearted place. The whole world will know about the corruption here. About how you ignore the law! And then, gentlemen, chances are we'll get physical. Did I say 'physical'? Is this a threat? No, I wouldn't do that. But up till now, you haven't heard a word we've said, and I'm beginning to think that maybe you understand action better. Maybe we ought to *do* something that you can't ignore." I saw their faces harden. "I'm not saying it *will* happen, gentlemen. But you can expect a new phase in our campaign to begin very soon. When or where? You be the judge of that. But at some point you can expect divers in your waters. You'll have to be on guard, watching the water's edge . . . night and day. And we will come—when you *least* expect it!" I smacked the table and shouted at the top of my lungs: *"Least!"*

They didn't like that. Even I felt that it was a bit overdone. Slapping the table to make a point is okay. Shouting a single word, that's okay, too. But both together? And the wrong word? I don't think so. I should have shouted "Freedom!" That would have made more sense. They said nothing about it, but their eyeballs glazed over, and I was not surprised when they no longer invited me to the negotiations. Now they spoke only to Joe Roberts. By phone. They also replaced the fence to the lagoon with thick steel bars, which they monitored day and night by video cameras and off-duty police.

We never negotiated directly with Mr. Lindner himself, but at one point the word got out that Mr. Lindner, in order to comply with the law, had decided to let the public in. This outraged many members of the Ocean Reef Home Owners Association. The whole point of ORC is to keep the public *out.* So the association bought the club from Lindner for a price of $56 million. Bob Ambridge, general manager, now represented the home owners and negotiated with us.

Publicly, Ambridge announced that ORC would never let the dolphins go to the activists, but privately something must have stirred in the heart of ORC. Ambridge called Joe Roberts and asked which facility was the best to send them to. Joe Roberts called me and I told him that the simplest, most straightforward plan was to build a pen or halfway house at the Indian River Lagoon, where they were captured and would be released. We could take the dolphins there. But officials at ORC had asked NMFS what to do, and officials there said the dolphins should be transferred to another public-display facility.

Several such facilities had bid for the dolphins, including Steve Wynn's Las Vegas Mirage Hotel, the Dolphin Research Center (DRC), Dolphins Plus, Key Largo, and Theater of the Sea. The DRC, which in my opinion ought to stand for the Dolphin Riding Center, made a strong pitch for them, but we objected. Letting Bogie, Bacall, Molly, and Lady go there would be like from the frying pan to the fire. We told the DRC that if they got the dolphins, they also got us, which meant round-the-clock demonstrations. So they backed off. The main business of Dolphins Plus and Theater of the Sea is selling rides; both are just as mercenary, but maybe a little less hypocritical by not pretending to do research. Dolphins Plus is up a long canal from the Atlantic and has one large cage, where customers swim with the dolphins, and several other cages on both sides of the canal where six or seven dolphins are kept. Residents in the area have frequently complained about the rampant commercialism. Theater of the Sea began as a rock pit of several acres and is now connected with the ocean through a pipe. But it's not big enough, and the water is often full of algae. The "theater" probably has more billboard advertising than all the others combined, offering to let you swim with the dolphins and "be a trainer for a day." The grounds are beautiful, its shrubbery trimmed to look like dolphins, and sticking out over the old rock quarry is the prow of a fake Spanish galleon, where the trainer orchestrates standard dolphin tricks.

None were acceptable to us, and Ambridge wanted to know where we would put the dolphins if we got them. We knew about a small, unlicensed facility on Lower Sugarloaf Key, just east of Key West. Lloyd Good III was director and in charge of the only dolphin there, Sugar, the family pet. Everybody connected with dolphins in the Keys knew by now that we were winning our fight with ORC, and Lloyd was delighted when we asked if he wanted to be a part of what we were doing. He didn't have a public display permit for Sugar because he didn't need one. Sugar had been captured before the 1972 law requiring permits. But since NMFS insisted that we take the dolphins to a place with proper permits, Lloyd agreed to get a permit for the new dolphins and to turn them back over to us when we had built a halfway house for them at Indian River.

Most of us like to think that the law covers everything that might happen, but it doesn't. There was always some talk about needing a permit to release dolphins, but there was no actual law on the books. We all knew that. Lawyers told us that, and when we asked NMFS and others to cite the law, they couldn't. There were laws requiring permits to capture dolphins because that was done all the time. But dolphins were never released, not officially, so there was no law to cover it. And who has money and time enough to run it through the courts? So we went along with it.

o   o   o

Sugarloaf was small but had potential. Lloyd's show with Sugar three times a day put him squarely on the other side in the captivity issue, but I thought he could be turned. He was in his early thirties, a big bear of a man with an open face, blond hair down almost to his shoulders, and a light-brown beard. He was laid-back, at home in the Keys. In the old days the Keys attracted people who were on the run or had suddenly realized how very precious each day is, or they were just stumble bums with no place else to go. All that is a fading memory now. Talk to any of the old timers and they'll tell you that the Keys were ruined when the first bridge was built. Nowadays, the Keys are overrun with overachievers, people on the run from their own lives. Not Lloyd, though. He belonged there. He usually wore a T-shirt promoting Sugarloaf, but sometimes he changed into one showing a bleary-eyed drunk crawling across the beach that read, "See the Lower Keys on your hands and knees."

I realized early on when I finally moved down there that Lloyd was a complicated guy. I had known him earlier only as a member of the captivity club. I exposed him regularly, bringing reporters and others in the media to see the Sugar Show as an example of what happens to captive dolphins living in isolation. I didn't know it then, but he had also regularly butted heads with the captivity industry. So he was getting it from both sides.

Even before I went down and became a part of it, I had misgivings about Sugarloaf: How were we ever going to call it a dolphin sanctuary with Lloyd doing the Sugar Show every day? If I was there, old friends in the anti-captivity movement would be coming by all the time. How could I explain my toleration of this, this travesty of the very thing I detested and had dedicated my life to changing? At the time, though, before I knew what I was getting into, I still thought it possible to get Lloyd to see things my way.

In 1972 Mr. Good had bought much of Lower Sugarloaf, planning to develop it like a lot of people were doing in the Keys in those days. He purchased about two hundred acres from bridge to bridge, as they like to say, west of US 1, the highway running down the east side of the Key. The motel is at the center of things. It's at Mile Marker 17, which means it's seventeen miles from Key West, about 130 from Miami. The houses along the Atlantic and east of US 1 are privately owned, but Mr. Good owns everything else, including the fifty-five-room motel, restaurant and bar, marina, service station, general store, airport, and all the other houses. The airstrip, which has figured in two movies (*Drop Zone* and *License to Kill*), achieved notoriety for its part in the Keys' drug problem back in the 1970s and '80s, which the Goods had no involvement in.

Mr. Good was a short, gruff, bulldog a man with a full head of graying hair, neatly cropped. He usually wore short pants, a tennis shirt, and Top Siders with no socks. Unlike his carefree son, Mr. Good seemed to need challenge, a world where he could prove himself. He would have been excellent as an explorer in earlier times or a captain of industry in, say, the early twentieth century. I thought of him as a natural-born exploiter in a time of environmental awareness, and it was evident to me that he despaired of the dead-end world at Sugarloaf and its fragile environment. I felt that he would have sold it all in a minute if not for his family. But I'm not sure of that. We never talked on a personal level; he didn't seem to like me. Mr. Good was a straight-shooter and didn't play games. As an environmental activist, I was part of the environment to him.

My interpretation of Mr. Good's attitude was that he had bought this land and it was cursed, that instead of his owning the land, it owned him. He could sell it, yes, but if he did he would have lost his family. They wouldn't have stood for it. Mr. Good was stuck here, a captive in this strange, gnarled, marginal world. Like Sugar. And his beloved son, Lloyd, was slipping away. Lloyd had a Huck Finn life, fishing, swimming, living in the water with his dolphin. Walking around barefoot, never shaving. Mr. Good must have wondered what he had done to deserve this.

I felt sorry for the man. He had all the elements of a wonderful life: A beautiful, understanding wife, children he could be proud of, money, class—everything. Mr. Good's wife, Miriam, was tall and willowy, good at artistic things like landscaping and painting. They were married, but lived in separate houses. Mr. Good lived in a modest one-story house east of US 1, Miriam in one of the four houses in a row facing Key West across the bay with three of their children, all in their twenties and thirties: John, Caren, and Catherine. Lloyd, a loner, lived in a houseboat that he built when he was sixteen. During the Christmas holidays, Miriam and the children put up lights on the four houses in a row across from Key West that say "Ho! Ho! Ho!" After Christmas, they change the lights to read "Ho No Mo!"

This is hurricane country, and Hurricane Donna came through in 1960, covering everything with three feet of water. But nothing was hurt much because nothing much was there at the time. Hurricane Georges went through in 1998 and messed up Key West, but there was not much damage on Sugarloaf.

The most interesting structure on the whole island, a little-known tourist attraction, is the Bat Tower. Constructed of almost indestructible Dade County Pine, this fifty- or sixty-foot edifice was built during Florida's romantic boom of the late twenties to attract bats. The theory was that the tower would become home base for a certain kind of migrating bat, who would feed on the swarms of mosquitoes that made these islands all but uninhabitable. But it never worked. Shunned by bats, the tower stands in all its pristine glory, humming with mosquitoes that have taken over. Mosquitoes were the dominant species in the Keys till the invention of DDT during World War II.

Mr. Good's plan of development failed too, because before he could get the first of his bulldozers rolling, a marsh bunny was found smashed to death on US 1 near the motel. It was not just any old roadkill, this rabbit was of an endangered species, and environmentalists rose up to protect the few remaining members, as well as the Key's dwindling race of silver rice rats. Thus, Mr. Good's dreams were dashed. He fought to overturn the ruling in federal court, but an appellate court ruled against him eight years later. When you buy a swamp, justices said, that's what you get. I wouldn't be surprised if Mr. Good developed contempt toward the world he lived in, including the dolphins. He must not have liked the idea of a *sanctuary* for dolphins at his motel. Nevertheless, he let it happen. Sugar was part of the package when he bought the land. The kids all loved the dolphin. And Mr. Good loved his family very much.

Later, when I was working there, I noticed that though Lloyd and his father often engaged in pitched verbal battles, Mr. Good always gave in to Lloyd. Both of the daughters, Catherine and Caren, had been married and were divorced. They both had children, Catherine two young daughters, Caren one. Catherine is very tall, like her mother, and plays tennis and the stock market, both quite well. She helped her father run the trailer park. Caren, the eldest, liked working with dolphins. She also worked in the restaurant. When the Goods first moved to Sugarloaf, John was only four and immediately began feeding Sugar. Lloyd, ten, saw what fun it was and took the dolphin away from John. And that's the way it's been ever since.

o   o   o

Word came through that we had all but won the campaign with ORC and we would be at Sugarloaf. Rick Trout immediately involved himself in the process of getting the dolphins to Sugarloaf and preparing a place to keep them. I think Trout had a plan. If Bogie, Bacall, Molly, and Lady were heading for Sugarloaf, then he, their old trainer, might be able to get his job back. As a dolphin trainer, Trout needed dolphins. It seemed he had already burned his bridges in the captive dolphin community, and I think he must have seen a new opportunity emerging. Instead of training captive dolphins, he could train "retired" dolphins, dolphins like Sugar who could never make it in the wild. There were plenty of those. He could train dolphins and be politically correct at the same time, and it must have seemed like a dream come true—except for my presence. Down the line, I thought he and I would clash—and so did he.

I also think Lloyd had a plan. Like Trout, I think Lloyd wanted to keep retired dolphins in captivity, but he also wanted to *breed* them.

6

THIS IS NO ORDINARY LOVE

Man who says it cannot be done
should not interrupt man who is doing it.
    —Confucius

IN LATE AUGUST OF that year, Hurricane Andrew blew through town and left Casablanca, the estate I was living on, in shambles. Huge spreading banyan trees a hundred feet high or more were uprooted all around, like a giant mixer had run over us. I found refuge with Yoko, our dog, in a closet. After that, I moved to a small, neat cottage in Coconut Grove with Lincoln, then twenty-two, and Yoko. When I'm not on the trail, I paint. I love painting. To me, painting is a perfect world, a world that never changes, and if I were not so often desperate for money, I would never sell them. While the campaign at ORC ground slowly on into the fall, all of us waiting for Bogie to be cured of hepatitis, I covered the walls with my paintings of dolphins.

In the middle of the room was the couch, and there Sabine and I would lie together. Sabine Dietrich, a marvelous woman, stayed with me when she was in town. I had fallen in love, a dreamy falling without end. Wanting it never to end, I basked in the warmth of something wonderful from her, and I assumed she felt the same way, that it would go on forever. She was everything I wanted, I thought, someone to stick by me and believe in what I was doing. That's important to me because I'm always on the go. I never stop. Home is just a place where I pay the bills. I drop by, read the mail—I don't even unpack most of the time. There's always another dolphin in trouble, and like a fire horse, off I go to the next campaign. This is fun for a while, exciting. But one day comes the piper, and suddenly you get the feeling that you've done it all before.

Sabine worked in the fashion industry as a photographer's stylist, the one who puts the finishing touches on models. But she was more beautiful, I thought, than any of the models she worked on. It's an unreal world in a sense, a world of tableaux, perfect moments in time where everyone is young and beautiful. She works in Germany, Jamaica, South Africa, and, in this country, usually on South Miami Beach.

I was older than she, but that was not a problem. I don't believe in age. Or even time. Despite appearances, things are what they are, and they don't change, not really. If this sounds odd coming from me, an environmental activist always agitating to change the way we treat dolphins, realize that I'm merely trying to get dolphins out of amusement parks and back to the sea where they belong.

I had met Sabine some years before, long before Hurricane Andrew, when I was living at Casablanca. She came to the door, a beautiful girl with a cleft in her chin and cool, blue eyes, standing there with a confident smile and saying that she loved dolphins and wanted to do a video about me and the dolphins. She had read my book, *Behind the Dolphin Smile,* and though she didn't say so, I suspected that she had formed an attraction to the character in that book. That's happened before. People, especially women, expect me to be the same person I was then, an enchanted youth with the heart of a poet living in the water with dolphins. It's romantic. And though that character is true of how I used to be and, perhaps, how I still am in my heart, it's not exactly me anymore.

Sabine had a four-year-old daughter, Heidi, and no husband.

o   o   o

It was one of those days when nothing works right. I had tried to paint something—couldn't. I thought about calling Sabine, who was back home in Hamburg, Germany, but I had already called her once that day. I opened a book, read a few meaningless words and closed the book again. I asked myself, "What should I be doing now?" I knew of several dolphin problems that could use my attention, including one that loomed like a Stephen King horror movie. It was the leaky tank for Lolita, a killer whale at Miami Seaquarium. Part of the tank was off the ground and they had hung plastic covers around it but if you pushed them aside you could see the water running out. I had written several letters to authorities about the leak and impending disaster, to no avail. I tried to look afresh at our war with ORC, but the only thing that would help was a miracle cure for Bogie's hepatitis.

Disconsolate, I was about to throw myself into bed when the phone rang. Andrew Dickson, chief executive of the World Society for the Protection of Animals (WSPA, pronounced "Wis-pa"), called from London about a captive dolphin in Brazil named Flipper. He asked how much I would charge him for rehabilitating and releasing Flipper.

This is what I had been waiting for. Because of Sabine and Heidi, my thinking was now long range. For years I had been looking for a permanent place to bring captive dolphins for rehab and release. Why not Sugarloaf? One problem with the rehabs and releases up till now was that they cost too much. But a lot of that had been spent learning how to do it.

"I've given this some thought," I told Andrew. "And as you may know, when I worked on the Joe and Rosie release, I was paid $25,000 a year. I'll do the same for you on Flipper in Brazil for the same money, pro-rated."

I knew that WSPA had already brought in a number of "experts" who had no idea what to do for Flipper. What they needed was some straight talk. "And Andrew, this is not going to take a year. If it takes six months, WSPA pays only half of the $25,000. Four months, a third. And so on."

"Excellent!" he said.

I hung up the phone and did a back flip. This was it! My whole life was beginning over again. I called Sabine in Germany, told her that this was the beginning of something big, that she and Heidi should pack and meet me in São Paulo, Brazil, a city of more than seven million people. She said they would be there, and when I hung up, I took a deep breath and thought, "At last, things are going my way."

Before I could leave for Brazil, Andrew called and said he was thinking about signing up a consultant for me, Dr. Randall Wells, who was affiliated with Brookfield Zoo in Chicago and the Mote Marine Lab in Sarasota, Florida. "He's in the captivity industry, you know."

"I know. And I wouldn't mind at all," I said. "In fact, it's exactly what I've been looking for. At some point I've got to get with them. We're not as opposed as some people think. And Randy is perfect—hell of a nice guy!"

This was truly the moment I had been waiting for, when I could work on the same project with someone on the captivity side, someone who could see firsthand that all I'm trying to do is clean up the mess that they have made. They capture dolphins, they use them, and then they don't know what to do with them. They can't get rid of them, so they leave them in tanks. I want to return all captive dolphins to the wild, but those that have been used and left in tanks, those in particular I want to save. Someone's got to do it, and up till now I was the only one who would talk about the problem. With all the resources the captivity industry has, if they would only help me instead of fighting me, this job would almost do itself. Randy knew what my position was. We've talked about it. Yet they kept fighting me. And deep down I knew why. They were in denial. They had to keep fighting me because anything less would be an admission that they had been wrong.

I met Randy years before at the Scripps Institute of Oceanography in LaJolla, California. He was delivering a paper; I was there to meet two Chinese marine-biology students about my forthcoming trip to the Yangtze to help save the Chinese River Dolphin, the baiji. Randy, who has conducted a study of dolphins in the Sarasota–Tampa Bay area for years, told me he became interested in marine science by watching *Flipper* on television as a child. We went outside that day and sat on the grass and talked about our projects, including his plan to release Misha and Echo, two research dolphins at Long Marine Lab. I liked Randy immediately.

I ran into Randy one other time. It was at Ken Norris's Long Marine Lab in Santa Cruz, California, when I was representing the Mirage Hotel in Las Vegas. I had tried to get Norris to come to Las Vegas to see for himself what I was doing for captive dolphins that were en route to freedom, but he couldn't make it. It was Thanksgiving and he had plans with his family. "If you want to talk," he said, "you'll have to come here." I told this to Steve Wynn, who let me take his personal jet, and when I landed, a long black limousine was waiting for me. I rode out to Ken Norris's place, which was about a thirty-minute drive from the airport, and told him I wanted him to become a consultant for the halfway house I was planning, a place where I could let captive dolphins adapt to life at sea again. I explained that this was our effort to clean up the mess left by the captivity industry, that we were going first class all the way and that's why I was talking to him.

We talked for an hour, he charged me for the whole day, five hundred dollars, and told me one thing of interest, that when we built the dolphin tank, the sides should be sloped ten degrees off vertical. This would reduce the problem of noise pollution when dolphins used their sonar.

When Andrew told me about hiring Randy as a consultant for Flipper in Brazil, I called Randy at Mote Lab in Sarasota to welcome him aboard. He said he was looking forward to it, and so was his wife, Michelle, a dolphin trainer. He said he would check with the powers that be at Brookfield and Mote. And that was the last I heard from Randy. But Andrew called about a week later and said that Randy had pulled out.

"Pulled out?" I was stunned.

"Yes. But we'll manage. We'll simply go it alone."

"I can't believe this," I said. I felt like I had been kicked in the stomach. "Did he say why?"

"As a matter of fact he did. He said officials at the Chicago Zoological Society would not give their approval for him to go to Brazil to work with Ric O'Barry."

o   o   o

So I went alone, meeting Sabine and Heidi there later. Seeing Flipper for the first time was a shock. I had never seen a dolphin in worse condition. His eyes were swollen shut, his skin pale and bumpy. At the base of his left pectoral fin was an ugly discoloration, mushroom white. I tracked down the man who had captured Flipper, a fisherman named Tito, who told me he had dragged the dolphin into the boat by that fin, dislocating it. I watched Flipper using his fins very carefully, and though he never regained full use of his injured fin, he learned to compensate. He was living in what looked like a cesspool. It was fifteen feet deep, but the bottom three feet were pure sludge. This was part of a dying amusement park, virtually a ghost town, in Santos, a beach resort. The Frenchman who owned it lived in a condominium not far away and stood on his balcony every day, watching me through binoculars. Flipper had been captured in Brazilian waters before a law was passed banning native animals from being displayed this way, and he was the last captive dolphin in Brazil. For this reason, he attracted heavy media attention all over the country and in Europe as well.

My team included Marco Antonio Ciampi, WSPA Brazilian representative; Sabine; Richard Dickson, Andrew's son and an enthusiastic diver in his twenties; several scientific specialists from the University of São Paulo; and a number of volunteers. We tested Flipper's sonar with a hydrophone—nothing. But that was not surprising. Dolphins in captivity usually shut off their sonar when their life is as empty as Flipper's was.

My plan for rescuing Flipper was first to get him out of that cesspool they called a tank. Marco Antonio and I scouted for a place to take him, and the best we found was the very bay where he had originally been captured: Laguna, three hundred miles south. I checked with Andrew back in London and told him we should get a helicopter to move the dolphin. Roads were bad and if we tried to move him by truck, it could be fatal. Andrew asked how much a helicopter cost. I told him $2,000 an hour. He said to do what I had to do.

We needed to build a large pen at Laguna. I got Richard started making it, first driving pilings down into the sand across the mouth of the bay, then nailing a plastic fence from one piling to the next. The whole village was involved, providing Richard with all the volunteers he needed. I returned to where Flipper was, began cleaning the tank, working on Flipper's physical problems, arranging for the helicopter, and getting ready to carry the dolphin from the tank to where the helicopter would land. The closest the helicopter could get to the tank was about one hundred yards, so we would need a dolphin stretcher. Dolphins are transported all the time on large stretchers. These are about eight feet long, very sturdy, and with hand-holds for six men.

When I'm on the dolphin trail, I often have to make my own equipment. So I prowled around and found a couple of long aluminum poles and a pile of sail cloth in the back of a shed. A dolphin stretcher must have holes specially constructed for the pectoral fins, so I trained Flipper to swim up on a deck where some of my helpers had spread out the sail cloth. He swam up on it and I traced around him with a blue chalk, taking care to mark exactly where the pectoral fins were. We gave the pattern to a sailmaker, who made the stretcher for us.

Getting Flipper to the helicopter was only half the problem. We couldn't just put him on it and take off because dolphins out of water can be injured by sudden stressful gravitational forces. The noise and vibration of the helicopter are just as bad. You don't want a dolphin to panic during a helicopter ride. So I make every effort to keep the dolphin calm. We made a large transport box that would hold water, a box large enough for the dolphin and me too. When I transport dolphins like this, I get in the box with them to comfort them. We put a six-inch foam-rubber pad on the bottom of the box and had it ready where the helicopter would land. When it landed, we put the box inside the helicopter.

We also needed some water in the box—not much, just enough to cover the pad by an inch or two—and the best way was to get the local fire department to have their truck ready so that they could supply the water quickly. It was fresh water, yes, but this is not a problem for dolphins over brief periods. We also had a garbage can of crushed ice ready to cool the dolphin down with. Their normal body temperature is the same as ours, 98.6 degrees Fahrenheit, but when they're out of water, it rises, so we always have ice available. With everything in place—the helicopter, the box, the water, and the ice—only then did we capture the dolphin and put him in the stretcher. Six of us took hold of the stretcher and we walked him over to the helicopter, hoisted him up, and gently lowered him down into the box.

This was a big event in this small village, and a thousand people crowded around all along the way to watch and to be a part of it all. We landed a few hours later near the pen at Laguna and carried Flipper down to the sea again. It took three weeks to do all this.

o   o   o

When Flipper got back in the natural sea water, he began getting better every day. His skin, which had been cracked and bumpy, sloughed off, and the new skin underneath was like a baby's. His eyes cleared up. We tested with the hydrophone, and yes, he was using his sonar. His pen was next to the channel, which was used by a number of wild dolphin pods. He was swimming back and forth just for the fun of it, and the wild dolphins were coming up to his pen to see what was going on inside.

I reported to Andrew every week by phone, and toward the end he flew down from London to see for himself. We were at my tent pitched on the shore of the lagoon at Laguna watching Flipper chase down live fish. It was evening, a gorgeous Brazilian sunset of red and orange was beginning to light up the sky. Dairy cattle wandered freely everywhere and in the background were mountains. I was still in my tank suit, straw hat, and T-shirt; Andrew was in long white pants, sneakers, and a white shirt with sleeves rolled up. We sat and watched Sabine in a wet suit tossing live fish to Flipper, who was learning once again how to catch his own meals. Sabine was in the water up to her waist, tossing the live fish out of a small floating bucket, Heidi sitting on a nearby rock, watching. Sabine suddenly stuck her head into the water, then came up, pushing her blond hair back. She grinned and yelled up at us: "He's using his sonar. I can hear it!"

I gave her a thumbs-up sign.

"That's what it's all about, isn't it?" Andrew asked. "If he's using his sonar and catching fish, that means he's about ready for release, don't you think?"

"He gets better every day," I said. "Look at him go! I've got the banner ready—Andrew, you'll love it. It says, 'Good-bye, Flipper! Have a Great Life!' and it's signed WSPA. Then in Portuguese, it says, 'Seja Feliz! Laguna, Brasil!'"

"That's marvelous, Ric, simply marvelous."

"When Flipper takes off, it'll all be on video. Documented. The healing process and the method we used, all this documented for National Geographic TV. Remember what Flipper was like when we got here? All that's on video."

We watched as Flipper splashed the water vigorously. Some of this was showing off, like kids or frisky dogs. But in this case, Flipper was showing off not only for us but also for a pod of wild dolphins who had wandered into the area, curious about what was going on in the pen. "This makes a nice ending for you, doesn't it?" Andrew asked. "Returning Flipper to the sea again?"

"Yes, it's a wonderful ending," I said, "and I do love good endings."

I was walking on air. How lucky I was to have the confidence of the key man at WSPA. This campaign had been storybook in every way. "But it's not the end, Andrew. It's the beginning. There are a lot more captive dolphins out there. From here we go to Sugarloaf Dolphin Sanctuary in the Florida Keys and do the same for Bogie and Bacall. It's all planned. We're a team, Andrew, you and I, Sabine and Heidi. We're unstoppable!"

There was a long silence. Andrew was shaking his head. "I don't know about that, Ric. I'm afraid I've got a bit of bad news. This will be the final dolphin rehab and release project for WSPA."

Talk about bolts from the blue. I was completely taken aback. I sat upright. Could this be a joke of some kind? I stole a glance at Andrew. He was frowning, looking down. I knew it was not a joke. I ran my fingers through my hair. I started to say about five things at once. Nothing came out. Sabine was waving from the water and laughing. I waved back but I was dazed by what Andrew had said. "I don't get it, Andrew. This is working great. What's the problem? Money? We can talk about it."

"No, no, Ric. If it was up to me . . . but I got out-voted, you know. Simple as that."

"The veterinarians?"

He nodded. "Sorry, Ric, but they seem to think that what you're doing cannot be done."

Sabine was running in the surf, splashing water, Heidi right behind her. We watched for a moment. I felt like all my plans were going down the tube. "This is absolutely crazy," I said. I balled up my fists. "It's a cop-out. What *reason* do they give? No, don't tell me. I already know. Disease. That's what they say, isn't it? That it'll spread disease from captive dolphins to the wild."

This was not new. The captivity industry has used this pretext for years to stop the return of captive dolphins to the sea. "You could tell them that they're wrong, that it won't happen." I stopped for a minute. Why was I explaining this to Andrew? He already knew what I was saying. But I had to go on with it. "I'm more careful about this than they are. You know that. We take blood samples and cultures at every stage. We check and double-check. You could have told them that."

But what was the use? Contamination was not the problem. *I* was the problem. I was a threat to them, to their jobs, their homes and families, their very existence. They were opposed to me and everything I stood for. They thought that I was trying to return *all* captive dolphins to the sea again. But I was not. I wanted to return only those who would definitely make it. That's why I say that captive dolphins are *candidates* for release. Unless they're 100 percent healthy, they stay locked up unless we know for sure that they would make it in the wild. We don't just release them and forget about them. We track them until we're absolutely certain they've made it.

When you release a dolphin, you want everything to be as natural as possible. All along we're setting up a tracking team made up of people who live on the water, fishermen, and boat operators. We talk to them in person. We tell them what we're doing at every stage, especially about the freeze-brand we'll put on the dorsal fin when we release them. (The freeze brand is a painless method of marking the dolphin for future identification. We put the freeze brand in liquid nitrogen—320 degrees below zero—then we press it on the dolphin's dorsal fin for twenty-three seconds. He doesn't feel anything. In about ten days, the mark turns white.)

The fishermen and boat operators are not part of the dolphin's captive world, they're part of the sea, the habitat where the dolphins will live. If you tell the fishermen what's going on, they become part of it. They know the dolphins they see every day like they know their own children. Later, when we finally release the captive dolphin, when they spot him swimming, they report it to us and we record it. We record who spotted the dolphin, where and when, what direction he was headed and with how many companions. Most especially we're interested in any unusual behavior. If the dolphin is begging for food, for example, that doesn't mean failure. That means we have to keep people away. When the dolphin is first released, this is a very crucial time. He goes through a period of adjustment. He might even miss a meal. Up till now we've been feeding him regularly, all he wants. He's fat and sassy. Now he's having to feed himself. That's the main adjustment for the dolphin. And we must get out of his way and let it happen.

That's the whole point of rehab and release, to let this crucial moment happen. At first we get reports of his whereabouts every day. Sometimes several reports. We put it on a chart, trace his movements. He's here on the chart one day, there another. We see patterns. That means the dolphin is developing a life of his own. And after a while—if we leave him alone—he'll establish a new home range, a natural life in the wild again.

Using local fishermen to track the dolphin's movements might not seem like the most scientific method, but I think it's the most humane. We could put an electronic transmitter on him and monitor him every minute of the day. The Russians have done that. Randy Wells did it with Misha and Echo in Sarasota Bay, but in their case it worked for only a few hours. To put a transmitter on the dolphin, you drill a hole through the dorsal fin and bolt the transmitter on. At the dolphin's first chance, he swims straight to the bottom and tries to rub it off. The transmitter is designed to fall off after a time, but what about the ugly, painful hole that's still in his dorsal fin? No, I would never use that kind of equipment—not as it is now. It's better to use sightings by fishermen. We need people, and they want to help. Why not let them?

After a while sightings drop off. That's how it should be. If the dolphin has not been in trouble, has not been doing tricks at sea, or coming up to strange boats begging, then it is time to declare victory and move on. Just because we haven't had a report, it's not time to jump in a power boat and go looking for them. That's not tracking, that's stalking. We don't panic if the dolphin loses a little weight either. The dolphin returning to the wild will lose weight because he's having to hunt his own food. It's natural. He's not being fed the fatty fish he gets in captivity. Slim is healthy in a dolphin. All this I had explained already to Andrew.

"I know," he said, his voice gentle. "What can I tell you? I guess this is the World Society for the Protection of Animals—Except Captive Dolphins."

o   o   o

When Andrew returned to London, we prepared for the release of Flipper. The freeze-brand on his dorsal fin was the "world" symbol in the middle of the Brazilian flag. I wanted everybody in Laguna to be a part of the release. It sounds like the ending, but it's not. It's the beginning of a long process. At least a hundred people in the village came down to watch. Wearing a wet suit with fins and face plate, I held up a bolt cutter to the crowd and entered the water, then swam over to the fence and cut a big hole in it beneath the farewell sign, all documented on video. And then with Flipper at my side, we swam out. This took awhile because Flipper was confused and afraid of going through the hole. But finally, swimming next to me, he went out where the water was quite cold and swift. Then suddenly he was gone. We saw him later swimming with local dolphins. I left Dr. José Truda Palaza, one of Brazil's leading marine scientists, Dr. M. A. Carnaro, veterinarian, and Dr. Mario Rollo, marine scientist, in charge of tracking Flipper. I told them not to worry if Flipper lost a little weight. This was normal, I said, and it was also normal if he came up to people and begged. He's used to being fed by people and he's hungry. But he can do it himself.

o   o   o

We shook hands around, I kissed Sabine and hugged Heidi, and then we all split. Sabine had a photo shoot lined up in Hamburg, so she and Heidi flew home. I returned to Coconut Grove. I needed to recuperate. Early on in the project, I had slipped on the edge of Flipper's slimy tank and had broken two ribs on the left side. I had to keep going, though, and my ribs still weren't healed. In the middle of all this, I had caught a cold and every time I sneezed it was like a knife in my side.

Back home I was getting reports about Flipper every day from Marco Antonio. He was becoming concerned about Flipper coming in to the beaches and mingling with swimmers. We were not the only ones tracking Flipper. So was the media. As he swam south from beach to beach, playing and sometimes taking fish offered by swimmers and surfers, the media reported it. Our tracking team could virtually follow Flipper's journey south by simply reading the newspapers along the way, and by now, according to Marco Antonio, Flipper was at Guarda Beach, one hundred kilometers (sixty miles) south of where we had released him. I tried to reassure him on the phone that they could handle this, that this behavior would pass with time, but they insisted, so I flew back.

They met me at São Paulo. I got in a Jeep with Dr. Carnaro and Marco Antonio, and we drove to Gamboa Beach, where Flipper was last sighted. Up and down the beach we went with binoculars. "There he is," I said. I could see his dorsal fin with the distinctive freeze brand. We followed him, day by day, from beach to beach, telling swimmers and surfers and people in the media all along the way that this was completely natural, that Flipper is making the adjustment to a life at sea again, that if he loses a few pounds that's okay, that we should expect this when he's trying to establish his own range and live on his own. Our job, I said, is to respect this period of adjustment and help him by not feeding him or calling him to boats.

In news reporting, there's always the "other side," so a debate was raging in the media. The people who used to own Flipper wanted me to fail because now that Flipper was healthy again, they hoped to recapture him. IMATA and the Alliance of Marine Parks in the United States joined in denouncing the release. But the release was working. And the people of

Brazil seemed to understand what I was doing and that this was an important part of Flipper's rehabilitation.

Once more I returned to Coconut Grove, still trying to let my broken ribs heal. Forty-two days after Flipper's release, I got an urgent call from Brazil that Flipper was in trouble. Dr. Carnaro, our vet, called to report that he'd just seen Flipper. Dr. Carnaro was a dog-and-cat vet, doing the best he could with a species he wasn't familiar with. "I think he beached himself," he said. He's got these marks on his side, white marks. Like he's been scratched by rocks."

"Describe the marks," I said.

"Ric, I'm at the beach right now . . . at a pay phone. I'm squatting down in the sand, drawing a side view of a dolphin. Got it?"

"Yes, go on."

"I take the fingers of my hand and run them along his side."

"How long are they?"

"The marks? Six inches."

"Okay," I said, relieved. "That's good. He hasn't beached himself. Those are rake marks. This is okay. Nothing to get excited about. When dolphins play or fight, they grab each other with their mouths, and their teeth leave these marks. It means that Flipper may be establishing a relationship in a pod of dolphins—or trying to."

"You can be so sure thousands of miles away?"

"I could be a million miles away and it wouldn't matter. I've seen this before."

He said they still thought they needed me down there, so back I flew to Brazil, then down to Bombinhas Beach, about a hundred miles south of where we first released Flipper. It's a good surfer's beach, six foot waves. The beach was three hundred feet of golden sand up to the edge of the jungle where the landscape was littered with twenty-foot boulders. I stood on one of the boulders with binoculars and watched Flipper surfing the waves with people on boards all around. "Looks okay to me," I said. "But I'll go out and check him personally." I got on a surfboard and paddled out to where Flipper was. Other surfers were all around, I kept among them so that he wouldn't recognize me, and I was careful not to make eye contact. I got very close and confirmed that the marks on his side were, in fact, superficial rake marks. Otherwise, he was in excellent shape and showed no signs of weight loss. While I was there, he got bored, swam off, and began hunting for fish to eat. I stayed with the tracking team for a couple of weeks, then flew back home again.

o   o   o

Meanwhile, back at ORC, Lady died of a long-term liver problem. It was reported in the media and, while laid up waiting for my ribs to mend, I checked in with Sugarloaf to express my sympathy and to see how the Welcome Home Project was going. Trout, who now seemed to be in charge, said he had received a call from a woman in Argentina, a Mrs. Martha Gutierrez, who had called about a dolphin abandoned in the Buenos Aires Municipal Swimming Pool. Trout said she had heard about the Sugarloaf Dolphin Sanctuary and wanted to know if the dolphin could be sent there. I didn't know Mrs. Gutierrez personally, but she was part of the grassroots of the animal welfare industry. Without her and hundreds of others like her all around the globe, people who are not financially involved with animals but simply care about them, nothing could be done. I work with them all the time. They demonstrate with me, they write letters to the editor for me, they give money and, best of all, they know the right people in their communities and how to get things done. It's like an underground movement of people who dedicate their lives to doing the right thing by animals.

I called and discovered that this was Cheryl, a Russian dolphin, one of about a dozen that apparently had ended up in this part of South America. I had no money for the rescue, but maybe, I thought, WSPA, despite its position on dolphin releases, would help once more. I rang up Andrew in London and told him that I would go down and try to get Cheryl to a lagoon in Colombia if he could scrounge up some expense money.

"This is not a release," I told him. "This is a transfer. I merely want to move Cheryl from a dead-end swimming pool to a natural sea-pen off the coast of Colombia. I've heard of this place—the Rosario Islands—but I need to check it out personally. You're my *only* hope, Andrew."

"How much are we talking about?"

I had already talked to a travel agent about plane tickets and tried to figure the cost of housing, renting a boat in Colombia, and so on. "This is a guess," I said, "but if all goes well, $5,000 should do it."

"Five-thousand dollars?" he mused.

"We can make a difference, Andrew."

"Consider it done."

I talked to Lloyd and Trout about bringing Cheryl to Sugarloaf—that would have been much better than taking her to Colombia. In fact, Mrs. Gutierrez had managed to get a free flight for the dolphin to Miami. But Lloyd and Trout were not interested, so I let it drop.

I flew down to Colombia and found a spot for Cheryl—a beautiful lagoon on San Martin, Rosario Islands, just off the coast of Cartagena, Colombia—and got permission to bring her in, at least temporarily until I could figure out how to get her to the Black Sea. Then I flew to Buenos Aires and met Mrs. Gutierrez, a large gray-haired woman of enormous energy. Like most animal-welfare volunteers, she works from her kitchen table with more love than money, newspapers and clippings about animals everywhere in her small house.

She took me to see Cheryl. It was gruesome. Cheryl was one of the most beautiful dolphins I've ever seen, but she was struggling in a pool covered with some kind of white foam. Probably detergent. Dolphins eat about twenty pounds of fish a day. This means they produce lots of waste. The ordinary swimming pool filter system doesn't work. Someone probably tried to clean it with detergent and left this ungodly mess on top of the water. I thought she might be successfully returned to the sea again if we could work quickly with her, but I couldn't be sure. Every effort is made to return dolphins to the same waters they were captured in. But Cheryl, like most other Russian dolphins, was almost certainly captured in the Black Sea, and both the cost and logistics of returning her there were prohibitive. Even now I had run out of money.

We got custody of Cheryl. Mrs. Gutierrez picked out a local judge who was sympathetic to animal causes. He confiscated the dolphin and gave us custody. I was beginning to see a pattern here with all these captive Russian dolphins suddenly popping up everywhere. With the collapse of the U.S.S.R., hundreds of former military dolphins were now available. Their Russian owners were trying to sell or rent these dolphins around the world. Technically these dolphins were still owned by Russia and the Ukraine. Cheryl, I thought, was a civilian dolphin, probably illegally owned and smuggled out. Because she was young and strong, she had an excellent chance of making it in the wild again. Mrs. Gutierrez and I and some of her animal welfare friends in Argentina staged a campaign that resulted in laws prohibiting the importation of any more dolphins into the country.

I went to the pool just before I had to leave and shot a video of Cheryl, beautiful Cheryl, struggling to swim in that godforsaken scum. I said to her and to myself, "I'll be back, Cheryl. Hang on."

7

NO BURNING BUSHES NEEDED

In Israel, in order to be a realist,
you must believe in miracles.
—David Ben-Gurion

WHEN I RETURNED FROM Argentina I spoke with Mary Mosley about Joe Roberts. "He's already taken over the Bogie and Bacall project," she said. "He's put me down as an advisor in his organization, but I'm getting out of that. And I would suggest, Ric, that you get out, too."

I said that I needed to keep tabs on what was happening. I asked about things at Sugarloaf.

"No change," she said. "There's still Bogie's hepatitis. That's hanging on. And Lloyd has applied for permits to put up fences from the county and the Army Corps of Engineers. But it's a waiting game."

"If I were there would it speed things up?"

"Nothing can speed up bureaucracy."

"That's okay with me," I said. "I've got another campaign heating up overseas."

For days I had been talking with Robi (pronounced *Roe*-bee) Damelin, a tall woman with a crew-cut and a South African accent who runs an advertising agency in Tel Aviv. She and Benny Schlesenger, a Tel Aviv restaurateur and animal lover, got me involved in their campaign for Russian dolphins who were being abused at a nearby defunct dolphinarium. She is the head of Noah, as in Noah's Ark, the umbrella group of seventeen animal organizations in Israel. An aggressive, sometimes feisty woman, Robi called Benny and they checked out the dolphins, then in a shrill encounter with the Russians demanded that they abide by Israel's animal welfare laws. But the Russians got their backs up and refused even to listen.

When Robi and Benny decided they needed some heavy fire-power, Robi got on the phone and fax with high-profile animal-welfare/environmental organizations like International Wildlife Coalition, Greenpeace, World Wildlife Fund, and the Humane Society of the United States. A story by Reuters appearing in the *Jerusalem Times,* the national English-speaking newspaper, reported that she told these organizations and a dozen others about the plight of the dolphins, and nothing happened. Next on her list was the Dolphin Project. She faxed me the same information she had sent them and suddenly I was in Tel Aviv, popping videos in their VCRs to show them what I was about.

o   o   o

Six dolphins originally captured by Russians in the Black Sea had been exported to the Tel Aviv Dolphinarium, where for about four years they were a circus act. When that project went bust, both the dolphins and their Russian trainers—five men and one woman—were left high and dry. They hadn't been paid in months and their supplies were dwindling. There was no going back home. Mother Russia was in chaos, and they were stuck here in this land of turmoil, a land whose language they couldn't speak and which seemed to place little value on the one thing they could do. Their only hope was in Haim Slutzky, who owned Luna Park and who wanted to rent the dolphins and put them back to work. So the Russians figured, quite correctly, that anyone who threatened Slutzky's plan also threatened them.

That's exactly what we were doing because Slutzky's plan was barbaric. He had bought a steel water tank for the dolphins and was planning to put it under a roller coaster.

I arrived just before dawn at the Tel Aviv Airport. Benny met me, helped me with my bags, and hustled me into his combination van and pickup truck. It was the vehicle he used in his animal shelter work and it was covered with signs in Hebrew. "You won't believe your eyes," Benny said softly. He was smoking one cigarette after another and driving with hyperactive intensity. That time of day there was almost no traffic. "Or your nose either," he added.

"Pretty bad smell?"

"*Pretty* bad? No. Not pretty at all."

He didn't park at the entrance, but along the fence. I dug around in my bag for the video camera. "This may come in handy," I said.

He found a hole in the fence and we crawled through and crossed the grounds, which were littered with trash, then went inside where the dolphins were. His description of the place didn't even begin to tell what it was actually like. It was gloomy and wet, garbage everywhere, the air heavy and full of the smell of death. Something had definitely died here. I thought it might have been a dolphin or sea lion. Mixed with that smell was the odor of chlorine so strong it burned my eyes. The electricity had been cut off and a generator was grinding noisily. When we got to the show tank, I was not prepared for the sickening sight. The tank itself was only half full, the water filthy, and lying there on top like flotsam were the six dolphins, five of them together in a group, one off to the side all by himself. That one was Mark, and I knew with a glance that he was doomed. As the dolphins became aware of us, they opened their mouths, begging for food—all but Mark. I began shooting the scene with my video camera.

When Robi clashed with the Russian trainers at their first meeting, she and Benny sprang into action, Robi going to the media, Benny to his mobile phone. This is not a casual interest for either of them. A little earlier, Benny had gotten wind of a plan to round up stray dogs in Tel Aviv and ship them off to the Philippines where the Filipinos would have them for dinner—not as guests, as

Benny might have done, but as the main course. In the Philippines, dogs are considered delicacies. Fifty dogs were involved, and this was to be only the first of many roundups. When Benny called government officials, he got the bureaucratic brush-off. Shipping stray dogs to a foreign country was not in itself against Israeli law, they said. So Benny hired an attorney who dug up an old law from British days about mistreatment of animals and squashed the plan.

When he and Robi first saw how the Russian dolphins were being treated, Benny protested to the Minister of the Environment, who appeared sympathetic, according to Benny, but his hands were tied. "What law are they in violation of?" he asked Benny. "You've got to be specific. You say that they are mistreating the dolphins, but how do you know? You're not an expert, are you? You need an expert. And besides, what's wrong with a dolphin in a dolphinarium?"

Benny figured that if they wanted an expert, he would get an expert. That's when Robi sent me her fax about captive Russian dolphins in Israel. I was intrigued by the Russian connection. First Cheryl, now this. Coincidence? I was beginning to realize that Russian dolphins were in trouble everywhere.

After Benny and I had snuck in and got video footage of the Russian dolphins in the Tel Aviv Dolphinarium, Robi took copies of it around to the TV stations, and they ate it up. For several days that was the big news in Israel. TV and newspaper reporters interviewed us, the Russian trainers, and government officials on several levels.

o   o   o

The next day, Benny got an interview with the Minister of the Environment, Yossi Sarid, a short, balding man in his sixties who smiled and peered at me through round glasses. He smiled when we shook hands, then leaned back in his chair comfortably and said in English with a thick Hebrew accent that he had seen the video. "Very impressive," he said, then offered to watch it again if we wanted him to. We did, and then, with his permission, I showed him the video Sabine and I had made of Flipper's release in Brazil. "This shows not only the problem," I said, "but the solution." Then I said that what I had seen at the dolphinarium would be against the law anywhere on earth.

He agreed that something should be done, but in Israel, like most places in the West, it's quite legal to keep dolphins in captivity. "It's a business," he said. "You know, free enterprise." Then he smiled with a touch of irony and gave a little shrug, waving his hands, palms up.

I'm not given to public speaking ordinarily—maybe I'm shy—but something quite strange comes over me at times, and I stood up and said, "A business? Yes, it's a business. And so was slavery. That doesn't mean it's right, though, does it?" I took a few steps—but not many; it was a tiny office. His office is in downtown Jerusalem, but not in the ancient city. It's a two-story building on grounds the size of a football field. The building is surrounded by several layers of razor wire, coils of it all around, and it's patrolled by armed guards with German shepherds. Because of recent death threats to Minister Sarid by Israeli right-wing extremists, we were searched when we entered and everything we had with us was closely inspected. Hovering around Yossi Sarid were two soldiers in civilian garb holding Uzi machine guns and trying to look inconspicuous.

"My job is not about right or wrong," Minister Sarid said, "it's about following the law. And the law is quite clear in allowing these people to operate. That's what I meant when I said it's a business. Unless I can show that they are not following the law, my hands are tied. What I need, Mr. O'Barry, is evidence that they are breaking the law." He smacked his hand down on his desk for emphasis and said, "Scientific evidence."

I had sat down while he was speaking, but I stood up again at this point. I once wanted to be a marine scientist, but that was long ago. Now, to my sorrow, I realized that scientists are like lawyers and you can buy whatever scientific evidence you want. It's not that they're liars, it's that they're very clever at customizing their findings to the needs of whoever is funding the research.

When we first entered the building, I saw a huge mural on the wall depicting a scene from the Holocaust. That nightmarish specter is always with the Jews. I blurted out, "We're missing the point! This is not about science; this is about ethics! Show me *scientifically*, Mr. Sarid, where it's abusive to stack a dozen Jews on a shelf meant for one like they did at Auschwitz and

I assure you, sir, that I could find a scientific authority who would say that there is no compelling scientific reason to find that this is abusive."

I was jabbing my fingers into the air. "Please do not misunderstand me. In no way am I suggesting that the plight of these half dozen Russian dolphins compares with the Jews of the Holocaust, but I assure you, sir, that I am not merely talking about a half dozen dolphins." I was leaning toward him and speaking softly but very clearly. "I'm also talking about 200,000 Israeli children every year who will go through that facility and be told that what is being done to these captive dolphins is okay. You don't need a burning bush to tell you that it's wrong, Mr. Minister. You know it's wrong. "

Minister Sarid had heard enough. He called in his secretary and dictated a letter giving me the authority to inspect the dolphinarium. A few minutes later, the secretary came in with the letter, he signed it and said that he would do whatever he could to alleviate problems at the dolphinarium.

o   o   o

In high spirits, Robi, Benny, and I drove back to the dolphinarium. I walked in waving the paper that gave me the right to check their facility. The Russians met us at the entrance en masse, their backs up, their faces hard. A small immigrant Russian Jew wearing a black leather jacket acted as interpreter, even though the Russians understood enough English to know what I was saying. Nevertheless, the big Russian named André never looked at me even when he was speaking to me. He focused on the little interpreter.

"Tell him," I said, "that this paper gives me the authority to check the whole facility." I needed to check the fish house. That's the key to how well these dolphins were being treated. I could tell in a minute whether it was okay or not. Already, I could see that they had put in some long, hard hours cleaning up since I had first seen this place. The grounds around the dolphinarium were as filthy as before, but inside it was immaculate. They had drained the pool and replaced it with clean water—though the odor had not changed. The air was still heavy with the stench of something dead and the acrid sting of chlorine. The dolphins were still the way they were the other day, five of them floating lethargically in a group, one of them, Mark, off to himself.

The interpreter relayed my message, then he and Andre talked back and forth in Russian, and the interpreter said, "He says to tell you that he knows who you are, that it could even be said that you inspired him to become a dolphin trainer. But he also says that he sees no point in this, that it ought to be obvious to you that these dolphins are well cared for and that with your background in marine mammals, you ought to know also that these are very happy animals."

I hate it when someone tries to con me about dolphins. Through clenched teeth, I asked, "Does he know why I'm here? Does he know that I was here the other day with a video camera, that I know what it was like here then and that so does all of Israel—"

"He knows all that," the interpreter said, waving his hands.

"Then tell him that I *know* these dolphins. I can read their body language. I know a sick dolphin when I see one, and I say to him—you *tell* him this—that that dolphin there," I pointed at Mark, "is practically *dead in the water*." I don't know what it is that makes me sound like a professional wrestler at times like this, but now to my amazement I was shouting in a hoarse voice and gesturing broadly. "And by God," I said at the top of my voice, "tell him that this place is a *disgrace* and I want to see the damned fish house—*now!*"

Even before I finished speaking, the ridges in André's muscular face hardened and his eyes glistened with hate. Two of the Russians had the same first name, André, and I had been told that one of them was a former KGB agent and a black-belt in karate. Now I knew which one it was. He was wearing a bulging T-shirt with CCCP on it and beneath that the Russian hammer and sickle. I've had a few lessons in karate myself (I'm a white belt), and I recognized from my training that he had assumed a stance from which he could have decked me with either foot and either hand.

I stepped back, bumping into Benny. Maybe it was the sudden danger or something about the way these Russians always went around like this, like a pod, the group forming a semicircular backdrop for one of their members, that set off a bell in my head. Could these guys have been dolphin trainers in the Russian Navy and were these the dolphins they had trained for military service? Since the late 1950s, both Russia and the United States had captured dolphins and trained them to do a variety of things, such as guard naval installations, retrieve things lost at sea (like dummy warheads on practice missiles), attach transmitters to enemy submarines for tracking, kill enemy divers with the "swimmer nullification system" (a device placed on the dolphin's snout that could inject a spear or a 45-caliber bullet), or blow themselves and enemy targets to smithereens with a bomb strapped to their backs.

As the *Jerusalem Times* reported, these were indeed Russian dolphins of war, and the two Russian trainers named André (André Abramov, thirty-four, and André Kolganov, thirty-three) had trained them for military service. The others were circus trainers. When the U.S.S.R. folded, Russians scattered to the winds with dolphins for hire. I later learned that about one hundred of their dolphins had been taken to Chile, Malta, Vietnam, Hungary, Argentina, and Israel.

Though I was spoiling for a fight, I could find nothing wrong with their fish house. I opened several boxes of frozen fish. All of them were fresh. "All right," I said through the interpreter, "now I want to watch the dolphins being fed."

That's the other key to checking dolphins. Sick dolphins do not eat. And I knew that at least one of these dolphins, Mark, would not eat. But even before my message was translated, André folded his thick arms on his chest and spat out, "Nyet!"

I stormed and fumed and waved my letter of authority, but in the end it did no good. He insisted on using Slutzky's own vet to check the dolphins and I insisted on using mine. So we agreed to call in an outsider, settling finally on Dr. Manual Hartman of the Pieterburen Seal Hospital in Holland. We flew him in, he tested the dolphins and declared that Mark and two others were suffering from stress in the form of stomach ulcers and skin problems.

Soon after that, Mark died. And in the dark of night the Russians packed up the other two sick ones and sent them back to Russia.

Now there were only three.

∘   ∘   ∘

Benny and I pulled up chairs to Robi's desk to lay plans for the next step. She has a two-room office in an old building on Mapu Street, a block off the main drag in Tel Aviv. Robi uses the small room, the larger one is where the secretaries work and models and photographers wait. Pictures of models were on the wall, and piled up here and there were clippings from newspapers and magazines, products to be promoted, and various promotional stuff.

Benny and Robi didn't want me to leave. They wanted me to stick around in case something else came up. But that would take time. I needed to see Andrew Dickson and do something about Cheryl.

"The problem now," I said, "is that steel tank. We've got to keep Slutzky from putting the dolphins in it. I know what a steel tank does to dolphins." "I've seen it and it's horrible."

Any tank is bad for a dolphin, but a steel tank is the worst of all, reverberating like a bell with every passing truck, with every breeze or sneeze. In the sun, it becomes a boiler, no place to hide, nothing to do. The dolphins float on top in the sun, their skin blisters and soon, perhaps mercifully, they die.

"You're thinking of Flipper?" Benny asked with sympathy. "The one who died in your arms?"

"Actually it was Kathy," I said. Suddenly I felt exhausted. I was so tired I felt weak. I swallowed hard and said, "Yes. I'm always thinking of her. To me, every captive dolphin is Kathy."

"No way will we let Slutzky put those three dolphins in that steel tank," Benny said. "I know where he got it. It's a recycled water tank. He got it from a dolphinarium at Haifa. And I know something else. That is a death tank. It has a history of killing dolphins."

"I know what we can do," Robi said. "Lawsuit. This is wrong, what he's trying to do, and we can stop him in the courts."

"Good," I said, standing up. "That's what I like to hear." I walked around the office briskly, rubbing my hands together. "You don't need me for that. Yossi says he'll do what he can. I think he will. And that means I can get on with the project at Sugarloaf." I was also thinking of Cheryl in that filthy municipal swimming pool in Argentina, trying to swim in that foamy scum on top of the water. And I wanted to see Andrew again in London, to set up a press conference about all these Russian dolphins of war being transported around the world. It was almost Christmas and I was tired of Israel. I was tired of everything. Bone tired. I had been on the trail too long. Most of all I wanted to see Sabine again. But Andrew said he would set up the press conference. So I flew to London, where Andrew said everything was ready. They already knew about the problem, he said. In fact, Chris Stroud of the Whale and Dolphin Conservation Society had been researching it for a while. At the press conference, we put our heads together and issued a press release to the media deploring what had happened.

o   o   o

When I returned home near the end of January, Robi called again and said that the Russian dolphins were still in trouble. There were only the three dolphins now, but nothing was happening, she said, and nothing would happen unless we could put the pressure on one final time.

"We've been through this," I said. "What about the lawsuit?"

"That didn't work."

"Didn't work? What do you mean it didn't work?"

She took a long breath. "The law is simply not on our side."

"Then what can I do about it? I've done everything I can think of."

"Have you thought about a hunger strike?" Robi asked.

"A hunger strike? No, not really." I had been on a hunger strike once before and, yes, it worked, but I had told myself I would never do it again.

"Well, think about it. A hunger strike will work, Ric. It might be our last shot."

"A hunger strike . . . I don't know." I hated the idea. "What does Benny say?"

Suddenly Benny was on the phone. "Yes, Ric, I'm here, and I do agree with Robi. You may not realize it, but we've got hunger strikes going on over here all the time. And for a very good reason. Sometimes it's the only way to get their attention."

There are no guarantees in this business, but I knew Robi and Benny well enough to know that they were almost certainly right. "I really don't want to do this, but I will. You'll be in it with me?" I asked Benny.

"If you want me to, sure." He said that he had frequent flier miles available and would use them for a ticket in my name.

"Beginning now," I said. "No more food, Benny."

"My lips are sealed."

We talked on the phone about where it should be staged, whether in Jerusalem in front of the Minister of the Environment's office, at the Tel Aviv Dolphinarium where the Russians and their dolphins were, or at Luna Park where Slutzky was trying to bring the dolphins. Benny opted for Luna Park because of the traffic. I told them to get the tents ready.

I had just got word about a lagoon in Fiji that might be available as a dolphin sanctuary. Tony Robbins, the motivational guru, owned Namali, a resort, and his agent in San Diego mailed me a couple of tickets to check it out as a possible dolphin sanctuary. I planned to take Lincoln, who was helping me more and more in these projects. I didn't see the place in Fiji as a halfway house. I would not have released Atlantic dolphins or Black Sea dolphins in the Pacific. Until further research is conducted, it's considered too genetically risky. But it might have worked as a place for retired dolphins like those now at the Hagenbeck Zoo in Hamburg, Germany, or others languishing at the Antwerp Zoo in Belgium. With our protests, we were able to close the dolphin show in Hamburg. And now I was committed to a hunger strike in Israel. I called Trout at Sugarloaf and asked if he wanted to go in my place. Though he and Lynne had been planning a vacation at St. Thomas in the Virgin Islands, Trout jumped at the opportunity to visit the luxury resort in my stead.

o   o   o

I was one day into my hunger strike when Bubba Jones dropped by on his bike. A native of these lands who lives on a twenty-seven-foot sloop, the *Hallelujah!*, in the Coconut Grove anchorage, Bubba sometimes holds my coat while I'm campaigning. He brought his bike inside with him, and I told him what I was doing.

"You're *what?*" Bubba was easily shocked by anything a little odd. "Did you say '*hunger* strike?'"

"Affirmative."

"Pardon me for being negative, but I don't like the sound of that."

"What don't you like about it?"

He looked at me for a long moment, puzzled. "I don't like the idea. To me it's crazy. Why don't you put a gun to your head. Same thing. It's unnatural—that's what I don't like about it."

"Is that it?"

"Not quite. I also think it's *wrong*. And worse than that, it's infantile and stupid."

Under my breath, I said, "Except for that, how do you like it?"

"What?" he said sharply. "Don't mumble."

"Nothing." I shook my head. He would never understand, but I tried anyway. "Look, Bubba, do you think I *want* to go on a hunger strike?"

He gave me a long, expressionless look, then, with a sad shake of his head, said, "Sometimes I wonder about you, boy."

"It's not like I've got options. I've *got* to do this. It's—"

"No! You listen to me, for a change." He was bent forward, his small eyes narrowed into slits and his mouth puckered up. "Listen, now, because this is serious. Doing a hunger strike in Israel is *crap!*"

I was sipping on a bottle of natural spring water. I took a long, thoughtful sip. Then I said, "But in Israel that's how things get done."

He shook his head solemnly. "Then why go there?" He got up suddenly and went over to his bike. He stopped, shut his eyes, and held up his hands, waving them slightly. "No. I don't want to hear anything more about it. That's it." He opened the door, pushing his bike out in front of him. I went out with him, he swung one long leg over the bike and got on. "Okay, then. You want to know what I would do in this situation?"

"Not really."

"Here it is anyway. Don't go. That's my advice. And don't do a hunger strike. Nobody understands stuff like that." He screwed up his face in distaste.

"Well, I would agree except for one thing."

"Yeah?"

"You don't understand the situation."

Bubba looked at me for a long moment, pushed off, and peddled away down the street.

Two days later, I was almost ready to leave. I had eaten nothing and I was weak. The first few days of a hunger strike are the toughest. Your stomach has a mind of its own and when you don't eat on time, it worries. If you can get through those first two or three days, you can go on and on. I felt like I had hit a wall of hunger.

∘   ∘   ∘

That's when Sabine came to town. She came over to the house and I told her about the hunger strike. She didn't like the idea. But that wasn't the big problem. Something else had happened. I could feel it. I tried to get us in one of our patterns. I always have something on the easel when she's in town, so I started painting. She was tired—it had been a long trip—so she lay down on the couch by herself. I glanced back and thought she had fallen asleep. I went to the linen closet and got a light sheet, spread it over her, then I started to go back to the painting. She stirred and opened her pale blue eyes. "We'll have to get some flowers for your room," I said. She loved sunflowers. When she was in town, she stayed at the hotel with the rest of the photography team, and I always brought her a bunch of sunflowers or roses.

I lay down next to her and ran the back of my hand lightly along the lines of her face. How beautiful she was. When we lay on the couch together, all the peace in the world descended into my heart. Everything stopped. The whole world, including myself. I was still. I held her closely, wanting this moment to last forever. It was not really sexual, it was beyond that. I felt at home with her, and though I didn't realize it then, looking back, I think that I saw in Sabine a way to live another time of my life over again.

"Richard," she said quietly. "Something I must tell you."

"Yes?"

"I have a roommate."

Even though a part of me had seen it coming, I was stunned. There was a silence and I don't remember what happened next. Then when I tuned in, she was still talking, saying that it was someone she worked with, someone she'd known for years. When her photography job was done, she usually spent a week or two with me. This time, she said, she wouldn't do that; she would move in with him.

I walked around the little house aimlessly, going to the kitchen window and staring out. Then I turned around and started to say something but choked. I opened the front door and looked out. It's a busy street. Cars use it as a shortcut from Bird Avenue to Tigertail. In fact Yoko had been hit by a car on that very road recently, her left front leg still in a cast, and she hobbled around as if on stilts. I looked out on this busy street and saw nothing. I went to the refrigerator, opened the door and gazed in. Lincoln had left a large slice of pizza. Olive and mushroom. Here I was on a hunger strike, staring at a slice of cold pizza. I shut the door and said under my breath. "Damn! At a time like this."

From the other room: "What? What did you say?"

I swallowed hard. "Nothing," I said, grinning foolishly and walking in. "I mean that . . . well, just when I need you the most!"

"Richard, listen to me. You shouldn't be on a hunger strike in the first place."

"But I'm on one."

"And?"

"And you're not helping."

"So this is *my* fault? Do you want me to *lie* to you?"

I bit my lip. I couldn't think of anything to say—I felt betrayed. I said, "Want to go to Janjos for pizza?" That was our favorite place.

"Yes," she said brightly, hopping up. "But you're on a hunger strike."

"I won't eat anything. I can't eat anything anyway." I faked a smile. "I'll watch you eat."

My car was in the shop again, so I called a cab. I tried to think of something we could talk about till the cab came but nothing came to mind. I didn't think she would want to hear about the dolphins of Tel Aviv again. And when the cab came I walked out with her and opened the door, she got in, and then I leaned down and said, my voice choking, "I'm sorry, Sabine, but I . . . I cannot go."

"Okay," she said.

"I love you, Sabine," I said softly. "I've always loved you."

"I know, Richard. We'll be in touch. Always friends, okay?" She reached out to touch me but at the last moment drew back her hand.

As the cab disappeared down the street, I was thinking that my whole life was changing, that I would never eat again. I hated food. I hated life. I hated everything, especially myself and how old I had become. I went inside and for the first time in years, I really looked at myself in a mirror. Was I really this gray? Someone had told me I was developing a bald spot. I twisted around, trying to see it, and a crazy idea popped into my head, that if Robi and Benny had suggested instead of a hunger strike that I crucify myself on that road by Luna Park, I might have done it. Would I ever find a woman who could live with me?

∘   ∘   ∘

It was day eight of the hunger strike and had been raining almost all week. Lying on an Army cot in a small, cheap, leaky yellow pup tent at the edge of an amusement park in Tel Aviv, I was chilled to the bone. I hadn't eaten since two days before I arrived here and already I no longer even cared about food.

Benny was in another pup tent like mine and the two were joined with a piece of plastic between them that was supposed to keep out rain. But it didn't, and there was a steady drip from half a dozen places onto the ground. The ground used to be yellow clay, but now it was yellow mud and the mud was on everything and all over me, in my eyes and in my mouth. I felt grimy. I hadn't shaved since the hunger strike began and I looked like a homeless person.

The tents were on the side of the Rokah Highway, a four-lane asphalt road across from Luna Park. People whizzed by in their cars between Jericho and Haifa. They all knew us. We were on the TV news and in the newspapers every day. In front of our tents were flags, both Israeli and American, streamers and signs in English and Hebrew saying that our hunger strike was for the captive dolphins and to honk if they love dolphins. So there was a lot of honking all the time, and when they saw us, they waved like old friends. "Free the Dolphins," the signs said, and "Import Vodka, Not Dolphins."

The two tents were joined, but they could also be separated with a zipper, and that's how I kept it most of the time because Benny and I are an odd couple—complete opposites. He's a chain smoker, for instance, sometimes with two cigarettes going at the same time, and I hate breathing smoke. Especially during a hunger strike. I had to keep the smoke out because it was making me sick to my stomach. I wasn't feeling very good anyway. In fact, I had the feeling that something bad was about to happen and I had to be prepared.

Benny, a short, middle-aged bachelor with black, short-cropped hair, is very social and outgoing, his tent was usually teeming with people, all of whom were also chain smokers. Since they spoke only Hebrew, which I don't understand, it would have been impossible for me to be a part of things, and early on I told Benny that I'm a very private person, that I would talk to people as a part of the campaign, of course, but I needed to conserve my strength and I wasn't here to socialize. Also, I didn't explain it to Benny, but my heart had recently been broken. So most of the time, while he had a crowd of people in his tent, all smoking and laughing and talking in Hebrew, I was huddled up under the covers against the cold in my adjoining tent thinking my own thoughts, mostly of Sabine and what I might have done wrong.

When his tent wasn't swarming with people, Benny was talking on his mobile phone, sometimes to Sabine, who was back home in Germany. I had given her Benny's number, and she would call Benny and he would try to get me to talk to her but most of the time I didn't want to.

Tel Aviv, the largest city in Israel, has a population of about a third of a million, and Benny seemed to know them all. Of the seventeen animal organizations in Israel that we were representing, the largest by far was Benny's "Let the Animals Live." With seven hundred members in his organization, he is the key to getting anything at all done for animals in Tel Aviv. Benny was born in Israel of German parents and runs a café/coffee-shop, the Nor Dau, noted throughout the land for welcoming patrons with their pets. He feeds them both, giving the pets, usually dogs, a selection of things to eat in their own dishes. The first time I saw this I couldn't believe my eyes—a sidewalk café with dogs all over the place! "Benny," I said. "How can you do this?"

In his velvety voice and heavy accent, Benny smiled and said simply, "I love animals."

"I know, but this is a restaurant. A sidewalk restaurant, but a restaurant nevertheless. What about the department of sanitation?"

"What about it?" he said with a shrug. "They care, but they don't really care. You know what I mean, don't you? Israel has so many problems, Ric. . . ." He shrugged. "Or should I say that it has one really *big* problem." He gestured around at several dogs with their owners in his café. "But look! Is this a good idea or what?"

°   °   °

I would have been content to lie in the dark and let happen whatever might happen, but Benny needed a light on day and night. He had a bare lightbulb burning in the middle of his tent all the time, and at night he had several lights burning outside, which made us look like a roadside stand. So the generator, much bigger than it needed to be, roared all the time, the noise and fumes of it making me nauseous. He yelled over at me once and asked if I was cold. I was all bundled up, shivering, and I thought it ought to be obvious. Then I realized that he was just trying to be sociable and that something was making me crankier than usual. "Yes, Benny," I said. "I've got a chill. I didn't know it got like this over here in January. And I must have packed the wrong clothes." Something ran across my face. I thought it was a bug and I flipped it off, but it was just a drop of water. "This is also the wettest tent I've ever been in. I'm very cold. My teeth haven't stopped chattering all day." Then I added sarcastically, "But I'm doing just fine."

"That's good. And not to worry. I've got an idea," he said brightly. Then he struggled to hook up a heater in my tent with the generator, but it never worked.

Trout and Lincoln called from Fiji. They had seen a story in the paper there about my hunger strike and Lincoln was worried about me. I assured him I was okay.

"Maybe I should be there with you," he said.

"I'll be okay," I said. "What about Fiji? What's it like?"

"Beautiful," Lincoln said.

"Will it work?"

"It works for them," Lincoln said. "They want dolphins, but . . . "

"But it's not for us?" After my experience in Las Vegas, I was leery of these types.

"They want the dolphins, but they're not really committed."

I felt a little dizzy. I was lying on the cot listlessly, no desire for food or anything else. I signaled Benny for the phone, he nodded, hung up a few minutes later, and passed it over to me and I called Lloyd to check in again at Sugarloaf. Most of the times I called, they were waiting for approval to do things or waiting for inspections. But finally something had happened. Lloyd said they had formed a nonprofit corporation. On the board of directors were he and Trout, two others, and me. Lloyd was director of the sanctuary, Trout was in charge of husbandry, I of rehabilitation and release. Even over the phone, I could sense that Lloyd and Trout had become very close.

o   o   o

We got lots of publicity every day all over Israel and in Europe, but as the hunger strike dragged on day by day, I watched Benny out of the corner of my eye and marveled at how much better he was doing than I. He looked great. Could he have been snacking? People offered me food all the time but I always refused. One woman in particular, a kindly middle-aged woman in an Israeli Army uniform, interviewed me on a tape recorder almost every day, and each time she tried to sneak chocolate bars to me. I wanted to explain to her about hunger strikes, but it's not something you explain. Either you know about it or you don't. To me it was obvious that if you're on a hunger strike, you ought to look the part. I was beginning to look like someone you didn't even want to come close to. It was like I was dying. When I moved, day by day, I moved more slowly and deliberately, as if I were doing T'ai Chi.

There's no faking a hunger strike. Maybe once you could fake it, but not now. In the hospital they check your blood and can tell more about you than you know yourself. But the public doesn't go for medical reports. The public likes to see it with their own eyes. Day by day, they follow it like a soap opera, your body locked in a death grip with your will. They want to see you losing weight, losing first the baby fat and pudgy stuff that's part of the soft life we live. Now we're getting down to business, they say to themselves. Next you lose the sparkle in your eye. And now it's getting serious. Your speech is slowed, somewhat disoriented. Later, virtually cadaverish, you're reduced to skin and bones, the skin shiny like slick paper, and the bones, now protruding, thin and brittle. Life itself is ebbing away. And this death-camp look scares people, especially in Israel. Your clothes hang on you like on a scarecrow. Your hollow eyes have a vacant look. Your voice is weak, so whispery that people must lean in very close to hear. If you can show signs of vitamin deficiency, hair loss, for instance, or boils, that's the best of all. But you know this with certainty only when people look at you and draw back with a gasp. All this is but prologue to the final touch, the moment when suddenly you fall in your tracks. Someone is always watching, so they rush to your side, they call the ambulance, and off you go on a stretcher to the hospital so that you won't die and embarrass everybody. That's how a hunger strike should go.

Later, when the hunger strike was over, I was told that professional hunger strikers boil vegetables in water and drink the water. You lose weight but you keep your health up. I didn't know about that then, and neither did Benny. But I don't think Benny needed to. Every day, he took off in his truck for his restaurant—on business, he said. He came back shaved, showered, wearing fresh new clothes and bursting with energy. So what kind of a hunger strike was this? At forty-four he was younger than I by almost ten years, but I'm in good shape and my resolve, which has always been borderline fanatical, is as firm as ever. After more than a week of sipping only water, I was getting weaker by the moment, fading in and out.

The hunger strike climaxed just the way I thought it might. About eight o'clock on the night of the ninth day, I was dizzy. I couldn't sleep. I hadn't been able to sleep the whole time I was there, but this night was the worst of all. My stomach was burning. I stood up to get a cup of water and simply keeled over in the mud. Next thing I knew I was on a stretcher, strapped down and being put into the ambulance. Benny was there and so was his tentful of friends. I was seeing strange lights, and it seemed to me that I had a choice between living and dying. I was seriously considering my options when I blacked out again.

The next thing I remember was seeing a doctor in the Ichilov Hospital speaking very clearly into my face. "You must eat or you will die," he said. I began to ponder the life-and-death thing again when Benny, who was finally beginning to show the effects of his hunger strike, urged me to eat something. "Thank God you're okay," he said. "You had me worried, Ric. I think we ought to declare victory and get the hell out of this. They're not going to admit you to the hospital if you refuse to eat. And it's crazy to go on." Before I could say anything, his mobile phone rang and he went off into a quiet corner to talk.

They had already given me several bottles of intravenous fluid, and the young doctor came by, took my wrist, and counted my pulse. He wrote something on a chart and then said, "These dolphins, are they worth dying for?"

The whole time we were in the tents, we knew that the Israeli government had planted a spy among us. Not that he tried to hide it. He openly spied on us. He listened in on phone conversations and wrote things down in his notepad. We had a visitors' list where well-wishers came through and signed in, he kept track of them all and the words of encouragement they wrote next to their names. But we didn't object. We knew that the government had to know if we were serious or not. And because we were serious, because many influential people had joined our cause, including Yael Dayan, daughter of Moshe Dayan and herself a member of the Parliament, Minister Sarid kept a running negotiation with Benny via mobile phone.

Suddenly Benny broke through the crowd of people in the dolphin movement hovering around me on the hospital bed. He was grinning and holding his mobile phone up like a trophy. "We've won!" he said. "We've won!"

All eyes turned to me. And I stared dully at Benny.

"We can't get custody," Benny said, "but I think we knew that all along. Those are still Russian dolphins. There's no way to fight them on that. But Yossi says—listen to this, Ric—Yossi says they'll never import another dolphin into Israel. Never! And we have his word on it."

Everybody cheered, but they were looking at me to see if I would agree. I lay there for a long moment. This was not really a success, but it was as good as we could get for now, and I was out of gas. I don't think I could have gone on even if I'd wanted to. So I said okay. We all went back to the tents, somebody got my stuff for me, and they checked me in at a hotel. At last, I thought, a real bed. I cleaned myself up, soaking for a long time in the tub. Several people were with me and somebody said we ought to have a victory party. Benny, who had been waiting for this moment, invited everybody to his restaurant, and they all showed up, including Yael Dayan. I was still very weak and got there late, but when I walked in, they stood up and cheered. Benny came over, we shook hands. Yael Dayan hugged us both. They gave me some fruit. I looked at the banana, turned it over. It was not a Chiquita banana—the brand owned by George Lindner, who also owned ORC—so I ate it. I took a bite of the apple but couldn't eat the rest. I was still weak. I needed sleep. When they got me back to the hotel, I went to bed, and all night I kept thinking that I no longer needed food or sleep or anything else.

8

IN BED WITH AN ELEPHANT

Avoid, as you would the plague,
a clergyman who is also a man of business.
— St. Jerome

I RETURNED HOME, DRAINED. Doing a hunger strike is physically and emotionally devastating. I didn't think to weigh myself before and after because I never have a weight problem, but I must have lost a few pounds. Worse than that, I had lost my taste for food. Didn't seem to need it. I was listless. No energy. Weak. Couldn't sleep. Couldn't think. I had the shakes too. I stretched out on the bed, spread-eagled, and was staring at the ceiling. Then it occurred to me that this was like the hunger strike. Was my body still on strike? Something was clearly missing. Was this a vitamin deficiency? Emotionally, I was a mess. Strange thoughts kept popping up. I thought I was dying. That was not the strange part. The strange part was that I didn't care. I should have gone to a doctor, but I didn't have insurance and couldn't afford one. I needed rest, the simple life. I listened to my breath going in and out, my heart pounding. How long this went on, I don't know. My log book is blank.

At one point, I noticed the phone ringing and thought I ought to unplug it. But for all the trouble it gives me, I cannot live without a phone. I got up, stepped over a pile of faxes on the floor and picked up the phone. It was Michael Lang, an old buddy of mine. He had produced the first Woodstock Music Festival, and now he said he was planning another one in six months, Woodstock '94. "Come on, man," he said, "it'll be like old times." He knew what I had been through. His daughter Molly attended school in Jerusalem and he had been following my hunger strike in the *Jerusalem Times.*

"Old times?" I said, repeating him. I thought about it. Did I really want to go' back in time? Go through all that again? Then it struck me that Michael didn't mean it literally, he meant the fun we used to have. What a long time ago that was. "Okay," I said. "I'll be there."

I had often talked with Lincoln about the first Woodstock, and he wanted to be a part of this one. He ordered Woodstock T-shirts with Dolphin Project logos to sell at the festival. We were several thousand dollars in debt and this was a way to make a few bucks and spread the word.

I called Sugarloaf and assured them that I wanted to get down there and see the facilities as soon as possible—but not now. I needed sack time, I said, time to heal, and mercifully they understood. In fact, as I hung up the phone, I got the feeling that they were relieved. I checked in with Joe Roberts in Melbourne. Nothing had changed, Bogie still had hepatitis. I said, "Thank you very much," then I fell back in bed.

Spiegel TV in Hamburg, Germany, called about the Russian dolphins in Tel Aviv. They asked what I was doing next and I told them about Bogie and Bacall. They said they wanted to document the release. The only problem, I told them, is that we needed $25,000 to make it happen. No problem, they said. They could pay that much for video rights. "Sounds like a plan," I said. They told me to come over and we would talk about it. They sent me an airline ticket and the next thing I knew I was in Hamburg, talking to Stephan Aust, Spiegel's executive producer. They gave me the first third of the $25,000, and for the first time I was sure that one day Bogie and Bacall would be free.

I flew back and turned the money over to Joe Roberts, who put it in the "Welcome Home Project" bank account we had set up. I returned home and fell into bed again. I was still exhausted. And still broke. A few days later

Trout called from Sugarloaf and said he had something interesting to tell me. "What is it?" I asked.

"I'm coming up that way," he said. "I'll tell you when I get there."

Why he couldn't simply tell me on the phone, I don't know. He drove up in his white Jeep and parked outside. He came in, sat down, looked around to make sure we were alone, then began talking in a voice barely above a whisper. I had to lean toward him to pick up what he was saying, that he had been in contact with people in San Diego about the Navy dolphins, that a TV show, *The Crusaders,* was going to launch a campaign to free some of the Navy's dolphins of war there. The United States had about a hundred dolphins trained to do the same things the Russians trained their dolphins to do. U.S. dolphins were trained at three naval bases: Key West, San Diego, and Hawaii. In military nomenclature, they were "advanced biological weapons systems" or, in short, "systems." When trainers took the dolphins out to sea and lost track of them, they reported back on the radio, "I've lost my system." An air/sea rescue helicopter and several boats using a "recall pinger" would be dispatched.

The pinger is an instrument that makes a sound (12 kHz) in the water that the dolphins were trained to come to and follow. Rear Admiral Eugene Carroll (retired), is on record deploring the possibility that dolphins were trained for much more devilish things, like placing mines on enemy shipping, killing enemy frogmen, or delivering bombs to a target and unwittingly blowing themselves up like a kamikaze.

"A TV show exposing the Navy dolphins-of-war program? Terrific," I said. "What does it have to do with me?"

"They want you on the show," he said.

I'm usually eager to jump into a campaign like this. But I was still trying to recoup. "Why me? Why don't you do it, Trout? You talk to them."

"I may be involved." He grinned and gave me a wink. "But they want you, too." He glanced around, scanning the room, then slipped me a piece of paper. "Here's the number to call," he said, almost whispering. "Ask for Elaine Sawaya, producer."

o   o   o

Jane Cartmill, president of the San Diego Animal Rights Advocates, was in charge of the demonstration. She and Trout had worked together when Trout was training Navy marine mammals for Seaco, and he used her and her organization in trying to bring down the whole Navy dolphin program. He told Jane everything he knew about the military dolphins at San Diego and maybe some things he only thought he knew. This took courage, I thought, and at the time I saw in Trout a possible ally, someone who understood what I was going through and could work with me. But Trout was not to be so easily judged.

The Crusaders put together a twelve-minute video, which aired nationally several times. It included shots of about a hundred people marching around in a park, chanting and waving signs angrily at the Navy dolphin pens in the background, an interview with me at the demonstration about the evils of captivity, interviews at Sugarloaf with Lloyd and Trout, and an interview in Washington, D.C., with Dr. Naomi Rose, marine mammal scientist of the Humane Society of the United States (HSUS), who accused the Navy of keeping their dolphins in "fetid" water. It was a powerful piece of advocacy journalism and put lots of pressure on the Navy.

Being back in the swing of things felt good. Then came word from people I knew in Switzerland, led by Noelle DeLaquis of the Swiss Working Group for Marine Mammal Protection (ASMS), that they were protesting the two dolphin parks near Zurich: Connyland and Kinderzoo. Wanting me to be involved, they sent me a ticket. I flew over and helped protest captive dolphins there, including Chispa, a Florida dolphin sold by the Dolphin Research Center with NMFS's blessing to Connyland Park, where she performed in a disco, techno-music blasting day and night.

For years I've had a love-hate relationship with the Navy, and I didn't know what to think at first when they announced that they were getting rid of their dolphins of war. I served proudly in the Navy for five years, but I hated what they had been doing with dolphins. Were they releasing the dolphins because of public pressure? That was part of it, no doubt, but there was more to it than that. The Cold War was officially over. Russia was shutting down its dolphin program, and Navy bigwigs explained that the dolphin experiment was not working, that it wasn't cost-effective, and they now had better ways of doing what the dolphins were supposed to do. They would therefore give their dolphins, or some of them, to qualified public display facilities.

The Navy set up a half-million dollar meeting in Santa Fe, New Mexico, invited as many people in the captivity industry as they could think of, and tossed them the problem of how best to dispose of the dolphins. In typical Pentagon style, however, they asked the wrong people—people in the captivity industry who already believed that capturing dolphins and turning them into circus animals is part of God's plan. Not one of them believed that it was feasible to return a dolphin to the sea after its captivity. When they say "feasible," they mean "cost-effective." Even if it could be done, they concluded, it would cost too much and wasn't worth the effort. The danger they always cited was that one of the captive dolphins might have contracted a disease in captivity that could spread to the wild population. They seemed not to notice, however, that these same Navy dolphins were trained to follow boats into the open sea where they constantly intermingled with the wild population. And at least nine Navy dolphins had escaped, Atlantic bottlenose dolphins into the Pacific, never to be found.

These conferees, assuming a lot they knew nothing about, decided that the Navy could warehouse the dolphins till they died at great expense to the taxpayer or give them to qualified facilities. In either case, the dolphins would continue to live out their lives in captivity. Though I have spent most of my life finding proper solutions to the problem of humanely dealing with captive dolphins and returning them to a life that is as fulfilling as possible for them, I was not invited to the conference.

o   o   o

The HSUS had reaped terrific publicity with Naomi Rose's appearance on the *Crusaders* program, and when they learned about the Navy's plan to phase out its dolphin program and find suitable places for them to go, they got involved behind the scenes. With two and a half million members, HSUS is the largest animal-welfare organization in the world. It is not related to your home-town humane society, though many of its members assume it is. When HSUS faxed me and set up a meeting at their office in Washington, D.C., to discuss the Navy dolphins, it was like getting in bed with an elephant. But who could resist?

This was made to order for us. We were the little guy on the block, the one everyone else was kicking sand in the face of. If we could get HSUS on our side, with its prestige, power, and money, what couldn't we do? Though the general public has an exalted opinion of HSUS, many investigative reporters and environmentalists who have looked into HSUS affairs are sickened. A segment of the animal-welfare industry plays watchdog to the rest, looking out for scams that could turn off the public's sympathy toward animals. When people donate money for animal causes, they expect the money to be used for animals in distress, not to feather some official's nest. The Obscene Salary Watch, one of these organizations, lists HSUS's officials as some of the greediest in the business. HSUS President Emeritus John A. Hoyt, whose doctorate is in divinity, reportedly knocked down an annual salary of more than $342,986 a year. HSUS President Paul Irwin, a United Methodist minister, got more than $239,202, plus other benefits, like $12,000 in insurance a year, according to columnists Jack Anderson and Joseph Spear. On top of that, Hoyt lived rent-free in a $310,000 house.

Lloyd and I flew to the nation's capital separately, he from Key West, I from Miami a day later, and when we met, I almost didn't recognize him. This was the first time I'd ever seen him wearing long pants. He also wore brand new gleaming white sneakers with white athletic socks. I was impressed. Hardly anybody in the Keys wears socks.

Drs. Naomi Rose, the marine mammal scientist at HSUS, and John Grandy met us with their lawyers in one of the conference rooms of their building in Washington, D.C. Dr. Rose is intellectually quite aggressive. When we first met, I spent some time presenting my background and experience with dolphins, then I asked about hers. "Oh," she smiled, "I'm from academe."

Dr. Grandy made it crystal clear about the money. HSUS would in no way provide funds for the Navy dolphin project. Though HSUS had $40 million in reserves, the money for the project would have to come from somewhere else.

Like two hicks from the sticks, Lloyd and I sat on one side of the table, Naomi Rose and John Grandy and their lawyers on the other. The meeting itself began with a flirtatious serenade of admiration, the lyrics all about our common goal and the benefits of snuggling up. I went into my get-acquainted act, showing them a couple of videos, including my latest project from Brazil where Flipper was pictured as I first found him in that horrible cesspool of a tank, then, a year later, swimming free like any other dolphin in the sea, and confirmed again nearly a year after that.

When it was over, the lights were turned on, and I said, "I want to use this same method on the Navy dolphins. It works."

"You have a protocol for this?" Naomi asked.

I looked at her quizzically. I knew what a protocol was, of course, but there is more than one kind of protocol.

"A *scientific* protocol?" she said. "You know, like a cookbook?"

Like a cookbook? She meant step-by-step procedures, instructions you can follow as in making a stew. But also *unlike* a cookbook. In a cookbook, an onion is an onion, but in untraining captive dolphins, each of them is as unlike the other as she and I were. "The only thing we've got is from the Joe and Rosie release," I said. "Also from Flipper in Brazil." Andrew Dickson's son Richard, a diver-writer, had joined the team in Brazil and produced a booklet about what we were doing. I had both of these booklets in my backpack and dug them out, tossed them on the table and said, "Here they are."

She thumbed through them both, looked up at me with a smile, and said, "But this isn't science."

"Okay," I said, "there's more. I can provide you with hours and hours of video tape, video records of everything we did." I glanced at her again, hoping to see some glimmer of appreciation.

She was shaking her head and smiling. "That's not what I mean."

I said, "I know what you want. You want a protocol about the rehab and release of captive dolphins *in general*, right? Directions for the rehab and release of any and all captive dolphins, regardless of circumstance."

"Correct. Do you have it?"

"No," I said, shaking my head. "I don't have that, and neither does anyone else."

"But you could produce one, couldn't you?"

"I could, yes. It's all right here." I pointed to my head. "I obviously know how to do it because I've done it. I've done it several times. In fact, I have a longer track record in this than anyone else in the world." I stopped here and glanced around the table so that there would be no doubt about this next point. "I'm not a scientist, though. If we need a scientific protocol, it's not a big problem. It's just a matter of writing it up scientifically."

Naomi Rose paused in thought, the smile fading. Then just as suddenly she flashed it on again. "We'll need the protocol," she said. "But I think we can work together on this."

"You can come down to Sugarloaf," I said, "get involved and watch what we do and write it down yourself. I'll answer all your questions, fully, completely. I want people to know what I do and to understand it. And when it's done, of course, it will establish guidelines for all future dolphin releases. We could publish the protocol together."

She thought again. I'm sure she liked the idea of publishing the protocol with her name on it. Scientists love to publish. She said in a musing tone, "A lot of this could be handled on the phone, don't you think?"

"Sure," I said. "But you would always be welcome at the sanctuary." I glanced at Lloyd, who was nodding assent.

She gave me a big smile and said, "This is agreeable."

We droned on, serenading one another, into the noon hour, when something happened that told me more about HSUS than all the harmony we had been producing. It happened at lunch. Or just after lunch. To save time, we decided to send out for something to eat. We ordered salads or politically correct vegetable burgers. Lloyd and I, guests from out of town having already spent $1,000 each on airfare (and more than that in Lloyd's case because of his new wardrobe, including socks that he would probably never wear again) just to get here and croon this tune of endless love—after all that you might expect that HSUS would pick up the lunch tab. But no, we all shelled out for our own, Lloyd's from sanctuary funds, mine from the Dolphin Project. All this was money contributed by people who expected it to be used directly for dolphin welfare, and you can argue that paying for our lunch was part of it, that we had dedicated our lives to the dolphins and we had to eat. HSUS could use the same argument on their own behalf, it's true. Their contributors didn't expect them to pay for our lunch anymore than ours did. But what about hospitality? It wasn't just the money—that was nothing compared with what we'd already spent—it was the predatory attitude. *That* I should have noticed. It should have told me that they were not really with us, that they were not into dolphins at all, but money.

I should have stopped the music, thanked them for their time, got up, and walked away. But I didn't. I couldn't. This was so close to the dream I've had for so many years, that I let it happen. I so much wanted their help, their influence, and their money. If only half of HSUS's two and a half million members contributed the price of a postage stamp, we could have built a halfway house off Mississippi, where most Navy dolphins had been captured, and freed *all* of them that were candidates—and Keiko (the killer whale of *Free Willy* fame), too.

Like many large animal-welfare organizations, HSUS was mainly into marketing. I knew that all along. The Navy was offering free dolphins, HSUS wanted some. Simple as that. They needed Lloyd because his dolphin sanctuary was ready to go and they probably thought they could control him. They needed me for my expertise. Lloyd and I were also new and pure, the Sugarloaf Dolphin Sanctuary making a virginal leap of faith for the love of dolphins, and HSUS needed to clean up its act. If they could be a part of a successful release of captive dolphins and then get the book written about how to do it, think of all the commercial huffing and puffing they could do, and all the money that would flow their way.

We had always questioned the government's power to issue permits for the release of captive dolphins, but since that was how things were done with Joe and Rosie, we decided to go along with it. HSUS would see to that. They would monitor the permitting process, they said, and if in ninety days they hadn't got it, they would land on NMFS's neck with a mandamus, a legal instrument that requires officials to do their duty. Imagine the sense of power flowing through anyone who can utter words like that! That's why I hadn't gotten up and walked out.

When the meeting was over, Lloyd and I shook hands all around, then went down in the elevator to the street. We were walking along the sidewalk, people flowing back and forth, when suddenly we stopped at a light, and though we'd never done anything like it before, we did a high-five, leaping into the air as if on signal and slapping our hands together.

We were the happiest guys on the face of the earth, Lloyd and I. Our dreams were coming true. My dream was a bit different from his, but not incompatible, I thought.

o   o   o

Less than a month later, the Navy notified us that we were to receive six dolphins. Lloyd, Trout, and I flew out to San Diego, planning to meet Dr. Naomi Rose of the HSUS there. Rear Admiral Walter Cantrell presided over the meeting. It was obvious to me that he did not enjoy the proceedings. To him it was like surrender. A big man in his dress whites with a chestful of ribbons, Admiral Cantrell was flanked by his chief officers, all in dress whites, facing Lloyd and I across one side of the table, Naomi on another. Though Trout had flown out with us, he spent his time giving interviews to people he knew in the media.

It was an uncomfortable meeting, but Admiral Cantrell gritted his teeth and went through the formality of explaining that we had been selected to receive six of the Navy dolphins. These six were to be chosen from a list of about twenty-five dolphins, which were itemized in terms of their serial numbers, date of capture, and estimated age. The list was given to Lloyd, he looked at it for a moment and gave it to Naomi; she looked at it and gave it to me. I studied the list and checked off five dolphins, not six, who were, according to Navy records, all relatively young, all captured in the same general area, and all the same gender, male.

Les Bivins, director of the Navy dolphins, was also sitting at the table with the naval officers. When I checked the dolphins we wanted, I gave him the list, he nodded and produced the files of the dolphins I had selected. I was especially interested in the training they had gone through and whether they had been the subjects of experiments. But the files included only their basic training, their learning to eat dead fish, for instance, to follow a boat into the open sea, and to respond to the Navy's recall pinger. Nothing about their roles as dolphins of war. Lloyd, Naomi, and I huddled and talked about the dolphins, then Les Bivins asked if we were ready to see them. I said okay, we all got up and walked out of the room and down the stairs to the docks, where the pens were. On the way, Lloyd asked, "Why only five?"

"These were the best," I said. "They've got the best shot at making it. We need quality," I explained, "not quantity." I stopped. They gathered around. "Look," I said, "if we're successful with these, we can always get more. Most of the dolphins on that list were not the best of candidates. I would have preferred female dolphins," I said. "They would have fit in better with the dolphins we already have and they're easier to work with. But the females on that list. . . ." I shook my head. "They were either geriatric, you know, or Pacific dolphins. My thinking," I said, "is that we might be able to set up a bachelor pod . . . let them all go at once."

They nodded. And we went on to the pens. I walked with Les Bivins to each of the dolphins I had selected. In their thirty-by-thirty-foot pens, the dolphins for the most part had nothing better to do than swim up and down, back and forth, like they were pacing. But as I stood next to Bivins, watching, we noticed a cloud of minnows entering the pen of the dolphin called Buck. Buck was getting under them and herding them to the top, where he caught them in his mouth one by one. "Did you see that?" I asked with excitement. Bivins nodded and smiled. "That's an excellent sign," I said.

"Yes. The water is excellent here," said Les Bivens. "When Dr. Rose said the water was 'fetid' and the dolphins lived in a 'cesspool,' well, look for yourself." He was referring to Dr. Rose's comments on *The Crusaders* show.

I glanced at him, then down at the water, and with a nod I indicated my agreement. But I think we both knew that you can't see the bacteria that makes polluted water polluted.

We watched Buck herding the minnows and eating them. Then Bivins said, "You chose the right ones, Ric. No reason you won't be successful with them. I've worked with each of these dolphins, and I know them. They were trained in Hawaii. I've seen them all catching fish on their own."

"What kind of training did they go through?" I asked.

He looked at me and frowned. This was secret information. I knew he couldn't say. "Their training," he said, "is in their records that we showed you. That's all I can tell you."

"If you can't tell me what their training background is, maybe you would do me a favor."

"I'll try."

"Could you put them all in the same pen together to see if they're compatible?"

"No problem."

We thanked the admiral, left, and joined Trout, who was upset about the dolphins I had chosen. He had given Lloyd a list of dolphins to ask for, dolphins he had worked with in the past. I had selected none of these. He also couldn't understand why I had chosen only five dolphins when they offered six. While we had been selecting the dolphins, Trout had been giving interviews blasting the Navy, Seaco, their dolphin program, and everyone else he could think of. He had set up an interview with me, too, he said, and, without thinking, I went along with it. The TV newsperson walked along the beach with me, the camera recording everything I said. Then in the editing process, they made it seem like I was confirming Trout's story about mistreatment of dolphins at the base. When the story aired, newspapers picked it up without checking with me and ran their own stories about it. By then I had returned home.

No sooner had I walked through the door than I got a phone call from Naomi, saying that the Navy wanted an apology from me. They had expected Trout to say what he said, but not me. If I didn't issue an apology immediately, she said, they would cancel the deal for the dolphins. I explained what had happened, how Trout had got me into this, but it didn't matter, they said, so I told them to write up an apology and I would sign it. Someone in the office wrote the apology, faxed it to me, I signed it and faxed it back. They sent it to the Navy and the dolphin deal was back on course. I resolved not to get involved in Trout's private battles anymore.

°   °   °

At the same time, I received a fax from Martha Gutierrez of Buenos Aires, saying that Cheryl had been kidnapped, stolen from the municipal swimming pool. I called her on the phone. She broke into tears. She said that Cheryl had been taken to Cali, Colombia, and sold to a man with a traveling circus.

"I'll go and steal her back," I said.

"No," she said. "Promise me you won't try that. These are very dangerous people."

I promised, then called Alvero Pasada, director of the WSPA office in Bogota, and told him about Cheryl. He said he would check on it, and the next day he called to confirm that a dolphin indeed was now in a swimming pool owned by a man who owns a traveling circus.

°   °   °

Needing to bring the Bogie and Bacall campaign to some conclusion, we held a council of war at my place in Coconut Grove. Lloyd, Trout, and Lynne drove up from Sugarloaf. Lincoln was there, and Joe Roberts drove down from Melbourne in his little Japanese car. We had the permits, the fence was up, and yet no dolphins. With the law so clearly on our side, we should have won long ago. Why was this thing taking so long? There was the hepatitis, yes, or the claim of hepatitis. But we must be missing something else. Was it something right in front of our noses? Or was it "out there," something beyond the four corners of our thinking?

We had worked the official level, Mary Mosley covering that with letters to all the proper authorities, and certain high-placed friends of mine in the world of animal activism had added their voices. We had negotiated like gentlemen at first, attending their hearings with jackets and ties and abiding respectfully by their rules of procedure. Later, when these procedures became self-parody, I allowed myself the luxury of righteous indignation, and some in our party had perhaps yielded to the barbarian within and become a bit rowdy, me parking the Dolphin Project's whale-emblazoned bus next to their stainless steel guard stations, for instance, others littering their property with pleas that they stop breaking the law and let the dolphins go.

With the siege we had in place, we would have won this campaign in due course, but lucky for us, Joe Roberts found a way to win quickly. "If what we need is a skeleton in their closet," he said, "I've got it right here." He was grinning and holding a video tape. We slapped it in the machine and there it was, Dr. Bossart with the capture team.

To the untrained eye, this was just a guy helping capture a pair of dolphins. But when you realize that it appeared they were capturing these dolphins to be held at ORC, a private club, and that their vet of record was part of it, there was a strong possibility of scandal.

When I saw it, my mouth fell open. I couldn't believe it. Good Old Joe, I thought. Maybe I'd been a trifle harsh in judging him. We were all jumping with joy. "This is dynamite!" I said. "Great work, Joe."

We high-fived all around. We talked about how best to use it, whether to send Bossart a copy or maybe send copies to the local TV stations. But I saw another possibility. "Let's not show it to him now," I said. "Let's *tell* him about it, tell him what we've got and that we're about to go public." I rubbed my hands and said to those assembled, "Let's let him stew awhile."

In the campaign against ORC, this was surely the coup de grace. But in fighting such evil, an enemy with the power to defy the law itself, is even blackmail enough?

Once again Joe Roberts came flying to the rescue. He had heard of a woman who might help, he said, an Indian shaman in Carmel, California, who had magical powers. Conventional groups would have greeted a suggestion like this with skepticism, if not howls of derision, but we listened gravely and gave Joe authority to follow up on it. We were in an all-out war where blackmail and magic beans were no different to us than the tortured logic of ORC's arguments and a suspicious diagnosis of hepatitis.

Joe Roberts called Sharman, the shaman, and asked if she needed to come here. No, she said. She could do it over the phone. Do you want some money? Again she said no. But she needed a picture. Joe overnight-expressed her a picture of Bogie, she did what shamans do, and the next time Bogie's blood was tested—less than a week later—she passed. No more hepatitis!

What was going on here? Coincidence? Magic? The video? Was our campaign that good? I have no idea. All I know is that suddenly the hepatitis was gone and we had the dolphins. Trout got the transfer ready. He called me about it, and I called Spiegel TV representatives, who arranged for a camera crew. We were all together—Lincoln, Joe Roberts and I, Trout and Lynne, and several volunteers—with the dolphins in back of a Waterfront Market refrigerated tractor trailer owned by Bucko Pantelis of Key West, who was driving. Bogie, Bacall, and Molly were lying on Sugarloaf Lodge mattresses. We were keeping them wet and comforting them, all of us heading toward Sugarloaf, where Lloyd was waiting, singing the praises of Sharman the Shaman, believing in her and in a world where prayers are answered.

When we got to Sugarloaf, we carefully carried the dolphins to the lagoon and put them in. Ringed by towering Australian pines, the lagoon itself was fifteen feet deep, nearly as large as a football field, and closed at the mouth with a fence. It was dug originally as a yacht basin or small marina, and was connected to a channel that swept across the back of the motel over to the bridge between Sugarloaf and the Key just to the north. With the dolphins frolicking around in their new home, we congratulated each other on a job well done and pushed each other into the water in celebration, yelling and screaming for joy. Then, with cameras rolling, Joe Roberts presented a $6,000 check to Lloyd to pay for the fish needed to feed the dolphins. A day or two after that, Spiegel TV presented us with the second third of the $25,000, which went into the Welcome Home Project bank account.

o   o   o

Of Shawnee background, Sharman was short, round of face and body, her long black straight hair braided on each side. Her face alone was enough to induce tranquillity. Lloyd, who had an abiding belief in mysticism, flew her in one day and she occupied the motel room next to mine. A door was between the two rooms. I knocked on the door, she opened it, and I invited her in to see some of my videos. If she was going to be a part of this, and obviously she was, then I ought to get off on the right foot with her.

I told her that there is no secret to what I do, no magic, that my method in untraining dolphins is merely to allow all trace of human contact to fall away so that they are whole again. I let nature heal them, I said, using the ebb and flow of time, the moon and the ocean tides. She nodded her head slightly. We understood each other. It was nothing you could write down, it was a feeling we both had. And later she would tell Lloyd that the Creator had chosen me to do this work.

You never knew what Lloyd was thinking because he kept everything bottled up. Then without warning he would erupt with sudden anger. Lloyd's autocratic style was often interpreted, in these politically sensitive times, as sexist. The usually soft-spoken Lynne, for instance, carried on a running clash with Lloyd, who one day, apparently fed up with it, fired all the women. When I heard about it, I told him that now he would have to get up at six o'clock in the morning to do their work. He quickly rehired them.

It may have been true that, with the possible exception of his girlfriend at that time who lived on another Key, Lloyd did not take women seriously. But it seemed to me that he didn't take *anyone* seriously. He seemed oblivious of others. He once boasted that when he was in charge of the restaurant's kitchen he had "gone through" twenty-three cooks—*fired* them! But maybe I'm wrong about Lloyd. If he were oblivious of other people, would he have kept score? No, I never figured him out, unless this was something he got from his father, the same intense drive toward the perfection of other people.

Sharman was a good influence on Lloyd. When she beat her animal-skin drum and marched or danced around the dolphins' pen singing those soft Indian chants and burning sage, we all felt better. She was full of positive energy. Everybody felt it and we liked having her around. We didn't know it at the time, but Lloyd was paying her with sanctuary funds, once including a trip to Paris. But Sharman herself, who had not a single materialistic bone in her body, was untouched by this. Later, when she returned to California, Lloyd drove there in his white Chevy pickup and returned with a couple of plastic garbage cans full of volcanic rocks that retain heat for his sweat lodge. The sweat lodge, he explained to me, was for the enhancement of positive energy.

I believe in energy, both positive and negative, but I don't know that we can talk about it much. To me, everything is energy. Some people call it New Age, but it's also very old, going back before history, accounting as it does for the mystery of life itself. You could say that there are good spirits and bad spirits, and if you have lots of good spirits, things tend to happen for the best. And vice versa. When somebody walks into a room, you can *feel* their energy, whether it's positive or negative, the energy flowing over everyone and becoming part of the whole. I can't draw a diagram of it and say that a certain spirit did this or that to make things happen as they did. But that's how it seems to work in my case. All of us at Sugarloaf working with the dolphins, despite our differences, tended to believe in some form of this, that there's a subtle plane of consciousness behind this gross level of physical stuff that we all share, and that essentially we are all only energy. Everything is energy! And sometimes when it's not used right, it can become what it became at Sugarloaf—a nightmare.

9

ON THIS SLIPPERY SLOPE

Sanctuary . . . a place of refuge and protection.
—Merriam Webster's Collegiate Dictionary

LINCOLN AND I SOLD some T-shirts at Woodstock '94, enough to break even and a little more. My moment onstage came one night between Aerosmith and Metalica, when I thanked the Navy for planning to release the Navy dolphins to us at Sugarloaf.

Back home, I wanted to fall into bed—still no energy—but I had a million things to do. I had to move down to Sugarloaf—my office, everything. Going back and forth, a three-hour commute, wasn't working. I needed to close down the place I was renting in Coconut Grove and store the stuff I couldn't take, including a thousand T-shirts we hadn't sold at Woodstock. As usual, I would practically live with the dolphins. That meant getting a proper tent. I would need my car, of course. And I would take the bus down, too. It was parked in a garage, which was costing money.

All this took several weeks, during which I was back and forth at Sugarloaf. I checked in with Joe Roberts by phone almost every day. He was handling the paperwork and was encountering roadblocks at every step. According to our contract with Lloyd, we were not to get the dolphins in our names until the pen or halfway house was built at Melbourne. And though none of us, including the lawyers of HSUS, believed that we needed a permit from NMFS or any other agency to release the dolphins, nevertheless we figured that just in case *they* thought we needed one, we should go along with it. I asked Joe if he had the forms for the permit.

"What forms?" he said. "There are no forms."

I asked him about building the pen. He would need an okay first from the Army Corps of Engineers.

"I've tried," he said. "They won't give us a permit for the pen unless we have papers on the dolphins."

It was a Catch 22: no pen without dolphins, no dolphins without a pen.

I told him to keep working on it, he said okay, and things rocked on.

Nevertheless, the halfway house for captive dolphins was almost a reality at Sugarloaf, which I could hardly believe. So often before I'd tried this, but each time something happened. In Adelaide, Australia, for instance, the captivity industry ganged up on us and we couldn't get the dolphins. In Las Vegas, the facility was—pardon the pun—a mirage. Usually, though, like in Belize, Sanibel Island, Florida, St. Croix, Virgin Islands, and Orange County, California, it was a money problem. Sugarloaf had a long way to go. In the cold light of reality, it was nothing more than a highway motel with a dolphin show out back. But it was the start, I thought, of something beautiful.

o   o   o

At the moment, Sugarloaf had people problems. And most of the people there seemed to think the problem was me. Each time I called or drove down, I got the cold shoulder. During the first few trips down, I managed to meet them all, including Kathleen Brooks, one of a half dozen or so volunteers and who later played a key role in saving Sugarloaf—at least for a while. Kathleen was a tall, leggy brunette, early thirties, reserved, and focused like a laser. She loved animals, and at Sugarloaf Dolphin Sanctuary she sometimes did the Sugar Show. She had grown up in Greenwich Village, New

York, married and divorced, and now worked at Sugarloaf Airport in the office and sometimes on airplane engines. She was learning how to fly.

Like everyone else at the time, she was loyal to Trout and made me feel like a leper. I was reading the logs in the fish house early one morning and she walked past me. She would have walked on by without a word, so I spoke: "How's Sugar doing?"

Kathleen stopped, shrugged, and said, "Oh, the usual." She started to go on and I said, "It would be great if we could get her some company."

She put her hands on her hips and said, "Well, you've got to talk to Lloyd about that." Then she turned on her heels and was gone.

Everybody was like that, even Lloyd. It was as though they thought they could ignore me and I would go away. But that was not about to happen. I was part of the act whether they liked it or not. The isolation at Sugarloaf drew me closer to Joe Roberts for a while, and we talked on the phone every day.

I caught a glimpse of Russ Rector at the motel a few times. But whenever he saw me, he scurried off. Everybody else was settling in—maybe a little too comfortably. During my absence, Trout had filled the void. Though his title was director of husbandry, he was now issuing press releases claiming to be director of rehabilitation and release—*my* job. Usually I wasn't even mentioned in his press releases except as an afterthought, my name sometimes listed in the last paragraph as "consultant." And what was he doing issuing press releases in the first place?

Friends later told me that Trout had been waging an all-out war of words against me behind my back, spreading rumors with everybody I knew. At first I shook it off. I've been slandered by experts, and the best defense is usually to ignore it. I thought I knew what Trout's real angle was, but I couldn't talk to him about it. I had heard rumors that he was shopping his "life story" around as a TV movie of the week. It was his account of his role in denouncing the San Diego Navy dolphins. And though he was not the first or only one to do it, he did add his voice in opposition to the use of Navy dolphins in the frigid waters of Bangor, Washington. Now, he must have figured, if he could take credit for releasing the Navy dolphins at Sugarloaf, his story might be worth telling. I couldn't talk to him about it because he didn't know that I knew about it, and if I accused him of exploiting the situation here to enhance his own reputation, he could just as easily say the same of me.

I thought things would surely change when I moved in. Meanwhile, wanting to get started, I made a few suggestions to Trout about how things should be done. He didn't take it well at all. For months now, he had been the resident dolphin expert. Anyone with a question about dolphins automatically came to him. Then suddenly I'm on the scene telling him that he's doing it all wrong. I would have kept my mouth shut or at least tried to be more diplomatic if that had been possible, but it wasn't. I'm not confrontational unless it matters and I'm right. And in this case it did matter and I was right.

Controlling captive dolphins is a function of their feeding, and Trout was having them fed as if they were still being trained. That's 180 degrees wrong. My system of *untraining* is the reverse of training. And the sooner I could get the dolphins fed properly, the sooner they would be ready for their freedom. Trout was in his Jeep, getting ready to leave when I hailed him and told him that his feeding methods were wrong. It must have touched a nerve because his face got red, he looked as though he was going to pop a vein. He turned on the engine, revved it up, and sped off, spinning his wheels.

I tried it again a few evenings later when I was about to head back to Coconut Grove. I went by the office and poked my head in. "Can we talk?" I said. I went in and sat down across the desk from him. "Look, Trout," I said, "let's get something straight. We call this place a dolphin sanctuary, but that means nothing. The fact that we put some signs up that say 'Dolphin Sanctuary' has no credibility. Credibility is something we have to earn."

He was seated at the desk and was giving me a half smile, as though this was all a joke and I was about to deliver the punch line. But it was no joke for me. "This place will have no credibility," I said, "until we have a *successful dolphin release* behind us. And to do that, we need your cooperation. Know what I mean?" I asked. "There's a lot of power in cooperation, Trout, people working together with one goal. Now I've done all this before, I know what I'm doing, and I'm asking you right now to help, to be a part of it."

This was his opportunity to rally round the flag. But Trout said nothing.

"Or if you can't do that, then at least don't get in the way. Go along for the ride. Let it happen. Who knows, maybe you'll learn something. Maybe you're worried about me," I continued. "Well, forget it. As you know, I've always wanted a halfway house like this. But not this one." I shook my head sadly. "When the release is finished, I'm out of here. That's a promise. I'm saying that it will be yours." I waited for him to respond, but he didn't even change expressions. "Right now," I said, "getting these dolphins ready for release—that comes first." I looked him in the eye. "That's what this is all about. You help me, then I help you. I know for a fact that some of the dolphins that come through here cannot be prepared for life in the wild. Those are the dolphins you'll have when I'm gone. Just hang in there, Trout."

At the root of our problems, I realized later, was a basic misunderstanding. From the very beginning, I was involved for one reason only: to free captive dolphins. The campaign at ORC, the alliance with HSUS, the Navy dolphins—everything was about turning Sugarloaf into a halfway house where captive dolphins could be prepared for life in the wild again. I assumed we were all working for the same thing, but at some point, that obviously changed. Looking back, I think it must have been while I was in Israel. Lloyd and Trout must have realized that they could manage without me, that they could have their own politically correct dolphin show.

Even if Trout and I had seen dolphins in exactly the same way, we probably would still have disagreed about their potential for life in the wild. I began with the idea that they ought to be free. In the case of Molly, for instance, I thought she should have a shot at freedom. Despite her age, I thought she was a candidate because of her intelligence. This isn't black-and-white for me. I see lots of gray. That's possibility. And I saw lots of it in Molly. Trout, who had worked with her for years, didn't seem to see the possibility of freedom for Molly. He had her doing the same show at Sugarloaf that she had done at ORC. To people watching, I heard him explain that she was too old to be released.

Later on I changed my mind about Molly. In working with her, I saw that letting her go might have been too risky. She had been captive too long and probably wouldn't have adapted to life in the wild. But I never changed my mind that it should have been considered.

o   o   o

For his part, Lloyd's dolphin experience was limited to Sugar, a single and very singular dolphin. In my opinion, his life-long love relationship with Sugar might qualify him to work with dolphins, but not to be in charge of them. Lloyd seemed incapable of delegating authority. He kept a stranglehold on everything that happened, especially information. Though he sought Sharman's counsel, her advice was usually so general that he ended up doing whatever he would have done anyway.

Since Bogie's hepatitis episode, Sharman was almost like a miracle worker in Lloyd's eyes. He flew her in as often as he could, she stayed a while, then returned to her home in California. I approved of all this with my silence and even encouraged it because she had a calming effect on Lloyd. When she was there, I noticed that he no longer smoked cigarettes and drank beer. When she was not at the sanctuary I saw little of Lloyd, and never before noon. We used to say that Lloyd doesn't do mornings.

Ironically, Lloyd's periodic episodes of optimism created another seed of friction at Sugarloaf. When Joe Roberts and Rick Trout first approached Lloyd about moving Bogie, Bacall, Lady, and Molly down to Sugarloaf, Mr. Good had gone along only with reluctance. Lady died before she could be moved, but Lloyd assured his father that it would work. It was a simple idea in the beginning. We would get the dolphins, prepare them for life in their own world again, and let them go. Easy in, easy out. How could it fail? When I got the first installment of the $25,000 from Spiegel TV, our money problems were seemingly over. Then with news of the Navy dolphins, Lloyd's vision grew. He wanted them too, and Mr. Good agreed to go along, provided we had enough money to get the job done. So the deal went through. Lloyd had the best of intentions, but they were limited to selling more T-shirts and setting out more signs around the motel soliciting donations for the dolphins.

o   o   o

Each time I dropped in on the sanctuary while trying to move down to Sugarloaf permanently, things got worse between Trout and me. We could hardly speak to each other without disagreement. We had gotten off on the wrong foot when we first picked up the dolphins from ORC. The time to get baseline data about dolphins—vital statistics like length and weight—is when you first get them. They're out of the water and you don't have to catch them again just for that purpose. Everybody does it that way. Everybody but Trout. As we were loading Bogie, Bacall, and Molly into the truck, I said we should weigh and measure them. Trout brushed it off. I tried to make up for that by using a string to measure them while we were driving down in the truck, but it didn't work. Bumping along the road, trying to write things down—it was impossible.

Before we put the dolphins in the water at Sugarloaf, I said we should freeze brand them. I don't think that Trout actually had the freeze brands. But that didn't matter. I think he would have objected to anything I suggested anyway.

From there my relationship with Trout and the others increasingly worsened. Little things, big things—everything. Lynne saw both sides, I think, and whether she agreed with me or not, she tried to keep things cool. I thought that the hostility would disappear if the others would simply listen for a minute to what I was saying, that all this negativity could be turned around. I praised their work, told them that they had done a good job setting up the sanctuary. Now, I said, our real job was about to begin, that we were moving into something new for them, something exciting and even fun. The main thing, I said, was that they should not think of themselves as dolphin trainers but as untrainers.

I know this is a difficult proposition for dolphin trainers. Their whole lives are dedicated to *training* dolphins. On the surface, it might seem as if the dolphin is a blank slate onto which the trainer inscribes his or her instructions. Actually, four out of five trainers come upon dolphins who have already been trained. Then it's the trainers themselves who must be trained to act like trainers. Even in what we call training dolphins, the behavior that we call a trick is many times invented by the dolphin himself. When captive dolphins get hungry, it's as if they go through a sequence of behaviors, some of which is amusing to us. When the trainer is amused, he tosses the dolphin a fish. It's a reward. And the dolphin—no dummy—does it again. He gets another fish, and so it goes. If the trainer wants to put several of the dolphin's behaviors together into a complex trick, the trainer withholds the fish until the dolphin does the right sequence of behaviors, then rewards him with a fish. In sum, the trainer's job is to reward the behavior he wants repeated.

From the dolphin's viewpoint, in order to be fed, he goes through his repertoire of behaviors till he finds one that triggers the trained response of the trainer, which is to give him (the dolphin) a fish. To the dolphin, he's training the trainer. Or, when you see both of them doing it to each other, you could say that it's mutual, the trainer and the dolphin both locked into this system of rewards and behavior.

When I come along and tell the trainer to stop thinking like a trainer, it's like telling a marathon runner that he must now try to come in last. You can explain this to dolphin trainers till you're blue in the face and they still think they must train a dolphin to be free again. But training a dolphin to be wild—what could that mean? It means nothing. It's a contradiction in terms. Train them to be wild? *How?*

It's just as hard to get the captive dolphin to stop thinking it's a captive dolphin. And that's because it is a captive dolphin. So how do you get it to think that it's not? You can't *train* it to think that. When I prepare a captive dolphin for life in the wild again, I'm working with a creature that's been trained to think that it will be fed three times a day simply by leaping out of the water and walking or dancing on its tail. The dolphin believes this as much as it believes in the water around it. But out there in the real world, that's crazy, and until the dolphin understands this, it's not ready for freedom.

I'm not trying to eradicate everything the dolphin has learned in captivity. I would if I could, but it can't be done. All we can know is whether they still do tricks or not and whether they have the skills necessary to make it on their own. Their sonar, for instance, is vital, but we can't train them to start using it. All we can do is set up the circumstances that encourage them to use it. The rest is up to them. If they have regained the skills of a wild dolphin, if they can feed themselves, stay out of harm's way, and refrain from doing tricks or other inappropriate behaviors in the wild, they're ready for release.

Not that they'll immediately resume their lives as wild dolphins. When finally released, each dolphin is on his own. And the first time he gets hungry and must catch his own fish is a critical moment. It's the moment he must become wild again. This is not easy for the dolphin. He's vulnerable. And it could go either way. We could destroy everything we've done in preparing him for freedom by simply giving him a fish. With one toss of a fish, we could make him a captive dolphin again. If not, he'll hunt on his own, which is what we want him to do.

Trout still treated these dolphins like pets, however, and as long as he did, they could never be free.

o　　o　　o

Even without the procedural conflicts, Trout and I were on a collision course because of how our jobs were set up. As director of rehab and release, I had to be in charge of feeding the dolphins. But as director of husbandry and the person in charge of providing the food, Trout presumed he was in charge of feeding. He was already there and had taken charge of the feeding buckets. Oddly enough, whoever controlled the feeding buckets controlled what happened at Sugarloaf.

Trout must have figured that since the dolphins were fed three times a day, they might as well do their act at the same time, just like at ORC. So he and his followers went down to the lagoon three times a day with their buckets of fish and, with a dozen or two tourists in tow, they tossed the fish to the performing dolphins. Often leading this group was Sue Vola, a sweet-faced girl in her early thirties. She leased the restaurant from Mr. Good and ran it. She loved feeding the dolphins, maybe saw it as a way to become a dolphin trainer. The dolphins were leaping out of the water, jumping over one another, and tail-walking, racing across the water with a grin and a flirting eye. Tourists, gathered round in awe, loved it.

Then Trout sold them T-shirts at $25 a whack. Trout also made a show out of the dolphins' medical inspections. Dolphins are taught to present various body parts so that, from time to time, blood can be drawn for analysis and their bodies inspected and sometimes massaged.

The first time I saw Trout doing this, I cringed. I vowed to put an end to it, not realizing that I would create a most formidable enemy in Sue Vola. But I had no choice. If my old environmental buddies had seen me here in the midst of this, they would think I had gone mad or sold out, or both. And if they'd seen me here with Sugar, they'd have been sure of it.

But I had made my peace with Sugar. She was not a candidate. She was blind in one eye, mentally challenged or at least psychologically crippled, and content, it seemed, to push a large black inner tube around her private lagoon with a dead palm frond poking out at an odd angle. Like Molly, Sugar was grandfathered out of the law that covered captive dolphins.

The dolphin act with Bogie, Bacall, and Molly, however, had to stop. I found Lloyd sitting on a stool in the Tiki Bar and gift shop between Sugarloaf Bay and Sugar's lagoon. I slid up on the stool next to him and complained about how the dolphins were being fed. He heard me out, but he didn't seem to understand my objections. Sugarloaf was making money from T-shirts, dolphin jewelry, and donations. Could this be bad? People loved the dolphin show. And if the dolphins had to be fed anyway, why not entertain people with it? Wasn't that what he did every day with Sugar?

Since I hadn't even moved in yet, I thought better about demanding that Trout be reined in. I told myself to take it easy, that the dolphins needed to adjust to their new world, and so did we. I had dreamed too long of this to throw it all away in a glorious flash of righteous indignation. And that, I saw later, was another misstep on this slippery slope. I should have jumped up and down and screamed to the sky till they did it the right way, but I didn't.

o   o   o

I was back in Coconut Grove packing the last of my boxes to be stored when I received a phone call about Trout's grandmother's death. Trout and Lynne would attend the funeral in Ohio for a couple of weeks and I was asked not to go down to Sugarloaf till they had returned. This was like a starting gun to me. I packed even faster, threw my belongings in the car, and made the three-hour drive in two hours. When I arrived, I didn't go to the office or check in with Lloyd or anyone else, I went over to the lagoon and counted the dolphins. Three. "Thank God," I thought. They were okay.

o   o   o

I sat down under the Australian pines, leaning against a trunk. How quiet here, and restful. I watched as a blue heron probed the water's edge. A balmy breeze whispered through the pines high above. These are the trade winds. They come off the Atlantic or the Caribbean, sweeping over this chain of islands into the Gulf of Mexico. The sky was dizzyingly blue. I took a deep breath, the first really relaxing breath since—I don't remember the last time. Maybe it was with—yes, with Sabine. What a *fool* I was. Pure fantasy! I've had enough of that, I needed someone real.

The dolphins were swimming around, unaware of me. Every twenty or thirty seconds, they were coming up for air, breathing slowly with a whooshing sound. It made me conscious of my own breathing. I was listening to them, keeping track of each one of them as I always do. This is an important part of knowing a dolphin. I want to know them without names. I want to know who they are in their own world. Each one breathes differently, they dive differently, they swim together differently and make different sounds. They have their own ways of doing everything, and they adjust, like us—or like we're supposed to—coping with the world around them. I wanted to sleep, to soak up the peace and tranquillity here in the open air, breathing slowly, deeply like in a trance, breathing with the dolphins. And healing.

As I sat under the trees watching the dolphins I felt someone watching me, then a burly suntanned man sauntered over and stood a few paces back. He was wearing a Sugarloaf T-shirt and camouflage pants. He said he was in charge of security. "I've been watching you," he said. I nodded. I told him who I was, that I was in charge of rehabilitation and release of the dolphins. "Oh, yeah," he said. "I heard about you." He stood there for a long moment, then told me he had been an antiterrorist instructor in the Army, a sergeant in Vietnam and the Persian Gulf. Then in a soft crooning voice he said that two guys had recently jumped him in Homestead, a small community south of Miami, and in the melee one of them was killed. He said he had grown weary of the paramilitary stuff and now wanted to get into wildlife rehab. That's why he had befriended Trout and volunteered at Sugarloaf.

I said something about his getting into the right field at the right time, that we were breaking new ground here with the halfway house for captive dolphins. He nodded gravely and said he approved of science and sauntered off to do security somewhere else.

o   o   o

Was it science? When I first started doing this, I thought it was science. I kept records, I could point to events that changed with regularity. I could reproduce effects. I could talk up a storm of statistics. And several dictionary definitions would justify calling what I do science. But I don't use that word anymore. Science is mainly interested in the *ideal* dolphin, the species, and there is no ideal dolphin, except in books. I'm interested in actual dolphins, the *individual* dolphin that I work with. It's the difference between writing music and playing it. There is no scientific protocol for the release of captive dolphins because each dolphin is radically different. This seems to elude the captivity industry. When they capture young dolphins in the sea, the dolphins are all alike. Peas in a pod. But once captured, dolphins go a thousand different ways, becoming uniquely different from one another because of the disparate worlds we put them in.

Science is about control. You could say that it's about understanding first, but then it's about control, controlling the world, training it or breaking it down and turning it into something else, something we can use. But I was doing the reverse of that, taking what had been made into something else and turning it back into what it was originally. What I was doing was more like art, a healing art.

Before you can readapt a captive dolphin and return him to the wild again, you must know what a dolphin in the wild is like. If you know that, you can easily spot the dolphin's learned behavior in captivity. Watch a typical dolphin show for five minutes and you'll see virtually all of it. When the trainer comes into the arena with a bucket of dead fish, the dolphin gets excited and swims in circles. He leaps out of the water with joy, comes down with a flamboyant splash or a spin, and lies on his back and paddles around with his flukes, flapping his pectoral fins as if he were clapping. When the trainer squats down to get a fish, the dolphin swims up and begs for food, making squeaky sounds and clapping his fins, bobbing his head up and down and showing no fear even if there are hundreds of people watching.

All of this behavior is learned. Dolphins in the wild never do these things because in nature such actions would be dangerous, irrelevant, and stupid. These behaviors become important to us now, though, because in preparing the dolphin to live once more in his natural environment, we can keep score as we "extinguish" these abnormal behaviors one by one.

To speak of extinguishing a behavior sounds like we're throwing water on a fire to put it out. But that's only metaphor. How would we ever know that we had extinguished every bit of the dolphin's learned behavior? We can't. And it really doesn't matter because all we really care about is keeping them from doing tricks at inappropriate times.

When I lead a team in rehabilitating a dolphin, I tell them that our basic job is to "empower" the dolphin. When the dolphin is captured, he loses his power. He's a prisoner. And it's our job to return his power to him.

Three things we should keep in mind:

1. Assume that you know nothing,

2. Maintain sustained observation, and

3. Consider the obvious.

Simple? No. These are subtle and very difficult instructions to follow, especially the first one and especially for dolphin trainers. Before trainers can extinguish learned behavior in the dolphin, they must first extinguish their own learned behavior. They must realize that we're not putting on a show, we're putting on a nonshow. And the *less* we do the better.

I make no secret of my untraining method. I want other people to do the same thing. Trout and others have watched me, at times, with unconcealed disbelief or disdain. They see me sitting near the dolphins. And as far as they can tell, that's all I'm doing. They think I should be training the dolphins to be free. But the problem with captive dolphins *is* the training. They don't need more training, they need untraining. When they say I'm doing nothing, I agree. My method, like a *Seinfeld* episode, is about nothing. Since dolphins have been trained to do certain behaviors in order to be fed, I reverse all that. When they jump around like circus clowns, I don't feed them. Only when they act like normal dolphins do I feed them. And then it's not as if I'm feeding them. I never make eye contact, and most of the time they never see me. To them, I don't exist. Trainers want to make bonds, I want to break bonds. I toss the fish to them from different places and at different times, but never when they play the circus clown, and slowly those behaviors become irrelevant—both here and in the world we want them to live in. There's nothing mysterious here. What the dolphin learns is like anything you might learn . . . a language . . . playing the guitar . . . typing. Use it or lose it.

Actually, I'm watching the dolphins like a hawk. There's no shortcut here. No formulas. This is not research, this is *doing* it. One must eat with the dolphins, sleep with them, and be with them constantly. I call this "dolphin time." How do you learn to do it? Not by reading about it. Not by following instructions. You've got to *experience* it. Like anything else, whether science or art, you learn how to do it from someone who already knows how. Then when you do it right, you can *feel* it. It's nonverbal. Like Zen. We lose ourselves and become the dolphin.

When I'm doing it, I live in a nylon igloo tent next to the dolphins, and I can feel myself become part of the scenery. I'm like one of the trees, a leaf floating on the water, or an egret who simply comes and goes. When I don't respond to the dolphins' learned behavior, after awhile they give it up. And that's what I want them to do. Everything I do is without words. I have to keep records, of course; that's the only exception, that and the few directions I sometimes give to volunteers. But living with dolphins on the silent level provides an insight into dolphins that is necessary to understanding them as individuals and helping them become who and what they are, their life beyond words.

Why go through all this? Because that's the only way we can assess their ability to survive back in nature.

o   o   o

Bright and early the next day, I felt better than I had in years. I felt alive again. I had been getting to know the dolphins by the sounds they made, that and the way they swam back and forth in the lagoon. I went up for breakfast at the general store. When I walked in, everybody stopped what they were doing and watched me out of the corners of their eyes. Nobody spoke. I poured my own coffee, got a muffin, then paid in deathly silence. They took the money without a word. Walking across the broad lawn were several of the volunteers, women heading for the fish house. I waved, they looked the other way. I finished my coffee and tossed the cup in a garbage can. Lloyd walked by, headed toward the office. I waved to him. He glanced at me and kept walking. I went over to the sanctuary itself, which had a seven-foot fence around it.

While Trout and Lynne were gone, the people at Sugarloaf gradually loosened up. Trout was calling Lloyd on the phone from Ohio every day, but Lloyd and I were working together now. One morning I was in a kayak, trying to lead Molly around without Bogie and Bacall following. Lloyd came down and stood on the feeding dock, watching us. I nodded to him, he watched in silence for a while, then he said, "You know that Trout figures Molly will stay." It's very quiet there, just the natural sounds of the wind flowing through the pines, and the sound of voices carries over water. We both were speaking softly.

"I know," I said.

"What do you think?"

"About Molly?" I was maneuvering the kayak into a certain position and I focused on that. Then when I got it just right, I glanced at Lloyd and said, "I don't know yet. She's supposed to go. We planned that from the beginning. She doesn't need to go up with Bogie and Bacall though. Maybe she can go up later."

I was leading Molly around with the kayak—or trying to. I wanted Molly by herself, but Bogie and Bacall kept hanging around. "I'm hoping she can go," I said.

Lloyd wanted Molly to stay of course, which kept him and Trout close. They both wanted Molly. And so did the volunteers. I could tell in the way they fed the dolphins, Bogie and Bacall as if one day they would be leaving, Molly the way she had always been fed, with big tricks and acting the fool. This could have been Molly's wish too, I felt, because she had mastered this alien world. And even Joe Roberts, when he presented the check from Spiegel to Lloyd for fish, had said it was for Bogie and Bacall. Was it a slip of the tongue to omit Molly? I was watching this kind of thing. I was not unaware that if I were to give up Molly, I would gain enormously in popularity, which I needed. So I had to decide about Molly, and yes, perhaps I was wavering.

Working with Molly now, I was exploring the possibility of something gray, a middle way between freedom and captivity. Maybe she and Sugar could team up. Legally it was okay. Molly and Sugar both were pre-Act dolphins, which means they were captured before the 1972 law was passed, and technically they could be released at any time. If they got along okay, they might make it together without a fence, living in the lagoon and the deep channel off Sugarloaf Bay that stretched a mile or more through the flats. They could live there and come back to the feeding dock to eat if they needed to.

When I told Lloyd what I was thinking about, it was electric. He dropped what he was doing, got some tools, and we made a gate in the fence at the mouth of the lagoon. But I couldn't get Molly to go through it, not without Bogie and Bacall. Molly would swim to the gate and stop. She knew what I wanted her to do, but she was afraid of going through.

o   o   o

Suddenly Trout was back. I saw his white Jeep at the office. I walked over to the feeding dock. I was in a black swim suit and a straw hat, sitting on a box, hanging out with the dolphins. Lloyd and Trout came down to the lagoon talking, then Lloyd, wearing baggies and aviator sunglasses, walked around the lagoon and out on the feeding dock with me. I looked up and he said very softly, "I don't know how to tell you this, Ric, but you aren't supposed to be down here alone. In fact, this fence was supposed to be locked."

I couldn't believe my ears. "What?"

"Trout says . . . I mean Trout and I think it's better—"

"That's it!" I snapped, standing up. "I've had it. I've had it up to here." I made a karate chop to my own neck. "And I'm not taking it any more. Look, man, this is not a game for me. This is my life. I brought these dolphins down here and I'm going to get them out of here. I want a meeting in the fish house. Everybody involved."

At one o'clock, we all gathered at the fish house. It was cool inside, the coolest place on the island. It was also an office with a steel desk, a chair and a phone. The floor and walls were tiled, everything clean. At the far end was the freezer for stacks of frozen fish. On one side was a matching pair of deep stainless steel sinks separated by a long stainless steel table to prepare the fish on, seven stainless steel buckets hanging from the ceiling, log books for each dolphin, and a locker for vitamins and first aid.

I sat down in the chair, Lloyd and Trout leaned against the sinks, Kathleen, Caren, and Lynne, the three volunteers, lounged around.

I gave them the "cooperation" speech, saying some of the things I had already said to Trout alone, that we had a long way to go and we must work together, that there is power in cooperation and that we could only hurt each other by not cooperating. I told them again that what we were about to do was historically important, that this halfway house for captive dolphins was the beginning of something brand new, and that everything we do was being monitored all around the world. "The first time you do anything like this, it's like entering a forest," I said. "But don't worry. I've been through it before and I know the way."

Never before in a campaign have I had to give a pep talk to my own people like this. I'm not a talker, I don't preach. And I don't give detailed instructions either. In a cooperative setting it's not necessary. What we do with dolphins you don't learn in a book or by talking. I show people what to do, and I expect them to learn what to do by doing the same thing. In the hostility at Sugarloaf, though, it wasn't working. I looked at Trout, grimly silent. "We must all work together on the same plan," I said. Then for the benefit of Trout and Lynne, who had been gone for a week, I explained what I had been doing with Molly, trying to get her to swim out of the lagoon, down the channel and into Sugar's lagoon. It was my hope to end Sugar's twenty long years of solitude.

Then I said: "I want to move Lady over with Sugar. We need to see if that will work."

Trout, who had been leaning against the sink, suddenly exploded. "Oh, my *God!*" he screamed. His hands went to his face as if in agony and he crumpled almost to his knees. He stood up again and said to everyone else, "Did you hear him? Did you hear what he just said?"

Everybody stopped and tried to remember what I had just said. His face turned red, and he was shaking his head back and forth. I thought he was about to start swinging at me. I braced myself. Suddenly he hit the door, banged it open, and rushed outside. Lynne rushed out to comfort him. The rest of us were dumbfounded. When Lynne returned, I asked her, "Was it something I said?"

"You said 'Lady' instead of 'Molly.' Lady is dead. Have you forgotten?"

I slapped the side of my head with my hand. "Damn!"

"He feels very strongly about that."

"I'm sorry," I said. "I misspoke. And I apologize. I'll apologize to him, too. It was stupid of me. What can I say?" I looked around for help in a pleading way, my hands out, palms up. Nobody moved. "It was a slip of the tongue," I said contritely. "I made a mistake and I'm sorry."

Trout came back in. His face was red. He looked like he had been crying.

"Sorry, man," I said. "I didn't mean to upset you."

Trout said nothing. He faced the sink and turned the water on, splashed it in his face, and dried his face with the bottom of the T-shirt he was wearing.

"I said that I'm sorry, Trout. And I mean it. But let's get a hold of ourselves. You're a walking time bomb, man." Trout had taken several deep breaths and was leaning against the sink again. "This whole project depends on each one of us—including me and maybe especially me—each one of us being at our very best."

Suddenly the meeting was back on track and I told Lloyd that it was a good idea to lock the fences, but I wanted a complete set of keys to everything in the sanctuary. "That you think I cannot be with the dolphins unless I'm chaperoned is completely insulting," I said, "and I won't go along with it."

Then I addressed the volunteers: "I've said this before but you've got to start listening to me. We're feeding the dolphins all wrong. We're feeding them from the same feeding station all the time, and they're bonding with it. That's got to change. We've got to feed them from different places. And we're too regular with the feedings. It's like clockwork: nine, one, and five. To them it's like show time. This is not a show. Maybe you don't get it, but watch me. Do what I do. I don't want to see any more dolphins doing tricks for food. We've got to continue keeping track of what each of the dolphins is eating, but we must feed them at irregular hours. This is how it's done in nature. In nature, they eat at all hours, even at night. And that's what we're trying to do, get them back to nature." I stopped, looked around at them, and said slowly, "If we're successful, we can open the door for many more captive dolphins. It's important to them and to us. And remember that the world is watching."

o   o   o

Maybe I should have taken my own advice, that we all needed to concentrate on the work at hand. But I'm like a fire horse myself. When somebody calls with a dolphin problem, I want to drop what I'm doing, whatever it is, and go help. Here I was working in the most crucial stage of the most important project of my whole life, and even though I had scheduled a demonstration with the Brigitte Bardot Fondation in Paris six months before, I should have canceled. But they were counting on me. It would take only three days, I figured, and what could that hurt? Sometimes I feel like my whole life is like sweeping back the tide. I work like mad here because I'm here and the water is rising, then I notice the water advancing over there and I drop things and rush over there. While I'm rushing there, I see that I might make a difference at the other end of things, so I'm suddenly dashing back. I'm trying to be everywhere at once, and I suppose if I were asked directly about it, I would admit that I was looking for an excuse to get out of Sugarloaf Dolphin Sanctuary anyway, and away from its internecine struggle.

French activists wanted me to organize and lead a protest at the huge dolphin show at Parc Asterix in Paris. They set up the plane ticket and a hotel room and I flew over. Then about thirty of us bought tickets to the dolphin show and sat scattered around with the other spectators. We had our banners rolled up under our jackets and at a certain point, I stood up and displayed mine, which said in big red English letters: "Captivity Kills!" That was the signal for everyone else to stand up and wave their banners, which were in French. They all had various slogans, like "Free the Dolphins" or the names of dolphins who had died at the park. This amusement park was notorious for its high dolphin mortality. The show was stopped, and the other spectators, who had paid to get in, were furious. They booed us, jeered, and said nasty things as only the French can. It took at least fifteen minutes for the security people to round us up and inform us that we could either leave quietly or be arrested for trespassing. We left and met in the parking lot where journalists, who had been notified ahead of time, interviewed us. Because of my Flipper connection, they always interview me, and one of the obvious questions was what effect the demonstration might have had. "Probably very little," I said. "I love Paris, but Paris obviously does not want its complacency disrupted."

o   o   o

When I returned to Sugarloaf three days later, they were feeding the dolphins like they always had, giving them fish for tricks. And I was not surprised. I went directly to the fish house, sat down, and checked the log books. Then I called Joe Roberts and asked him if he'd made any progress with the permit. He hadn't. He was in this project because of his connections, and now, when it counted, he couldn't connect. He said that as the head of a dive club, he could get any number of volunteers to build the pen, and they could build it in a day or two. I had given them the simple plans I had used in Brazil, a plastic fence along wooden pilings. But without the permit, we couldn't get started. Ironically, if we'd wanted to move the dolphins and put them in a show, that would have been approved immediately.

All this talk about the permit was soon dropped when NMFS replied to one of Joe Roberts's petitions with a list of questions like this:

• Prove that Bogie and Bacall both have their maternal instincts.

• Prove that both dolphins are capable of defending themselves from predators.

• How will the dolphins be protected from any potential problems associated with the press and media coverage, or the general public?

Joe faxed it to me—it was fourteen feet long—and asked his own question: "What does this mean?"

I faxed him back: "It means that they don't want us to have a permit."

○   ○   ○

Around this time I heard rumors that Trout was saying bad things about me. He was calling me "bogus" and a "moron." He complained that all I do is sit around watching the dolphins, and then dash off to Woodstock or Paris with Brigitte Bardot. The frustrating part is that with all this arguing, Trout and I were hurting everything we were trying to do at Sugarloaf. Exasperated, I went over to the restaurant, sat down, and glanced out through the glass. Lloyd was doing the Sugar Show. I had told Lloyd many times that this was the worst dolphin show I'd ever seen. He and his sister Caren took turns with Kathleen presenting the show, which was always the same, feeding after feeding. Sugar jumping through the hoops, Sugar finding the coins, Sugar kissing the trainer, and finally Sugar with a little wooden propeller that Lloyd had carved himself, spinning it on her snout like a helicopter. It was also seemingly the same little handful of spectators coming to bear witness.

I couldn't watch it. I got up and went back to my bus, which was parked just outside the sanctuary and served as my office. I started to think about what Lloyd had done earlier. At Trout's behest, an heir to the Dole pineapple fortune contributed $10,000 for the sanctuary's medical pen. She had flown in from Hawaii to Key West, rented a car, and driven up to inspect the sanctuary. Unfortunately, Lloyd must have been in an imperial mood. Her room in the motel was on the second floor and he refused to carry up her two bags. She struggled to get them up the stairs herself, got mad as hell about it, then carried them back down, put them in the car, and took off.

Eleven German photojournalists later came through in a group on assignments for various periodicals and television stations. They flew into Miami, then drove by van to Key West. They called me and I told them to check out of the hotel they were in and move into the Sugarloaf Lodge. The next morning bright and early I met them out front and took them down to the dolphin lagoon, and there were Lloyd and Jerry, the maintenance man, feeding the dolphins from a kayak. Lloyd knew not to feed the dolphins from a boat. I had told him that if they were fed from a boat at this stage of the process, they would more likely approach a boat for food in the wild when they were freed. But Lloyd was doing it his way.

I had told Lloyd about the German journalists coming through. They would be here for four days, I told him. But when he saw them standing around the lagoon, he feigned surprise and told them they could not take photographs without written consent. This was beyond bizarre, of course, because even tourists passing through were allowed to take pictures. But this was the kind of control he wanted over everything. The photojournalists checked out and returned to Key West.

"Maybe I've been missing the point," I told Caren in the bus. "My focus is on the dolphins. It never changes. Maybe sometimes I lose sight of what happens beyond the dolphins. You know, Caren, I think Lloyd could be turned around if he simply understood what I'm trying to tell him about the Sugar Show." I said, "I'm not Sharman. I don't do miracles. But if he could see that changing the Sugar Show is really an opportunity for him." I stopped suddenly. "Look at it like this. All up and down the state, it's one big dolphin show, all of them doing the same tricks. Don't you think it would be better if Lloyd could show the people something different? He could have the first anti-captivity dolphin show in the world by simply telling people what was really going on."

She smiled. "I'm doing the show tomorrow morning. What *is* really going on?"

Caren is very bright. She was in a blue one-piece swim suit, a loose white T-shirt on top of that, flip-flops on her feet. I was sitting in one of the bus seats, she curled up in another. I told her some of the things she could say that would be true, that Sugar is not an ambassador of the dolphins, she is a captive here, a prisoner. That Sugar was here when her family bought the place more than twenty years ago and by now she's so unlike real dolphins in the sea that it would be inhumane to try to free her. It's too late for that. She's a dead-end dolphin. And the best thing we can do now is keep her as happy and healthy as we can, and feed her. I also told her to say that when Sugar is fed, she does tricks because she needs the exercise. But the spectators shouldn't applaud. They should never applaud any wild animal doing tricks. That's a form of dominance that deprives the dolphin of dignity. I told her I was thinking about the children. The children don't know any better. They see something in public and they think it's the way things ought to be. They need someone to tell them the truth. At first Caren resisted, feeling a show without applause was like a funeral without flowers. But she eventually agreed to try the show my way, and my hope was that Lloyd would like it.

о   о   о

The crowd was not large, ten or fifteen people, a few others perhaps watching from the restaurant. They had no idea what was going on when Caren began the New Sugar Show with a simple statement:

"This is Sugar," she said, "but she doesn't belong here. She really belongs out there." Caren pointed to the flats of Sugarloaf Bay beyond the lagoon. "When my family bought this place, she was here. And we would free her if we could. But we don't think she would make it on her own out there anymore. She's been here too long, a captive. And that means she will probably live out her days here."

I was off to one side and I could see Lloyd sitting in his white pickup truck, watching his sister, frowning. And so were many of the people watching. This was no longer a frolic in the lagoon, this was solemn business. The premise of allowing dolphins to be kept at public facilities is that it's educational. And yet, these shows are all a fraud. Caren repeated some of the things I told her she could say, that Sugar was not an ambassador, that she's a victim, blind in one eye and very old. But Caren forgot to ask the crowd not to applaud, and when Sugar went through her tricks for exercise, some of the spectators applauded, some didn't. It was strange. Everybody had a frozen look. But they understood, I think, that this was a pathetic beaten-down dolphin going through a bizarre ritual in order to be fed. This was not a dolphin doing tricks, this was Sugar, and they were seeing her for the first time as she really was.

When Caren finished the show, I walked over with a big smile and told her, "Beautiful job. I loved it. Thanks."

Lloyd signaled her from the pickup. She went over, they talked a minute, then Lloyd slowly pulled away, glancing back at me. Caren walked back over to me and said glumly that she wouldn't be doing the Sugar Show anymore.

So I had failed in turning Lloyd around with an honest Sugar Show, Caren had lost her job as a dolphin trainer, Trout apparently was continuing to malign me, the Welcome Home Project had bogged down because Joe Roberts couldn't get the paperwork we needed to transport Bogie and Bacall back to Melbourne, and any day now we would be told that the five Navy dolphins were ready to be picked up. I glanced down at Sugar, who was pushing around her big black inner tube with the dead pine tree limb on it, and I wondered if what we were doing made much more sense than that.

10

BRICKS IN THE MIX

The best laid schemes o' mice and men . . .
—Robert Burns

IN MID-MAY OF 1994, a number of newspapers in South Florida and the Florida Keys began to take note of the brewing furor over the dolphins at Sugarloaf. It began, not unexpectedly, with the Dolphin Research Center (DRC) complaining about our plans to release captive dolphins. One reporter in the *Florida Keys Keynoter* noted the dramatic irony:

"It's like a scene from *Kramer vs. Kramer.* Two well-meaning parents are locked in a bitter battle over what is best for their beloved child. . . . "

Yes, it was, sort of. But the media had also sensed something much more to its taste, a lurid peek into the private affairs of the animal welfare industry. From the viewpoint of the media, these animal welfare groups, though mysteriously different in their attitudes toward animals, were all the same in being both tax-free and private. To the media this is an oxymoron. If they were collecting money from the public, their books ought to be public too, but they weren't. And the media, sniffing a scam, waited for someone on the inside to start blabbing about the others. And a wild and crazy notion took shape that this whole idyllic dream of freeing captive dolphins was perhaps but a house of cards.

When Bogie and Bacall and Molly arrived at Sugarloaf, it must have seemed like old home week for Trout and Lynne, as if their gig as trainers at ORC had been revived. Trout began setting things up as they had been in palmier times. I kept reminding everybody what our goal was and that this was not a dolphin show, but the moment I turned my back they reverted to form. Once again the problem was about feeding. Trout and Lynne and all their volunteers were feeding the dolphins as they had at ORC. I saw Lynne baby-talking to the dolphins as she fed them one day and I confronted her.

Lynne was the worst about baby-talking. She'd say the same things over and over in a sing-song falsetto. Things like, "Come on, girls, come to mamma. Come on, sweetheart. Do my baby girls want a fish?" and so on.

Is this really so terrible, baby-talking to a dolphin? It seems like a trifle, but it strikes at the very foundation of what we were doing. Even if the dolphins never noticed it, *we* noticed and it became part of our thinking. It's the wrong message. I don't mean the words. I mean the tone, the body language. When everything I'm trying to say to the dolphins is "freedom," the body language of baby talk is "captivity." When I'm rehabbing dolphins, I'm reading every move the dolphins make. I'm getting an insight into how they feel and what's going on inside. I keep track of these movements and compare what they do today, their patterns and behaviors, with what they did the day before. Then I compare all that with patterns made by dolphins in the wild. I want them to detach themselves from us, to live entirely in their own world, which is the world they will live in when finally we set them free.

At the same time, I'm watching every move *I* make, too. Ideally, they would never see me, and then my movements would never conflict with the world they find themselves in. But in reality, they do know that I'm there, and the best I can do is keep from sending body messages that could blur the one message I have for them: "Freedom." When I turn from reading the dolphins, I don't immediately click off the body-language mode I'm in. I don't especially want to. To me it's better than spoken language. It's truer; it never lies. It's almost like reading someone's mind. When I saw Lynne and the others baby-talking to Molly, I could tell they had no intention of freeing her.

Do *I* ever "talk" to the dolphins when I'm working with them? I talk to them sometimes, yes, when they're under stress, for instance, and I'm trying to calm them down. But I never use baby-talk. My talking is usually silent. I think the words. I don't mean "mind reading" or anything like that. I think the words in order to focus myself on the dolphins and the energy of my thought to help them be free. In a way it's like prayer.

When I was with Trout and the others, overseeing things at the dolphin lagoon, they fed them the way I wanted them to; when I was not there, others told me, they did it their way, undoing in my absence what we worked for when I was there.

°   °   °

Even as the APHIS inspectors checked out Sugarloaf preparatory to receiving the Navy dolphins, Lloyd was still on the fence about Trout and me. He wanted everybody to work together, to be a "family," as he referred to us. But with Trout and I locked in such a death struggle, Lloyd couldn't get anything to work, and it became increasingly obvious that he would have to get rid of either Trout or me.

He seemed to be seeking enlightenment from Sharman, and I noticed them chanting, burning sage, and beating their drums. I probably came across as an ascetic spoilsport. From their viewpoint, I must have seemed to be leading them down a new and dubious path that was not much fun. I was critical. I kept to myself, coming and going at irregular times and in virtual silence. And if I lent a hand on work details, I don't remember. Nor do I regret it if I didn't. My job, my expertise was in rehabbing captive dolphins, and my place was with the dolphins. Was I being aloof? Stand-offish? Sullen? I've been accused of that before. I used to explain that I was shy, and that's why I kept to myself so much. Now I'm not sure. I think it may be more complicated than that.

I would have understood his opting for Trout. They were pals. It was hard not to like Trout. And I'm sure Lloyd would have preferred his buddy around except that Sharman said that the Creator had selected me. I hadn't tried to talk to Lloyd much. I thought that Trout and I might still work out separate paths that would allow us to avoid conflict, at least till the job was done. At the same time, I wasn't sure what Lloyd would do if I called for a showdown.

So the day Lloyd and I sat down on the seawall together, it was not to talk about Trout. I saw Lloyd sitting there with a beer, gazing off into the Gulf. It was one of those very still days when the whole sky was like a huge white dome, disappearing without a trace into the water. I sat down next to him, we nodded pleasantries to each other, and since neither of us is much of a talker, we just sat there for a while, looking out over the Gulf. Then Lloyd turned slightly toward me and said, "You spent a whole week just sitting down there with the dolphins. What's that about?"

"I always do that," I said. "That's how I get to know them."

"Get to know them?" He gave a little laugh. "Well, let me introduce you, Mr. Dolphin Expert. That's Molly there." He pointed at one of the dolphins rising at that moment and blowing a plume of vapor. "And that one over there," he said, pointing again to another one, "that's Bogie. You ought to know that Bogie is not a male."

"I'm aware of that," I said, nodding.

"You are, are you?" He smiled as if he were talking to a child. "Well, and the other one there," he pointed again, "—that's Bacall."

"I think you know that Bogie, Bacall, and Molly are more than just their names," I said. "When we name something, we think we understand it. But there's more to it than that. You're amused because I spent some time just sitting by their lagoon, doing nothing—or so you thought. But I was getting to know them and who they are to each other. There are no shortcuts to knowing dolphins. You have to live with them, day and night. The one we call Molly," I said, "makes a sound like this." And then I made a whooshing sound, D-Minor, in and out.

"You're not saying that that's her signature whistle, are you?"

"No," I said. "The signature whistle is something else. This is just the way she breathes. It's in the tone of it." I stood up. "Come on over," I said. "Let's get to know them a little better."

He got up and we walked over closer to where the dolphins were, sat down on the sea wall again and watched for a minute. I made Molly's breathing sound again. Then Molly surfaced and made the same sound.

"The other two, Bogie and Bacall, are like this," I said. And then I made their sounds, A and A-minor, slightly higher and faster. About the same time Bogie and Bacall came up and breathed the same way I had breathed, quickly in and out. The sound they make in breathing is a function of their size. Molly, being larger, made a deeper sound than Bogie and Bacall.

Lloyd turned to me, smiling. Then he frowned suddenly. "But so what?" he asked. "What good is it?"

I gave a shrug. "When you know something that's true, does it have to be good for something else? If so, I guess you could say that I don't have to watch them to know what they're doing. I can 'see' them in the dark, follow them around the lagoon in my own mind at night, just by listening to the way they breathe. If one of them doesn't breathe in their rhythm, I know she's under water, maybe chasing a fish."

"Just by the sound you know she's chasing a fish?"

"I know the sounds they make when they chase fish in the daytime. When I hear the same thing at night, that tells me what they're doing. When I *don't* hear certain sounds, that tells me what they're doing too. When I don't hear them breathing, for instance, I don't know that they've actually caught the fish, but I know they're hunting fish. And if they're catching fish on their own, that means their sonar is working. The more fish they catch on their own, the closer they come to being free. And you know what they're free from, Lloyd? They're free from *us*. By listening closely I also know about their socializing, whether this one is with that one or the other, whether one of them is off to herself, sulking or maybe sick, or maybe just wanting to be alone. When I hear these things—even at night while lying in my tent, it tells me what I should check the next day."

Lloyd looked at me and said, "This problem you're having with Trout. What can I do about it? What *should* I do?"

"Right now? Nothing. I don't think it'll work, but I'm still hoping I can get through to him. We have a problem, Lloyd, because Trout is only a trainer."

Lloyd darted a quick look at me, frowning. Lloyd was "only" a trainer, too. I didn't mean "only" in a demeaning way. Training a dolphin gives the trainer a certain understanding of the animal. It's the same understanding that's achieved by working closely with anyone or anything, even a computer, and it's as intimate as a relationship can be. So Lloyd, I'm sure, must have been wondering what I was getting at, and whether I was taking a shot at him. "Now what exactly does that mean?" he asked.

I told him that I didn't deny that the trainer-dolphin relationship was sometimes wonderful, especially to the trainer. "To the trainer," I said, "it's a little like making love. But it's not love. Not even close. Love is between equals. And the trainer and dolphin are not equal. In training a dolphin, the trainer feels the thrill of controlling a fabulous beast, but the dolphin is a prisoner and what he feels is merely the thrill of eating another meal. When dolphins are captured, they lose their power. What I'm doing is the reverse of that. I'm trying to give them back their power, to *empower* the dolphins, to give them back their identity, give them options, decisions to make. And to do that, I've got to know who they really are, which has nothing to do with these phony names we give them. If the whole point of what we're doing here is to return these dolphins to the sea again and have them survive, they must become whole again. Real dolphins."

Lloyd was beginning to see things my way—or so I thought when he was with me. But when I noticed him with Trout, he seemed to be with him even more.

My problem with Trout was not always center stage. In the generally dysfunctional atmosphere at Sugarloaf, we were all having problems with each other. Mostly it was petty stuff, both real and imagined slights and misunderstandings, feelings of unfair treatment and so on. We were all running to Lloyd and griping about something—everything had to go through him. And yet, he had no idea what to do about it. So Lloyd was calling meetings almost every day to solve the problems. We gathered in the bushes about thirty feet away from the lagoon. The theory in group therapy is that airing grievances makes them go away. But in our case, these meetings were like throwing gas on fire. Everybody was blaming everybody else for whatever happened, misquoting and misinterpreting what others had said, all of us pointing and yelling about each other for being late or not filling in the log books, not cleaning up the fish house properly, and about purely personal things that had nothing to do with dolphins. Looking back, it was a farce, and I'm embarrassed to have been a part of it. But it was the best we could do at the time.

It finally got so bad I went to Lloyd again about Trout, warning him that this whole project might well go down the tubes if Trout kept undercutting everything I tried to do.

Lloyd was half in the water working on a fence. He looked up with sweat running down his face and asked me what I wanted him to do. I didn't know. I think Lloyd was trying to get everybody to work together. He talked about all of us at the sanctuary being like family, and that we were just having a family fuss, which should go away any time now. But it hadn't, and now maybe it was time to do something drastic, maybe like firing someone. But I didn't want Trout fired. I wanted to work with him. Unfortunately, I couldn't even talk to him.

I glanced back over the lagoon, the dolphins were swimming slowly in a lazy circle, Molly leading the others. "If we could get some other activists to sit down with him and arbitrate this thing. An intervention. That might work. Maybe then, if he'll listen, we can all get on with it."

o   o   o

About a week later the Gadfly Conference met at Sugarloaf. It was not just about the trouble between Trout and me, though. It was aimed at organizing everybody in the world of dolphin activism. The ugly dispute now leaking to the public between Trout and me was used as a cautionary tale. Rick Spill of the Animal Welfare Institute organized the conference. A few years later, Rick would be the subject of an investigation into his background as a possible "mole" for the other side: an anti–animal welfare organization called "Putting People First." After Merritt Clifton, editor of *Animal People,* made that charge in his magazine, Spill dropped out of sight.

About a hundred people showed up at the conference, most of whom I knew. In fact, I had personally gotten many of them involved in captive dolphin issues. We met one weekend at the firehouse next to the motel, and right off the bat Spill called Trout and me up to the stage. He put down two chairs next to each other like a talk show, we sat down and he said in his gruff way, "What's all this fighting about, guys? Can't you two get along?" He turned to Trout. "What about this business of throwing bricks at dolphins? What's that about?" He was talking to both of us when he said, "And let's stick to the facts."

Trout was grinning now. He said he had found an entry in the logbooks where I had written that the dolphins were bonding to the northwest corner of the lagoon. "And in that corner," he said, "I found the bricks."

Spill turned to me. "Is that so, Ric? What about it?"

"Did he find the bricks? Is that what you're asking me? He might have. But so what? I think he's trying to say that I had something to do with the bricks being there, that I threw the bricks at the dolphins to keep them from bonding with that part of the lagoon. *Nonsense!* The population of the U.S. is about 250 million people. I would be the very last in that long line of people to throw a brick at anything, much less a dolphin. Did I see the dolphins bonding to that end of the lagoon? Of course, I did. And I made a note of it in the log. This is not hard to understand. The dolphins are bonding there because that's where they're always fed. It had become their feeding station. If you look at the logs, you'll see that I also recommended that we no longer feed them only at that spot. We should feed them at no particular spot. We're trying to break all bonds the dolphins have with us, including that one."

Trout said, "It's an old trainer's trick, throwing bricks to shoo them away."

I got up from my chair and walked back and forth for a moment, my head down. I peered out at the audience and finally said, "That may be an old trainer's trick, Trout, and you would know about that because you have been a trainer all your life—only a trainer. And that's what you still are. But I've never thrown a brick or anything else at a dolphin in my whole life. And correct me if I'm wrong, but when you were fired from Seaco at San Diego, didn't you charge the other trainers with kicking dolphins and throwing bricks at them?" Before I was called to the front of the room, someone had given me a press release that Trout had prepared. "You want to know what this is really about? Here it is," I said to the crowd, waving the press release. "He's not in charge here. But he's putting out press releases claiming to be. It's as if he's doing this all alone, except down here at the bottom," I said, holding the paper up again, "that's my name, listed as 'consultant.'" I hadn't noticed the acoustics here before, but I was speaking very softly and yet my voice filled the room. "I'm not a consultant here. I'm in charge of rehabilitation and release. That's *my* title. I've done this before. And I'm the only one who has." I turned to Trout, who was grinning through it all. *"And you haven't.* I'll say to you here and now in front of this group what I've told you in private. Do your job, Trout, and learn. Learn a little humility, too. It will carry you a long way. Try to learn about the power of cooperation. When the job is done, I'll be out of here and you will have a successful release under your belt. Then you'll have credibility. Until then, you have no credibility. That's all you can do, Trout, and that's all I'm asking you to do."

Trout was shaking his head. "He misses the point. I found those bricks, just like I said. What about the bricks?"

Lloyd was in the audience and had been silent till now. He slowly rose to his feet and everybody fell silent. In a soft but commanding voice, Lloyd said that he had put the bricks there some time ago to hold down the aerator hose. The bricks had been covered by silt, but when the dolphins were put in the lagoon, their tail-flukes had dusted the silt away, revealing the bricks.

I was stunned. If Lloyd had known this all along, why had he waited till now to say it? And then I recalled something he had told me earlier when I complained to him about Trout's lack of cooperation. I told Lloyd that if he was in charge he ought to take charge and put a stop to it. Lloyd had shook his head and said that my problem with Trout was not his problem. "You guys are in a shoot-out," he said, "and when it's over, one of you will be left standing. That's the one I'll work with."

Trout wasn't backing down. "But the bricks . . . they were there," he said. He twisted around in his chair, talking first to Spill, then to the group. "It's open and shut. Don't you get it?" He was nodding his head, pointing his finger, and grinning like all this was a big joke. Ironically, Trout himself had once worked at DRC in the 1970s and was fired, according to DRC spokesperson Dana Carnegie, for kicking a dolphin and depriving it of food.

Captain Gary Elston, an intense man with longish hair wearing a Dolphin Watch T-shirt, rose from his chair and said in a booming voice, "If anybody in this room thinks that Ric O'Barry would throw a brick at a dolphin, hold up your hand."

We all looked around, but nobody held up their hand. It was a long moment that dragged on and on, and finally I said to Trout, "Come on, Trout. Hold up your hand." He just grinned.

Everybody in the room stared in stony silence at Trout. I had moved my chair around so that I could look squarely at him. Spill said quietly, "Try to get along, you guys. Think of the dolphins first."

Though that was the most dramatic part of the conference, its grand purpose was more far-reaching and more sinister than that. It had been billed as a conference to set up a coalition, an umbrella organization to control all dolphin activists. At first, this sounds like a great idea, getting everybody together, working toward the same goal. We would be more efficient that way, more effective. We could share information, speak with one voice. Focus ourselves. And there would be no more embarrassing public squabbles like the one between Trout and me.

But on second thought, it was not so good for me. I was doing okay on my own. To me it was a bunch of new people trying to take over, including marketing geniuses like Dan Morast. He and his International Wildlife Coalition ran an adopt-a-whale program, selling certificates of "adoption." Others in the coalition included armchair activists, people who had never worked with a dolphin. And now I would be expected to report to them for permission to do what I had been doing on my own the past twenty-five years. This made no sense to me. I would also have to fill out papers, submit plans, and spend time in meetings, reading reports and writing them, the kind of bureaucratic tomfoolery I had spent my whole life avoiding.

No, I didn't like the idea. I was a very active activist. I wanted to *do* things. And I didn't care to have my life and work funneled through Spill. While I was sitting in the audience, I couldn't tell how the others around me were reacting to this new plan. But when I went up on the stage I could see their faces. I noticed Naomi Rose, for instance, who was standing in the back of the room against the wall. I glanced around the stage, noticed a TV set there, pointed to it and said, "You see that? To me, everything I do is really about that: educating the public. Everybody's got a TV set, at least one. When I can tell people about my work on TV and show them what I'm doing, I'm getting the message out to millions and millions of people all over the world. And that's not the end of it. When they understand the message, never again will they buy another ticket to a dolphin show. That's the bottom line: money. Cut off the money and the whole thing dies. When people see these dolphin clown shows for what they really are, they'll never spend another dime on them." I glanced to the back of the room at Naomi Rose, and she was shaking her head "no."

After the conference, I hoped my publicly confronting Trout would mellow him out, and even if we didn't enjoy each other's company we could at least get on with the job. But Trout, like the Energizer Bunny, never stopped. My confrontation with him seemed only to inspire further animosity. And by now I was beginning to appreciate Trout's determination as a thing in itself, the teeth-clenching ferocity of it an absolute marvel. Some people view me as being somewhat hyper-focused, but this thing with Trout was on a whole different level. I had never seen anything like it.

o　　o　　o

I flew to San Diego and hooked up with three of the Navy dolphins—Buck, Luther, and Jake. Navy officials told us that the other two, Ikaka and Modick, were sick and unable to travel. Then I flew back to the Boca Chica Naval Air Station near Key West with the dolphins and their Navy crew. We were met by Lloyd, who signed for the dolphins, Trout, Spill, and Naomi Rose, who had her own professional film crew in tow, and about a dozen volunteers. We transported the Navy dolphins in the same truck we had used to transport Bogie, Bacall, and Molly, then put them in the east wing of the lagoon, separated from the females by a plastic fence.

This was a jubilant moment, our dreams coming true. Despite some hard feelings, the plan was working even better than I thought it would. Lloyd, Trout, and I and a crew of about a dozen volunteers were working full-time, and it was still important, I thought, that we work together. Caught up in the spirit of the moment, I said something like that to Trout, who was washing his Jeep with a hose. He glared at me, and I realized that nothing had changed. Because we were working on the same project, we had to talk from time to time, we had to get things straight about feeding the dolphins, for instance. *Feeding* again? Yes, it was always about feeding. I was sick of the subject, but it was crucial, and when Trout refused even to listen to me, I did the next best thing. I wrote a message down on a piece of paper:

"To avoid conflict in the future, please communicate with me through Lloyd, who will pass the information to me."

I had already cleared this with Lloyd. I put the paper on the hood of Trout's Jeep and walked off. I didn't look back, but I could hear him exploding like a trick cigar. I walked on over to the lagoon, dejected.

Lloyd, who had been watching, came over to me and said softly, "I've got to get rid of one of you. And since you're the only one who's done this before, I'm going to fire him."

"No, no," I said. "That's not the thing to do. 'Keep your friends close, your enemies closer.'"

He looked at me, half smiling. "Did you just make that up?"

"No," I said. "I don't think I made it up."

"That's pretty good, but I've got one, too. 'Friends are good, but control is better.'"

I didn't see how his saying related to mine, except perhaps in meter, and I didn't know what to say, so I just stared at him.

"Anyway," he said finally, "I've had enough. I've got to do something." He headed toward Trout.

Half an hour later, we heard police sirens, an ambulance, and a fire truck pull up outside. Someone had called 911. The emergency vehicles and crews had gathered at the water's edge. We looked out on the bay and there was Trout, walking across the flats in his clothes, cursing, and splashing water. He and Lloyd had been out in Lloyd's boat together. Now Trout was making his way back across the flats. We watched as he reached the mangrove swamps, then marched by us to his Jeep, his clothes dripping wet, his shoes muddy. He got in, fired it up, and took off with squealing tires. His story, which he soon spread to the world, was that Lloyd had knocked him out of the boat.

Lloyd called a meeting of the staff and explained that he had not laid a hand on Trout. He said he had fired Lynne, and given Trout a month or so off with pay "to rest up" and "get some help." At that point, according to Lloyd, Trout screamed obscenities at him, and jumped out of the boat.

With Trout and Lynne gone, at least for a while, I felt like a curse had been lifted. We were all out by the lagoon and I began picking up the women and tossing them in the water, Vanessa, Kathleen, Cathy, Caren, and even Guili Cordara, an officer of Prince Sadruddin Aga Kahn's Bellerive Foundation. Ken Peterson, a freelance filmmaker, was producing a documentary about the rehab and release of all the dolphins and was shooting the scene with his video camera. I jumped in the lagoon, a big cannonball, and we all splashed water at each other, laughing and cavorting around.

Ken and his girlfriend, Cathy Kinsman, a singer-songwriter, were from Canada. She had appeared in some of Ken's music-video productions. She loved feeding the dolphins, but disliked having to prepare the fish she fed them. And because she sometimes shirked doing the actual work, some of us—Caren, Kathleen and I—had to keep after her about it.

Jack and Vanessa Martini of Colorado, another Sugarloaf working couple, had recently lost their only son, the victim of a violent crime, and they were trying to cope with it and get on with their lives. Their arrival here was an interesting story. They had been driving down US 1 to Key West, she holding an urn of their son's ashes in her lap, and on the urn three dolphins swam. At that moment they happened to be passing Sugarloaf and noticed that it was a dolphin sanctuary. As if drawn by a higher power, they pulled the car into the lot, parked, and went over to see the dolphins, Bogie, Bacall, and Molly. Could it have been more obvious to them that this is where they belonged? They didn't think so. They rented a place on a canal nearby, Vanessa began working as a volunteer with the dolphins, and Jack took a job in Key West.

Ken and Cathy, Jack and Vanessa were all loyal to Trout when Trout was in charge, they switched their loyalty to me when I seemed to be in charge, and even later, when winds came from yet another direction, Ken and Cathy switched their allegiance again. When Trout was told to go on vacation, Jack came to me and explained that Vanessa's volunteer work with the dolphins was better than therapy, and I assured him that Vanessa was welcome to stay on as a volunteer. There was always a ready supply of volunteers, whom we called "caregivers" to distinguish them from trainers.

◦   ◦   ◦

Now that I wasn't challenged by Trout every step of the way, I was trying various things with the dolphins, like getting Molly in with Sugar, and keeping Luther from fighting with Buck and Jake.

Meanwhile, Trout teamed up with Russ Rector and the two of them kept up a steady drum-beat of complaints to USDA/APHIS. The charges were reported in the *Miami Herald*:

"Some of the most prominent activists in the movement to free captive dolphins from marine parks and military programs are now fighting one another. . . . The problem: Trout and former Flipper trainer Ric O'Barry disagree about how to prepare the dolphins for eventual release."

Joe Roberts was quoted saying, "Trout is too emotionally attached to the Ocean Reef dolphins he once cared for exclusively. Trout is full of rage and guilt and has been making life at Sugarloaf miserable for the staff there. They [at Sugarloaf] feel like a black cloud has finally passed over and the sun is shining since Trout left."

Naomi Rose was quoted, too: "The dispute is an internal personnel matter and does not mean there is any trouble with the pioneering project to release dolphins. . . . It's not affecting the dolphins at all," she said. "There's been some disagreement . . . and Mr. O'Barry is the man with the experience. He knows how to do it. He's done it before successfully."

An animal rights group in Ohio called Lloyd and sent him a tape of a message Trout had left on their answering machine with shocking charges full of invective against Sugarloaf, Lloyd, and me.

At the end of Trout's thirty-day furlough, Lloyd called a meeting of the board and Trout showed up. Lloyd asked him if he had been bad-mouthing Sugarloaf. Trout denied it, Lloyd played the tape and fired him. The board of directors upheld Lloyd's action except for Dr. George Baker, a friend of Trout's, who abstained. A veterinarian, Dr. Baker soon quit the board, and so did the lawyer and his wife, who were fed up with all the turmoil. So Lloyd and I, the only two remaining members of the board, thought it politic to name several of the more prominent members of the newly created Gadfly Coalition as their replacements. We selected Spill, Mark Berman of Earth Island Institute, and Robert Schoelkopf of the Marine Mammal Stranding Center.

Trout stepped up his accusations against us. In a *Miami Herald* story of December 17, Trout and Lynne Stringer said that they were calling for a government investigation of the facility. "These guys aren't doing their jobs," Trout said. "They say they're going to release dolphins. They haven't even applied to release the Navy dolphins. They've become just another captivity facility. That puts them under the scrutiny of activists and federal agencies who have expectations . . . [and] those expectations aren't being met, even at the most basic levels."

The newspaper article continued: "In his letter to the USDA, Trout said the husbandry and training skills of former Flipper trainer Ric O'Barry are 'outdated and abusive,' . . . that someone may have thrown a brick into the dolphin pen, hitting Molly. He is challenging staff qualifications, the inappropriate placement of a large net at the mouth of a lagoon where the dolphins live, poor to nonexistent record-keeping and fiscal irresponsibility. . . . Trout said he still believes in the mission—to release captive dolphins or provide a restful retirement for those that can't be released. But O'Barry and the Goods are the wrong people to direct that effort. 'That's why I'm working real hard at setting up another one someplace else.'"

Lloyd called a meeting and asked all of us for our resumés. Then, in an effort to soothe troubled waters, he sent a heartfelt note to Trout:

"At such a time when you are once again happy, receptive and free from whatever is causing you horrible pain, and you can replace your hatred with love, this is your home. Please realize that something is wrong, and that you need to fix it. All of us working together will be magical. When you are well, you are welcome back."

We soon had no time for such gestures. We were involved in almost continuous inspections. APHIS inspects captive dolphin facilities periodically—once a year or less at the larger dolphin shows. But they also inspect when they receive complaints. And they were beginning to get lots of complaints. That year they inspected Sugarloaf more than thirty-five times. Number of violations: none.

Trout stepped up his attacks on us in very personal ways, saying things on radio talk shows or to newspapers and TV stations that he was in no position to know, things like what we were planning to do next and exactly where Sugarloaf money was going. Sugarloaf had no secrets to speak of, but this was not public business. I suspected someone was peeking into our account at the local bank. This was the only way that information could be obtained, and later I plugged that leak by getting some people discharged.

Besides the war with Trout and Rector, and the wounds they opened almost daily in the press, two key things were happening at the same time. One was Naomi Rose ratcheting the pressure on me to do a scientific protocol about the rehab and release of captive dolphins. The other was that Sugar wasn't eating.

11

IN CHAINS

Trust me.

—Joe Roberts

SUGAR HAD NOT BEEN eating, which in any other dolphin would indicate a health problem—possibly serious. But in Sugar's case, you can throw out the norms. She was different. She was old, or she seemed old. Actually she was twenty-six or twenty-seven, which is old for a captive dolphin, but not for a wild dolphin. If she had lived in the wild, she would have been middle-aged. What made her seem so old was that she lived not only in captivity but also in isolation. She was being bored to death. And because of this, she was depressed, losing interest in almost everything, including food. I call this Captive Dolphin Depression Syndrome (CDDS). It wasn't surprising to me that from time to time she would refuse to eat. And each time, I thought this might be it, that she would die. I mentioned to Lloyd that I had seen other dolphins like this, and that Sugar was depressed. But Lloyd insisted, "No. This is not depression. She's meditating. She's like a monk, peaceful and calm."

Just looking at Sugar, you couldn't tell whether she had eaten or not. Most of the time, she just floated on top of the water. Was this because of her age and isolation? Partly, perhaps. But this is how other captive dolphins live, too, even young and energetic dolphins in captivity. This is the part of dolphin clown shows they don't show you. When you go to a dolphin show, you see the happy clowns with the big grins, their joyful leaping about and eagerness to please. This is how they're depicted in the world of advertising, and you expect them to be like that all the time. But what you don't see is what happens to the dolphins between shows. When the crowd is gone, the dolphins have nothing to do till the next show, so they just lie there, floating on top of the water, waiting.

I didn't know that Sugar was going through another eating crisis till I asked Caren one day where Lloyd was and she said, "He can't be bothered now. Sugar hasn't eaten in more than a week."

More than a week! That's not just a lack of appetite. But what is it? A problem? You never know that it's definitely a problem until blood is drawn and analyzed. Then if technicians find indicators of a certain list of possible causes, a name can be put to it and steps taken toward a cure. But many times, you never know for sure. And often it clears up by itself. That was Lloyd's strategy now, waiting. At first, it would be noted in the log that Sugar hadn't eaten. If we had had a resident vet, he would have been notified. Then the vet would have joined Lloyd and some others in watching Sugar, trying to assess the cause. But since there was no vet on the premises, Lloyd stood watch alone. By the fourth day, Lloyd wouldn't have been able to keep his eyes off his beloved pet, while she floated with disinterest around the lagoon, her eyes closed. For Lloyd, it was almost unbearable, because not only was his pet apparently sick, but her fate was also in his hands. Trying to decide what to do, Lloyd watched with growing anxiety, hoping to catch the first glimmer of a response from her.

What he was actually looking for, what everybody was looking for, was to see Sugar looking at the dock. That's where they always fed her, and when Sugar glanced at the dock, that meant she was hungry. When someone saw her glancing at the dock, they would say, "She's looking." Then Lloyd or someone else would go down and feed her. That would be the Sugar Show. Now, though, Lloyd was watching Sugar from wherever he might be, from the restaurant, from the Tiki Bar, from his pickup truck, or from the edge of the lagoon, sitting with his legs drawn up and his arms around his knees, watching in silence for Sugar to glance toward the dock.

When the vet, Dr. Baker, was finally summoned, he said she had to be force fed. A doctor is not necessary for this; we do it ourselves when we need to. But this was what he prescribed, so we got ready for it. If all goes well, this takes about an hour. Ten people were involved, six of us got in the water with a net and ran it around the floating dolphin. Using the capture net we forced her into the stretcher. Then we put a couple of towels in her mouth so that we could hold her mouth open when the time came. With the stretcher, we walked her over to the bank where Dr. Baker, Kathleen, and a few others waited. They already had the lubricated three-foot tube and a gallon bag full of "soup" that would be gravity-fed into her stomach. The soup was composed of fish, water, electrolyte, and blue-green algae, all chopped in a food processor to about the consistency of apple sauce. The most important ingredient was the water because the immediate problem was dehydration. Their only source of water is from the fish they eat. We carefully pushed the tube down Sugar's throat about two feet so that the end of it was in her stomach. It's a straight shot from mouth to stomach. There is no gagging, not even a possibility of that, because a dolphin breathes only through its blow hole. The soup was released and down it flowed. While Sugar was still in the stretcher, a sample of blood was drawn for analysis. We floated her back out into the deeper water of the lagoon in the stretcher and let her go. If she held the food, she would start feeling better very soon and eat on her own again. So we all watched to make sure she didn't throw up. If she did throw it up, we would have had to do it all again.

o   o   o

When Sugar's crisis was settled, Molly acted up, refusing to go into Sugar's lagoon. A few days later, Sugar had to be pulled again. We were all feeling the tension, and little things got to us. One time, for instance, as volunteers were feeding the dolphins, one of them noticed a rake mark on a dolphin, and asked where the gentian violet was. This is an antiseptic for slight skin injuries to the dolphins. Nobody spoke up. Later, though, after feeding the dolphins, Cathy Kinsman went over to the dolphin and applied the medication herself. She had it all the time and had said nothing. The others were furious. Adding to the normal tensions of caring for dolphins was the endless pressure of the media. It was like a giant eyeball staring at us all the time, newspaper stories, TV reports, and moralizing local radio talk shows. Gradually a siege mentality emerged, some of us drawing closer to each other. Others, however, were feeding information to the other side, hoping to cause our downfall.

And yet we were not anxious to answer every charge against us. The charges were negative, and negativity tends to rebound against those who produce it. We wanted to be positive or, failing that, negative only about their negativity, which theoretically would be positive. Lloyd had the volunteers drink a concoction of blue-green algae, an antioxidant, and summoned Sharman.

On her arrival, the California shaman detected negative energy at once and went to work, beating the drum, burning sage, and easing tensions. That evening, she read Tarot cards in her room for some of the women, including Kathleen Brooks and her mother, Shaney Frey, a talented writer of Boynton Beach, Florida, who recalls with amusement her first meeting with Sharman: "Who is this little Humpty-Dumpty wrapped in fox furs with a tom-tom and with ribbons and feathers in her braids?"

Kathleen told me she was amused by Sharman. It was a good act, she thought, Sharman saying that Molly feels this and Bogie thinks that, but could she really read their minds? Kathleen thought not. This was confirmed one day when she and Sharman were swimming in one end of the lagoon together, fifty yards away from the dolphins and separated from them by a fence. Suddenly up popped Buck, the most gentle of the Navy dolphins, right between them. Sharman shot out of the water like a Polaris missile, obviously terrified. Kathleen later wrote in her journal: "I guess she didn't know what Buck was thinking after all."

o   o   o

Armed with information from NMFS that all we needed for the permit was a scientific protocol, Naomi Rose and Rick Spill flew down to Key West from Washington, D.C., rented a car, and drove to Sugarloaf. They arrived around five o'clock in the evening. I had finished for the day, showered, and put on some blue jeans and a T-shirt. I was waiting for them in the bus with several others, including Cathy Kinsman, Lloyd's mother, Miriam, and Lincoln.

Since Naomi Rose and I had talked several times about doing a scientific protocol and had reached the same impasse each time, Spill said he wanted to give it a shot. Wearing his usual black tank top and thick dark glasses, Spill slapped his hands together like a judge banging a gavel and asked me if I could explain to him, *mano a mano,* exactly what I was doing.

"Can I explain what I do? Of course," I said.

"Then let's go to your room, you and me, and get to the bottom of this."

We went to my room, Cathy Kinsman tagging along. Spill sat on the edge of my bed, Cathy was in a chair against one wall taking notes in a little pad, and I sat up on a chest of drawers.

To Spill, like Naomi, this was simply an administrative thing. Plug in the right people and things get done. To them, the only question was whether I was the right person. And since I was the one in charge of doing it and the only one who could do it, they figured writing the protocol was my job. Their problem, however, was getting me to do it.

To me, it was also very simple. A scientific protocol, even if it could be written, would be useless. And even if I had time for it, never in a million years would NMFS accept a scientific protocol from me. For ten years or more I had been NMFS's severest critic; less than three years earlier I had called for an investigation of NMFS's basic conflict of interest before Congress.

I thought I could avoid a lot of misunderstanding and frustration if, right off the bat, I could explain to Spill that they were making too much of the cookbook idea. I said, "You know, Spill, rehabbing a captive dolphin is not brain surgery. It's more like trimming a Christmas tree."

"Wait a minute!" Spill said. "Let's get down to cases. Can you actually prepare captive dolphins for life in the wild?"

"Of course I can. I've done it. That's what I do. I'm not the only one. Randy Wells has done it too. But I'm the first to do it and I've dedicated my life to this one thing. You know all this."

"Okay, okay. No speeches. Just answer the questions. If you can do it, why can't you write it up?"

"As a cookbook?"

"Yes, as a cookbook."

"I don't have time for that, Spill. If you want to come down and do it, be my guest. You can watch me do what I do, you can write it down yourself. I'll even tell you what I'm thinking as we go along. I told Naomi the same thing, but she wouldn't do it. She wants *me* to do it. I've offered to help. I'll cooperate in every way. But I've got a full load as it is."

"Does that mean you won't do it?"

"The cookbook? Right. It's a fool's errand, and I won't do it."

"Are you a biologist?" He cocked his head at me.

I knew where he was going with this. "You know I'm not a biologist," I said. "So what? What I'm doing is not science."

He made fists of both hands. "Then what the hell is it?"

I looked around in frustration. Cathy was scribbling, trying to keep up. "Spill," I said, "it's more like Zen."

He shook his head. "Now what the hell does that mean?"

"It means that it's a piece of life and a very delicate thing."

"Good God!" he snapped, frowning. "Can we come back down to earth here? Tell me this: What is it you do when you prepare a dolphin for life in the wild? I mean basically."

"Basically?" He wanted the whole thing in one sentence. I threw my head back, thinking. Then I said, "What I do basically is extinguish captive behavior in dolphins."

"Excellent!" He flashed a smile of victory. "Now, do you see just what happened here? We're making progress." He rubbed his hands together. "This will be easy. Now tell me this: How long does it take?"

"Extinguishing captive behavior in dolphins? Different times, depending on the dolphin. And depending on the behaviors that I'm extinguishing."

"Different times, hey?"

"Right."

"Then give me a range of times."

"Some can never be released."

"Never?"

Bogie and Bacall.

Ric O'Barry (top) with his son, Lincoln; dog, Yoko; and the Dolphin Project bus.

Lloyd Good III doing the Sugar Show.

O'Barry with Flipper in Brazil.

Flipper being loaded aboard a helicopter.

Flipper close to freedom.
COURTESY OF DAVID HIGGS

Benny Schlesenger (left) and O'Barry during the hunger strike in Israel.
COURTESY OF ROBI DAMELIN

Buck catching his first fish.

Rick Trout (left) and Ric O'Barry.

Ric (left) and Lincoln O'Barry transporting Buck and Luther to freedom.

Sharman the shaman.

The Navy dolphins being released.

Stephania arrives on Albuquerque Island.

Helene and dolphin Stephania.

Helene and Ric in front of their home on Albuquerque Island.

"That's right, never."

"Okay. So that's infinity at one end of it, I believe."

"You could put it that way, yes. Think of Sugar. She's at that end."

"And the other end?"

"Some have very few behaviors to be extinguished; it might take very little time for them."

Spill asked, "Based on what?"

I looked at him, puzzled. "I'm not sure—"

"What *criteria* do you use?"

"What criteria?" I looked at the ceiling in thought. "What criteria do you use when you trim a Christmas tree?"

"No!" he said angrily, shaking his head. "I don't want to go down that path."

"Okay, what criteria do you use when you like a song? Or an apple— anything! When you like a song, you don't run through a checklist to see if it meets certain criteria, do you? Of course not. Same with rehabbing a dolphin. This is not mysterious, Spill. Do wild dolphins tail-walk and clap their pectoral fins to get fish? No! Do they swim up to boats and beg for fish? Hell no! That's what I'm trying to get captive dolphins to stop doing, that and any other behavior they learned in captivity. When they have stopped that, and when they can catch their own fish, they're ready."

"What about Bogie and Bacall right now?"

"They're definitely ready. I've been working several months with them. They catch their own fish and I think they'll make it. I wouldn't just dump them, of course. We move them up to their pen in Melbourne, I observe them for a while—maybe a week while they get used to the water, the tides, and so on. Then—if all goes well—we open the gates. We follow up with them for a month or two, then—if all still goes well—we celebrate and go home. The job is done."

"About a week, huh?" He was rubbing a big paw through his beard.

"If all goes well, yes. Might take longer. I'll know when I see them up there. And more important, Spill, I'll know when they know. That's the important thing. They'll know and then I'll know."

"Can we write this cookbook?"

"For Bogie and Bacall? Sure."

"I meant for all dolphins."

"All dolphins? No," I said, shaking my head.

"But if you can do it for Bogie and Bacall, why not others?"

"You're talking as if they're all one dolphin. Each one is different."

"Let me get this straight," Spill said. "Didn't you just say that you could write the cookbook?"

"That's right. Each dolphin has his own cookbook."

"That's not what a cookbook is."

"I know that," I said simply.

He gazed at me for a long moment. "If they're all so different, each of them with his own cookbook, why would you release Bogie and Bacall together?"

"They need each other for survival. They may not stay together once they're freed, but they need each other at first."

"And that's in *their* cookbooks?"

I nodded.

Suddenly, he stood up and said gruffly, "Okay, Ric. I think I get the drift. And I think . . . I think it can be done."

He got up, we shook hands, he walked to the door, and, as he was about to leave, I said, "All we really need, Spill, is common sense and a goal. That's what I meant by the Christmas tree."

His hand went to his grayish beard. "No," he said finally. "We've got to have it written scientifically."

"I'm here to help," I said.

Cathy gathered up her stuff and followed Spill out the door.

o   o   o

From her office in Washington a few days later, Naomi called and said she and Spill had had lunch with Ann Terbush of NMFS, and there was a way to get NMFS's permit. I thought this odd because up till now we had assumed we didn't need their permission. "And how is that?" I asked.

She said they would give us a permit if I would "step aside." I could hardly believe what I was hearing. Were they serious? This was a sell out. For a long minute, I said nothing.

"Ric," she said finally, "are you there?"

"Yes," I said weakly.

"Would you do that for the dolphins?"

"Step aside?"

"For the dolphins, yes."

"Yes," I said in almost a whisper. "If that's the only way—"

"It's the only way. Will you?"

"Yes," I said. "Of course. I'll get out of it right now. It's important that these dolphins be freed, but it's not important that Ric O'Barry free them."

I don't think I had ever spoken of myself in the third person like that before, but it seemed appropriate because it was like I was talking about someone else. Back in my motel room, I got ready for bed and turned in. But I was wide awake. I lay there, tossing around and going over and over what was happening, trying to make sense of it. *But it made no sense!*

Finally I got up, slipped on my short pants and walked down to the lagoon. It was very still outside, no wind, a bright, silvery night. I didn't want to bother the dolphins, so I ambled over to the Australian pines and just stood under them. I felt like I had been slapped in the face. I was also mad as hell that they thought they could get rid of me this way. If stepping aside was the right thing to do, I would do it. But this was stupid. I was the only one here who could do what we were here to do. And wasn't this discrimination, refusing to issue a permit because I was involved? How could NMFS do this? The irony almost made me laugh. Here I was trying to expose their hypocrisy and conflict of interest, and they had almost gotten me to go along with it. If I stepped aside for the sake of these two dolphins, what about all the others? I went back to my room, fuming, hurled myself into the bed, knowing I could never sleep. And yet, somehow, I did.

The next morning I called Naomi and told her I had changed my mind, that instead of my getting out, we should file a lawsuit against them, exposing their methodology, conflict of interest, illegal captures, and discrimination.

o   o   o

About a week later, at the end of the day I finished work with the dolphins, went over to the dolphin bus and fed Yoko, sat down in the driver's seat, put my head on the steering wheel, and closed my eyes. I was dog tired. Not physically. The work was not demanding and I was in good shape. But the psychological pressure was exhausting. I took a deep breath and began to relax. Then I felt a pair of eyes on me. I looked up and there was Joe Roberts at the door, smiling uncertainly. I told him to come on in, gesturing to a seat.

"Tired?" he asked, sitting himself heavily on a bench across from me.

"Not really," I said. "What's up?"

Joe Roberts was hemming and hawing. Obviously he had something on his mind that he didn't know how to bring up.

"Okay, Joe," I said finally. "What's eating you?"

"You ask me, I'll tell you. But I don't like doing this."

"What is it, Joe?"

"There's been an impropriety."

"A what?"

"This," he said, producing a flyer about a benefit I had been a part of in Munich, Germany. "You're collecting money for Bogie and Bacall and putting it in your own pocket."

"That's ridiculous!" I was in no mood for this. I may not keep the best books in the world, but I keep the money that comes in straight and I don't like trying to explain it to anyone but my accountant.

"I don't think so, Ric. Look, it pains me to say this . . . believe me . . . but here it is." He waved the flyer in front of me, frowning.

"That's nothing," I said. "You don't know what you're talking about."

"Oh, no?" He spread the flyer out in front of me. "What about this?" He jabbed a finger at part of the text. It was in German and neither of us could read it, but he was pointing to words in English, *Bogie & Bacall.* "To me," he said, "that's proof."

"Proof of what?"

"That you're making money off Bogie and Bacall, money that ought to come to the Dolphin Alliance—to me! And it's not. What's going on, Ric? You've got some big explaining to do."

"No way," I said. "That benefit was for the Dolphin Project, not the Dolphin Alliance. See here?" I pointed to the same flyer where the Dolphin Project was spelled out in English. "I've been doing this for years. If I do a benefit for the Dolphin Project, that doesn't mean it's for the Welcome Home Project. This fund raiser was mainly about Israel."

Joe Roberts was fuming, shaking his head and muttering. "This is definitely an impropriety, Ric." Suddenly his manner became very cold. He dug in his pocket and came up with a letter. It was typed, a very formal letter from the Board of Directors of the Dolphin Alliance. I read it quickly. They were *firing* me!

"Have you lost your mind?" I asked.

"You're out, Ric. We need a permit to release these dolphins, we can't get the permit without a scientific protocol and we can't get you to do it. We can't deal with you. You said you didn't have time to write it down, so I sent you the tape recorder—remember that?—and I told you we would write it down, that all you had to do was tell us what to write. You wouldn't even do that."

"First of all, Joe, you can't fire me. I don't work for you. I started this thing, remember?"

"Okay. I thought you would say that. We'll keep you on as a consultant—*paid* consultant. How's that? And that'll all be written down."

"Written down, hey? And what good is that? Everything was written down already, and look what you're trying to do now."

"Ric, please. The only way we can get the job done is if you step aside."

"If I stepped aside, that would be admitting I'd done something wrong. And I haven't. Ask yourself, Joe, why is all this happening? Why are you accusing me falsely, merely to get me out of the way? Don't you see what's happening, Joe? What they really want is the dolphins, and I'm in their way. If you would simply build the pen in Melbourne, we could move the dolphins up there and release them."

"Without a permit? I don't think so."

"Permit schmermit!" I said with exasperation. "We don't need a damned permit, Joe. Haven't we been through this?"

It seemed clear to me that Joe had already joined the other side.

o   o   o

Since the three new members of Sugarloaf's board of directors controlled policy, new things were beginning to happen. Cathy was assigned to make weekly reports about Sugarloaf activities to the board, to Naomi, and to Joe Roberts. Because of this new assignment, she was relieved of her work in the fish house, which meant that it fell on others to do. And the others complained to Lloyd, who could do nothing about it. He shifted people around, trying to make it work or to balance energy levels—whatever he was doing. But this is not an exact science. Even Lloyd's sister Caren frequently opposed him. Meanwhile, the war of rumors and accusations was bearing fruit. APHIS and NMFS inspectors were checking Sugarloaf almost every week.

In a desperate effort to stop Trout's accusations, Lloyd instructed members of the Sugarloaf staff to write down their recollections of working with Trout. In one of the reports, Kathleen Brooks wrote:

"When Mr. Trout personally prepared fish to be fed to the dolphins it was not sufficiently cleaned . . . and it was often not completely thawed.

"[He] insisted that only a few select people were qualified to feed Molly, which included himself, his girlfriend, a friend with no dolphin or animal husbandry or caretaking experience and an eleven-year-old child.

"It was my feeling . . . that he had no agenda other than to maintain complete control over the dolphins and to eliminate his imagined opposition. He lied to and manipulated the staff to conceal the truth, thereby creating a very stressful work environment. . . . And since he proudly spoke about sabotage against former employers, we wait daily to see what he will instigate next. I see him as a disgruntled former employee with very little qualification to waste taxpayers funds initiating investigations against the Sugarloaf Dolphin Sanctuary."

Lloyd gave these reports to APHIS officials, then drove to California for a week-long retreat.

o   o   o

The new board also hired Mary Lycan, who held a bachelor's degree in psychology and had worked as a trainer at ORC with Trout and Lynne, and now was working as a trainer at Theater of the Sea. Naomi Rose and John Grandy of HSUS arrived with her, and announced that Mary, as a "behaviorist," would write the scientific protocol. Grandy, wearing an expensive gray suit, strode the grounds of Sugarloaf like a visiting emissary, coming to a stop at the edge of the dolphin lagoon. Lloyd, wearing a sweaty T-shirt and smelling slightly of fish, was down on his knees working on a float. When Grandy approached, surveying this pastoral scene with a little smile, Lloyd put down his tools and brushed his hands together, then walked over and greeted Grandy. "Have you seen the signs around the motel?" he asked.

"You mean the little signs asking for donations?"

"That's right."

"Yes, I've seen them. Very nice." He eyed Lloyd up and down. "Did you make them yourself?"

"I made them myself, yes. How about it?"

Grandy cocked his head, puzzled. "How about what?"

"How about a donation? I thought we were in this together. We're doing all the work down here. We're putting up the money. Now what the hell is HSUS doing?"

"Our good name is involved."

"Your good name! We need more than that."

They went off together, and about an hour later, Lloyd came back with a $5,000 check and showed it to me.

"That'll help some," I said.

"Yeah," Lloyd said. "About two weeks."

o   o   o

When Mary Lycan arrived to take over the rehab and release of Bogie and Bacall, I offered to help. After all, I had been in charge of the dolphins' rehabilitation up till now and the process was ongoing. I thought she might want to take that into consideration, especially since she had never done anything like this before. "In this transition period," I said, "I'll help in any way I can."

Mary gave me a sardonic smile and said, "Too many cooks spoil the broth."

But still, I thought, since we were supposed to be doing virtually the same thing and working cheek by jowl both at the lagoon and in the fish house, she and Cathy with Bogie and Bacall, I and the others with the Navy dolphins, surely, I thought, it made sense for us to cooperate. I offered again to help, and she said my help was not needed. She wanted no interference, no suggestions, no nothing from anyone at Sugarloaf. Nevertheless, I mentioned the blue-green algae that I had been putting in the dolphins' food. "They're used to it," I said, "and I would suggest that you not vary their diet." She reacted with silence.

In a memo to Lloyd, Naomi Rose outlined Mary Lycan's job description in the "permitizing" process and the rehabilitation of Bogie and Bacall. In her capacity as coordinating chair of the Scientific Steering Committee of the Welcome Home Project, Naomi said that Mary Lycan would be getting "baseline behavioral data, including activity (time spent resting, socializing, feeding, etc.) and association patterns (time each dolphin spends alone or with one or two penmates, and time orienting with humans)." She also wanted detailed data about each dolphin's feeding habits and a host of medical procedures like making ultrasound measurements and drawing blood, taking tissue samples—on and on. This was of course aimed at writing the protocol of the actual rehabilitation, showing loss of show behaviors and their replacement by behaviors favoring survival in the wild. About half of Mary's time would be devoted to rehabilitation and writing the protocol, according to the job description, and the rest would be involved in feeding, medical procedures, and record keeping.

In a letter to his six-person staff, Lloyd issued a warm welcome to Mary Lycan as behaviorist, saying, "Hopefully, Mary's employment will better enable us to release dolphins."

Within a day or two, Mary had formed an alliance with Cathy Kinsman, and together they undid all my work with Bogie and Bacall. They were baby-talking to them, petting them, and reinforcing all the old dolphin-trainer relationships. Working at the other end of the lagoon, I could see what was happening, and it felt like a part of my life was being torn to shreds before my eyes. Again I tried to explain my method of rehabbing captive dolphins, but Mary did not seem to care.

o   o   o

Personnel harmony was never at symphonic levels at Sugarloaf, but now everybody was playing his own tune. The discord began when Mary Lycan and Cathy realized that they had too much to do. They informed Lloyd that they could no longer work in the fish house preparing fish for the dolphins. Lloyd was upset, he told me and I was upset, too. Someone had to do the work, and if they refused, who would it be?

Lloyd began writing down his thoughts, sometimes to answer allegations in the media, sometimes to clarify his own thinking.

" . . . I was concerned that the desire of Cathy Kinsman and Mary to work together exclusively would cause separation of our small team resulting in dysfunction," he wrote. " The sanctuary staff is too small for any kind of hierarchy. The six people here must work together in order to reach our goal. . . .

"Unfortunately, my instructions were ignored and Cathy and Mary immediately paired off to form their own team, excluding Ric, Kathleen, and Caren Ward. . . . On April 30, Mary came to my office and told me that her workload was too heavy and that she and Cathy could no longer do any fish kitchen prep (the only tedious physical labor required of sanctuary employment at Sugarloaf). Mary instructed me, her boss, to replace them with volunteers. But all of our volunteers are busy in the gift shop (the sanctuary's only means of income) or already helping in the fish kitchen.

"If the team is not unified, I will dismiss Cathy Kinsman from the staff and thereby force Mary to either leave the sanctuary team or join it. . . . [The protocol] should be more of a cooperative effort between the sanctuary team and the so-called Scientific Steering Committee. This, after all, will be the guideline by which the sanctuary will operate in the future."

o   o   o

These people problems were discussed in reports, phone calls, and faxes throughout the far-flung management of Sugarloaf, where it leaked to the other camp and then onto the World Wide Web. Then the May 1, 1996, *Keynoter* ran a story stating that I had called for a boycott of Sugarloaf Lodge. They based this story on a forged fax with my letterhead and name, which I believe came from Trout. I had to drop everything and prove to the paper's editor that I had not sent the fax. On May 5, 1996, the *Keynoter* ran a counter-story reporting my stance that the fax was a fake and that I had never called for a boycott.

I complained to Michael A. Barber, chief investigator in the state attorney's office, Key West, about Trout's behavior, showing him the forged fax and giving him copies of several tapes defaming not only me but also half a dozen others on my staff or working with me.

At the same time, I was in the midst of studying the complicated social dynamics of the Navy dolphins. Something was clearly wrong. They couldn't get along. They were fighting too much. I was trying several ideas, but I couldn't get a handle on the situation. Finally, I had to put Luther in a pen away from the others.

One of our worst staff meetings occurred at this point. Everything got thrown into the fan. During the melee, Caren discovered that Cathy, in one of her reports to Naomi, had said something that Naomi interpreted as "animal abuse," and that Lloyd, her brother, knew about it and did nothing.

Then, as all the planets slipped with sinister intent into the wrong houses, Sharman arrived with disastrous advice for Lloyd. "Follow your heart," she told him. That very day Lloyd had an ugly scene with Caren, and I, fed up with all of it, informed Lloyd that if he didn't fire Cathy, I would.

Cathy and her boyfriend, Ken, were both dismissed, and Kathleen was assigned to help Mary. But Mary, who had been assured that Cathy would be back, wouldn't even talk to Kathleen.

And indeed, Spill ordered Lloyd via fax to reinstate Cathy, threatening to call a board meeting and "scorch the earth" if we didn't. He would kick both of us out, he vowed, on grounds of physical endangerment of the dolphins.

John Grandy entered the fray by seeking to go over our heads, speaking directly to Mr. Good. Mr. Good advised Grandy to stay away, that he would not allow anyone on his property who had attempted a coup against his son.

◦   ◦   ◦

I had to get away from the madness. I felt like I was in the eye of a hurricane, focused only on the dolphins while all around me the flotsam flew. I went back to my place in Coconut Grove that weekend. When I returned, Kathleen greeted me with the news: "Sharman told him he's a shaman too."

"On, no," I said with a groan.

"She told him he's a chief—and he believes it."

About twenty-five feet from the dolphins' lagoon, Lloyd had built an igloo-shaped sweat lodge with the limbs of trees and heavy carpeting. Outside lay the skull of a killer whale. When he got it done, he asked me if I wanted to look inside. I shrugged, said okay, and started in. "No!" he said sharply. "Not like that. You have to go in clockwise."

"Sorry," I said. I backed out and entered properly.

Inside it was carpeted around the edges where you sat, and in the middle was a sandy spot with a circle of rocks. The idea was to get in there and sweat out the evil spirits. They heated the rocks outside and moved them in with deer antlers. Even a few of the rocks would have turned it into a sauna. Lloyd seemed to like contraptions like this, mystical bridges between this world of mere appearance and something he believed was much more real.

◦   ◦   ◦

Meanwhile, I got a call from Ben White, a pioneer in the fight to free captive dolphins. An arborist by trade, Ben was middle-aged with long hair, braided in back, and had a dark, grayish beard. He formed the Dolphin Rescue Brigade, known in captivity circles for taking direct action. A single parent, he lived with his two daughters on an island off the state of Washington, but he worked on behalf of captive dolphins on both coasts. One long-standing dolphin activity that particularly irked him was Randy Wells's "research" off

Sarasota, Florida. Yes, the same Randy Wells who signed on to help me in Brazil and then reneged when his bosses warned him not to work with me. Randy captures dolphins in the bay periodically with the help of fifty or sixty people who have paid for the privilege of doing something for the environment. As far as I can tell, what they do is capture the same dolphins year after year, measure them, and compare them with their previous year's measurements. What irks activists like Ben and me is that they appear to never do anything with their data. It's all meaningless, except for the money they collect. But in Sarasota, Randy is an environmental hero. And worse still is that the research is so violent—captures, inspections, pulling of teeth, drawing of blood—that surely, we think, it drives some of the dolphins away. The next year, when those dolphins are not around, they are presumed to be dead, which skews the data about life expectancy of wild dolphins, making it support the claim by those in the captivity industry that dolphins live as long in captivity as in the wild.

When Ben called, he asked if I would help him disrupt the netting of the dolphins. I told him I was up to my eyeballs in the mess at Sugarloaf, and couldn't leave it now. "Why don't you try your friends in Gadfly?"

Three days later, he called again. He had tried them all, none could help him. He asked me again to join him. He said he thought they had been tipped off to his plans and he needed help. I hopped on a plane, he met me at the airport, and we drove down to where he had rented a boat. The plan was to follow their boats—about twenty-five of them—out into the bay and when they set their nets, we would jump in the nets with the dolphins and tear the nets down, freeing the dolphins. That sounded like a brilliant idea to me. But when we got there, the place was swarming with police boats. They knew about us and had us under surveillance. Newspaper reporters closed in too, wanting to know why we were opposed to Randy's dolphin research, so we told them. And because we knew that police would never let us get close enough to the nets to jump in, we changed plans. We got a few heavy metal pipes and were going to jump in the water near the pods of dolphins and beat the pipes together under water to run them off. But when we pulled out in our boat, the marine police surrounded us and forced us back to where

Ben had rented it. Our demonstration had failed to prevent the netting, but perhaps it helped open people's eyes to this type of questionable research.

            o   o   o

Lloyd told me that when his spiritual leader advised him to follow his heart, she also confided that Molly wanted a mate and a baby. And while I was in Sarasota fighting a lost cause, Lloyd seized the moment by setting the dolphins free. Or rather, giving them a chance to leave. They left the safety of their pen, sniffed Sugarloaf Bay, and quickly returned. Word quickly spread that the dolphins were swimming free, and suddenly there was Trout, sitting in an inflatable boat off Sugarloaf, watching for an opportunity to lure one of the dolphins away.

This surveillance of Sugarloaf was conducted by Trout, Cathy, Ken, Becky Baron of the Florida Keys Wildlife Rescue, and others who took turns in a kayak and inflatable boat, spying on us through binoculars, taking notes, and videotaping whatever they could see us do. They wanted these dolphins and I suppose they hoped to witness a violation of some rule that they could use in court to get them. Mary Lycan's last day at Sugarloaf came abruptly when Lloyd discovered her using a cellular phone to communicate with the spies. He terminated her employment, calling it a "leave of absence."

I had been in Sarasota, Florida, only a couple of days and hadn't kept up with the latest media feeding frenzy in the Keys, so when I got back, I went to the fish house, checked the log, rubbed my eyes, and checked it again. I couldn't believe what I was reading. Following his misguided heart, Lloyd had let Luther, a sex-crazed male dolphin, in with three eager females, two of them on the verge of returning to the wild. The name for this is captive breeding. Captive breeding is at the heart of our opposition to the captivity industry. It's the horror, the scourge, the most hateful thing they might do. I had spoken to Lloyd about it quite often.

I went over to the lagoon to see for myself. And there they were: Bogie, Bacall, and Molly with Luther, swimming in a pod. Were they happy? Oh, yes. Blissfully so. It felt *good!* And why not? It was natural. And they were delighted to be together, to swim around as a family, a pod of Lloyd's creation.

But in twelve months, what then? What about the baby dolphins that would be born in captivity? In Australia, these are called battery dolphins, dolphins in breeding programs kept like chickens to lay eggs. These dolphins could never be *returned* to the wild because they had never lived there. I know of only one dolphin born in captivity that has successfully made the transition: Annessa, who escaped from DRC during Hurricane Andrew. She's been spotted from time to time near the reef off Key Largo by fishermen. But her case is unusual, perhaps unique. The last thing I wanted was to be responsible for even one dolphin more whose entire life would be condemned to the role of clown for the amusement of human beings or as an experimental animal who lived at the pleasure and curiosity of science.

I stormed back to the fish house, threw myself into the chair and felt a wave of nausea sweeping over me. My energy, my life was draining away. I couldn't move. Kathleen came in, saw me, and said, "Oh, you saw what happened."

I nodded.

"What can we do?"

I shook my head in despair. "Nothing," I said softly. "It's done."

Suddenly I felt like confronting Lloyd. I got up quickly, ran to the Tiki Bar where he was counting T-shirts, and asked him if he realized what he'd done.

"They're a family, Ric. This is a beautiful thing. We should leave them alone."

I stared at him a long moment. Was this a sarcastic shot? Did he know that when I speak to groups, that's the message I leave them with, that we should simply let them alone. But I'm talking about *wild* dolphins. I searched his face for a hint of amusement, a flicker of merriment around his eyes or at the corners of his mouth. But Lloyd was in his most solemn of moods and there was no sign that he was goading me.

I turned on my heel and left. The only thing I could do was go over his head. When I had driven up to the lodge, I noticed Mr. Good stepping out of his new white Cadillac and walking toward the lodge. I dashed through the front doors of the restaurant and headed to his office. He was working on some papers. He looked up when I entered and said, "Yes?"

"Mr. Good, I need some help."

"Is it about the dolphins?"

"Yes, it's about the dolphins."

"Lloyd is in charge of the dolphins. Have you talked to him?"

"Mr. Good, talking to Lloyd is like talking to a coconut tree."

He shook his head, put down his pen, and rubbed his eyes wearily. I knew what he must be thinking, that this whole thing with the dolphins and with me had been a nightmare for him and his family. Softly I said, "I'm sorry."

During my whole career working to free captive dolphins, I've been passionately opposed to what Lloyd had done, allowing captive dolphins to breed. If it got out that I was involved in this, people would never believe me again.

I went back to the fish house. Kathleen was still there. "I might have been a little hasty before," I told her. "Maybe there is something I can do. I need to do some damage control—fast! And maybe you can help."

"Sure."

We composed a statement of policy and we sent it to all the various media in South Florida and the Keys.

o   o   o

In the *Miami Herald* of June 7, 1995, Lloyd said, "I'm defying the jurisdiction of any government agency when it comes to the freedom of dolphins. There is not a law anywhere on any book on this planet that governs the release of dolphins to the wild."

Ann Terbush, chief of permitting for the NMFS, responded that that wasn't true. "Releases into the wild require a scientific research permit."

Lloyd countered, "Nowhere in the Animal Welfare Act does it say that you can't let your animals out of their cages. All they can tell me is what my cage should be."

As if on cue, the net to the dolphin lagoon was mysteriously cut, and Lloyd's little pod, all four of them, swam in open water for seven hours. Lloyd called this "an act of vandalism." At feeding time, the dolphins returned to the lagoon on their own.

Lloyd took the dolphins' open-water swim as evidence that they were ready to move on.

As the *Miami Herald* reported in the same article: "[Lloyd] Good pushed aside the gate [and said,] 'They're all going from here as a family—on a gradual basis. They can come and go as they please until they have the courage or the stamina.' But the dolphins did not leave . . . [so] Lloyd pushed the gate closed again and said he would try again."

Responding to Joe Roberts's statement that he wanted to get Bogie and Bacall up to Melbourne, Lloyd said, "They're talking about breaking up the family that's formed now to return them to a family they haven't seen in seven years. It's ridiculous. . . . My colleagues are foolishly applying [for a permit] to the same agency that this year allowed the slaughter of 1,200 dolphins in tuna nets."

o   o   o

Sugarloaf's out-of-state board of directors voted via telephone to give Bogie and Bacall to Joe Roberts, and the three Navy dolphins and Molly to Trout at his new Marine Mammal Conservancy near Key Largo.

Blocking their path was Lloyd, who, as director of Sugarloaf and son of the owner, had custody of all the dolphins, including Bogie and Bacall. He had signed for them and, according to the original agreement, was not required to turn them over to Joe Roberts until a pen was built for them in the Indian River Lagoon off Melbourne, and the water was tested and approved.

There was one little loophole, however. In case of an emergency at Sugarloaf, the dolphins could be moved to better facilities. So they seized on one of Trout's standing accusations—that our water was polluted—and filed a lawsuit for custody.

From the *Key West Citizen* of June 8, 1995: "Despite warnings from the federal government and an active contingent of the dolphin-activist community, Sugarloaf staffers plan to continue allowing four of their dolphins to leave their secured lagoon."

When they interviewed me, I saw some hope of working this thing out, and said, "We're giving them a little breathing room, that's part of the re-adaptation process. This is the first time they've been able to swim in a straight line longer than 100 yards in years."

Rector, identified as a Sugarloaf critic, said the dolphins were being allowed free swims in the gulf to hide problems within the sanctuary. He claimed that the lagoon was contaminated by a "heavy growth" of bacteria harmful to mammals, and "it will take weeks of flushing to make that lagoon safe for dolphins. . . . Something is rotten at the Sugarloaf sanctuary."

Joe Roberts opined in the June 8, 1995, *Miami Herald,* "The people now running the place are unqualified and are doing great damage to the anti-captivity movement. Moronic stunts like this [letting the dolphins out as a pod] are exactly what the captive industry predicted from our camp." Then he added, "We're bringing the dolphins home."

In the June 9, 1995, edition of the *Miami Herald,* I was quoted in defense of releasing captive dolphins. "We're not defying the government," I said, "we're challenging them. There's a big difference. I would never let one of these dolphins out unless I were sure they could survive. My loyalty is to the dolphins themselves and to get them ready and to get them in shape to be released into the wild. I'm not being attacked by the captivity industry or the Navy—only by new and improved dolphin freedom groups who are trying to blow me away."

Lloyd summed it up about as well as anyone in the June 25, 1995, *Key West Citizen:* "[T]he whole situation has hurt the sanctuary tremendously. Nobody is buying sanctuary T-shirts anymore."

At the next meeting of the staff, I told them that I was ready for the battle of my life. I was in this to the end.

o   o   o

As a result of all the accusations, twice a month we were visited by Dr. Betty Goldentyre, APHIS inspector. She was stationed in Tampa, Florida, which is more than three hundred miles from Sugarloaf. In all her visits, Dr. Goldentyre and her assistant found not a single violation. She took specimens and samples each time and had them analyzed, but nothing turned up positive.

Because of reports we had heard about the government's plan to confiscate the dolphins, Joe Roberts arranged for a military helicopter to fly Bogie and Bacall to Melbourne, but Mr. Good notified the Air Force that they would need a court order to remove the dolphins. They backed off.

Dan Morast, of International Wildlife Coalition (IWC), left his office in Cape Cod to visit Joe Roberts in Melbourne, bearing gifts to help in Bogie and Bacall's release: a thirteen-foot hard-bottom inflatable boat with outboard and trailer on loan, a check of $500 for gas, a grant of $1,068 for camping equipment and supplies, and $800 worth of marine radio equipment.

In a letter to Lloyd and myself, Morast scornfully wrote: "I cannot stress more strongly my disapproval of what appears to be threats and challenges coming out of Sugarloaf. The two of you are being quoted as refusing to release Bogie and Bacall to the Dolphin Alliance; both of you are openly challenging APHIS and NMFS with pledges of premature release of Bogie and Bacall. . . . I can assure you that none of the Dolphin Alliance sponsors will tolerate your refusal to transfer the custody of Bogie and Bacall to Joe Roberts within forty-eight hours of his facility receiving the APHIS display license number. . . . "

Morast continued, "I am obviously putting the two of you on notice that the International Wildlife Coalition intends to monitor your actions closely and to provide an instantaneous local, state, national, and international protest should you further delay the transfer of Bogie and Bacall. These dolphins have suffered enough; you should never have begun using these animals as pawns in your unfortunate confrontations."

Kathleen responded with a touch of sarcasm to Dan Morast's criticism.

"It is very gratifying," she wrote, "to know that you were able to raise so much money ($2,368) and support for the two dolphins Bogie and Bacall. . . . It is very important for you to know that the Sugarloaf Dolphin Sanctuary has been caring for Bogie and Bacall for ten months, feeding them and attending to their health and incurring expenses in excess of $15,000 per month."

o   o   o

At the same time, it seemed that Lloyd's thinking had taken new form. He sent a long thoughtful letter to Linda Reeves, a reporter with the *Keynoter*, who never seemed to get Sugarloaf's position right:

"The dolphins should be released from Sugarloaf together in a pod and come and go as they please until they build stamina, courage, teamwork, and local knowledge. In this way, if they get tired, hungry, sick, hurt, or scared, they can find their way back. A kind and gentle release. Bogie and Bacall can no longer be thought of as a singular entity. They have lived with Molly, a matriarchal thirty-year-old for seven years. Now Luther, a third adolescent, has been adopted by the females to form a pod of four dolphins. When considering Bogie and Bacall one must consider them as part of a social group and the subsequent ramifications of separating them from Molly and Luther. These four dolphins should all be given the choice of freedom together. It is their best chance of survival."

Under the heading "Some Notes", he added:

· There are no rules or protocols for dolphin release.

· Then why can't a pregnant dolphin be released? Who says? Why is it being said that if a dolphin gets pregnant, then not only is she automatically sentenced to life imprisonment, but so is her baby?

· Why can't captive-born dolphins be released?

"Which is better for the dolphins? To release them with no government interference for $25,000 in three months, or to release them for $500,000 and have it take two years of choking on red tape. Red tape stuffed down our throats for dubious reasons."

Captain Ron Canning of Key West, an old friend of mine, called Lloyd after receiving disturbing messages on his answering machine from Trout. Because Ron was helping me, Trout threatened to destroy his business, Dolphin Watch, which took tourists out in his thirty-one-foot catamaran to see dolphins in the wild off Key West.

In preparation against future litigation, or perhaps just to understand what had been going on, Lloyd filed papers with the Marine Mammal Commission under the Freedom of Information Act for files about Sugarloaf; Dolphin Alliance/Joseph Roberts; Marine Mammal Conservancy/Robert Lingenfeller and/or Rick Trout; Animal Welfare Institute/Rick Spill; Dolphin Freedom Foundation/Russ Rector; International Wildlife Coalition/Daniel Morast; HSUS/Naomi Rose and/or John Grandy. We discovered that virtually all of Sugarloaf's harassment had come from just a few of these people.

Mr. Good had sought an exemption from NMFS in releasing the dolphins, and Ann Terbush of NMFS's permit division warned him:

"An unauthorized release would . . . be in violation of the terms and conditions of your public display permit. . . . No protocols currently exist for rehabilitating and releasing captive dolphins back into the wild. . . . It is the intention of the NMFS to develop scientifically sound protocols through the permit process which affords the opportunity for both scientific and public review."

She cited Public Law 103-335, which said, in part, " . . . the conferees direct the Navy to cooperate with the Secretary of Commerce and the Marine Mammal Commission in developing rigorous scientific protocols for experimental releases."

About this time Sugarloaf received an okay on its water from the Marathon Department of Environmental Protection, then announced with pride in a press release: "Our water quality meets human standards. However, it has come to our attention that the federal government is requesting $300 million for next year's budget to continue efforts to clean the polluted Indian River Lagoon."

I sent Morast a letter in which I corrected some of his most flagrant errors of fact and then concluded "that none of you care enough to actually come to the Sanctuary to see the dolphins and the work we're doing speaks for itself."

Morast fired back on June 26, 1995, in *Whalewatch*, an Internet newsletter, headlined: "Ric O'Barry fired from Sugarloaf Dolphin Sanctuary."

Captain Ron Canning wrote to Spill: "Releasing dolphins back into the wild is not just about science, it's about art. It's a quiet, day-to-day understanding of the individual dolphins and their psychologies. No whistles, no hand signals, no cute baby talk. Yes, science is an important factor, but not the only ingredient for a successful release. Wisdom gleaned from over thirty years of working with and for dolphins is a very valuable contribution, I thought you understood this. We are very fortunate to have an accomplished artist like Ric O'Barry leading this team.

"The three of you [board members] were supposed to lobby for support of the sanctuary, not try to destroy it. Lobbying is supposed to be your expertise. Dolphin untraining and release is Ric O'Barry's forte. But because of the concerted efforts of yourself and the other misled and misinformed members of the board, Ric O'Barry and those involved in the day-to-day responsibilities of preparing the dolphins for release have had to spend their days and nights defending themselves."

Morast issued a call for my harassment: "All anti-captivity activists," he wrote, "should protest, yell, shout and/or otherwise harass and attack Ric O'Barry until he releases Bogie and Bacall. The original concept for this entire program was the scientific readaptation and permitted release of Bogie and Bacall. This is beyond Ric O'Barry's capability; he must immediately give up Bogie and Bacall and let the Joe Roberts team onto the Sugarloaf property and move them to the new Indian River facility." Then he listed all my numbers—phone, fax, address—and Lloyd's, too, to make harassment easier. Two people responded: Rick Trout and Russ Rector.

We got together at my cottage on the key to prepare for the lawsuit that challenged water quality at Sugarloaf. Lloyd was there, Captain Canning, Kathleen, and several others including Gary Elston, who monitored Sugarloaf's water quality, and a new ally, Helene Hesselager.

∘   ∘   ∘

A Danish freelance journalist specializing in wildlife subjects, Helene had recently written a piece on the rehabilitation of wolves in Portugal, her writing was honest and carefully done. We had met on the phone about a year earlier when she called me at Sugarloaf to set up an interview. I told her not to bother coming to Sugarloaf, I would be in Paris in about a month. I was one of four speakers at a whale and dolphin conference at the Theâtre de Empire on Avenue de Wagram in the north end of town, and it would be simpler for her to meet me there. I had no idea what she looked like, but as I glanced out over the crowd of about 150 people, I spotted her immediately. She looked exactly like she sounded on the phone. Fair and with light-blond hair, she was sitting back in the crowd wearing a big brown overcoat with the sleeves rolled up. She's certainly not a slave of fashion, I thought. No makeup, either. Completely natural. How different from Sabine, I thought, and how refreshing. I waved to her, she waved back, then I went over to her, took her by the hand, and found a seat for her on the front row. Afterward we walked the streets of Paris, talking about Sugarloaf and dolphins, eating dinner and drinking wine.

I returned to Sugarloaf and not long after that, she called from her parents' home in rural Denmark to say that she had an assignment to do a series on the release of our dolphins. I invited her to Sugarloaf and told her that my cottage had an extra room, which she could use if she wanted to. When she stepped off the plane in Key West, she was carrying the same brown coat she had been wearing in Paris. The more I got to know her, the more fascinated I became with her quiet beauty. Somehow, it made her seem ageless. She was younger than I, but something mystical, something definitely spiritual was telling me that this was right, that this young woman and I were really meant to be. I needed her.

o   o   o

The judicial hearing on Plantation Key lasted until 8:00 P.M., and because the facts were on our side, the ruling was in our favor. Trout, who had financed the lawsuit, appeared against us, as well as Mary Lycan, Dr. Baker, and Cathy Kinsman and Ken Petersen. But the ruling was cut and dried. In a nutshell, the absentee board members were still absent. And since we could prove that our own water was good while water in Indian River Lagoon was and had been polluted, the judge ruled that "conditions at Sugarloaf did not warrant the animals' removal."

We had stopped them, but now we were all dead in the water. Nobody could do anything. They had the votes, three to two, but we had possession and could keep them off the property. Not that they wanted to go on it. Except for the Gadfly Conference, they had never stepped foot on Sugarloaf. And yet they wanted to micro-manage the place based on reports by people who would benefit only if Lloyd and I were replaced.

Ridiculous? Yes. It reminded me of two old ladies fighting with handbags.

Morast had often criticized me, so Andrew Dickson of WSPA faxed Morast about my work with Flipper in Brazil. "Mr. O'Barry did a first-class job," Dickson wrote, "and the absolute success of the project was largely due to him. . . . Some of the comments made about Ric's ability are absurd, as are the criticisms made about the Flipper project in Brazil."

Trout had talked to the media about Judge Ptomey's decision in the custody battle (also tossing in some invective about me), and now sent the judge a letter trying to wriggle out of it:

"A reporter from the *Keynoter* . . . wrote that I 'lashed out at the judge's decision,'" Trout wrote. "I am sending you a copy of that statement to show that if there was any lashing, it was certainly not directed at you. Rather it is directed at perpetrators of violations at Sugarloaf and those who misled you on the witness stand when they claimed that only one dolphin has been medically compromised and/or injured during Sugarloaf Dolphin Sanctuary's very short existence of ten months."

Shortly after that, Ben White called, suggesting a compromise. If Joe Roberts, HSUS, and the others were so hot to get Bogie and Bacall, maybe in exchange they would dump Spill and his two associates from the board. Mr. Good was for it, and so was I. Lloyd objected because it would break up his little dolphin pod, but finally he gave in and we agreed in principle.

That night, Joe Roberts called me at the cottage, an original wooden Keys house in the middle of Sugarloaf under an enormous royal poinciana in glorious orange bloom. Helene had moved in with me and we were cooking dinner. I was keeping one eye on the spaghetti and stirring a tomato-with-mushrooms sauce and she was cutting up tomatoes for the salad when the phone rang. She picked it up, spoke, and handed the phone to me. "It's Joe Roberts," she said.

I took the phone and Joe said he had just finished reading a piece in the *Palm Beach Post* that was making us all look very bad—like a bunch of spoiled brats—and suggested we put aside our differences. I agreed that it was time we all start acting like responsible adults; that we should go back to the original agreement about Joe getting the permit and building the pen in the Indian River Lagoon off Melbourne, then I bring the dolphins up and do the rehab and release. It was not a good time of year. It was cold up there, the water sometimes freezing, but everything else was perfect. I would be on a small island with the dolphins. The pen was ready, a tent for me, and I could stay as long as I needed to. I told Joe that I would be coming up in the truck with the dolphins. He faxed me an agreement covering everything and I said I would show it to Lloyd in the morning. Everything was fine with Joe. We were buddies again and the Welcome Home Project was back on course.

Or was it? I hung up the phone and felt like something wasn't quite right. Up till now there had been insurmountable problems, now suddenly everything was okay. When I asked about it he said I should trust him and that Naomi Rose had a way of cutting through red tape. The dolphins were practically ready for release and I could get on with my life.

I uncorked a good California wine, poured it, and we clinked glasses in celebration.

"Maybe I misjudged Joe," I said. "I've always thought that if you give people a chance, they'll do the right thing." I lifted my glass and said, "To Joe."

Helene lifted her glass, too, and we clinked.

∘   ∘   ∘

With the agreement in place, the agreement giving us control of the board and sending Bogie and Bacall to Melbourne for release, Lloyd and I became the only two members of the board. We needed someone else on the board to break tie votes, so Lloyd named Kathleen Brooks, probably assuming she would always vote with him. And at first she did. At our first meeting I moved that we free two of the three Navy dolphins—Luther and Buck—whether we had a permit or not. Lloyd voted against me and so did Kathleen.

Joe Roberts called to say that he and his crew would be down to pick up the dolphins, and Lloyd, still following his heart, was outraged by this. When Joe Roberts and his crew arrived in a rented air-conditioned Ryder truck and pulled to a stop in the parking lot, Lloyd banned them from the property, saying that he and his own crew would catch the dolphins and put them in the truck. Joe Roberts and his crew, including Steve McCulloch and his girl-friend Marilyn Mazzoil, Cathy and Ken, Mary Lycan, and Billy Cox, the newspaper reporter, moved their vehicles away. And Lloyd's crew, including me, tried all day to catch even one of the dolphins. Finally, late in the after-noon, Lloyd relented, allowed the other crew to help. Steve grabbed Bogie, we all converged and put her in the truck. Joe Roberts and the crew drove her up to the new pen and released her. The crew returned for the other dol-phin, Joe Roberts and Mary Lycan remaining in Melbourne with Bogie.

I had packed for a month's stay in Melbourne, my dive bag and another bag with two pairs of blue jeans, shorts, underwear, tooth brush, and log books. This was a new log book because, in his anger at losing the dolphins, Lloyd refused to turn over the log books for Bogie and Bacall, including their med-ical records going back through their years of captivity at ORC. I tried to reason with Lloyd, that the log books and medical records were not his, they belonged to whomever had the dolphins, that it was a breach of decency as well as common sense not to turn them over. But Lloyd refused.

The truck and the crew returned for Bacall about noon the next day. We caught her almost immediately and got her into the truck. I was on one end of the stretcher and hopped out of the truck to get my bags, tossing them in the back of the truck. Then Ken and Steve closed ranks against me and said I was not to go back with them. When we were on the point of fisticuffs, Billy Cox invited me to drive up with him, but I insisted and finally got on the truck. I rode in the back with Bacall and the three crewmen Joe Roberts had sent down: Ken, Cathy, and Steve McCulloch.

It was a six-hour drive in a cold truck, so I had taken off my wet suit and put on something dry. But when we got close to Melbourne, I put my wet suit back on. It was still wet, but I was ready to go in the water with Bacall. When we finally stopped, we backed up about ten feet and the doors of the truck flew open. There was a crowd of people, including Jay Temple, a member of Joe Roberts' Dolphin Alliance. Flashbulbs were going off, TV cameras grinding. Joe Roberts, seething with anger, got on the truck followed by two uniformed law officers. I was at one end of the stretcher. Joe Roberts came up and yelled in my face.

"Get off my truck!"

"Are you kidding?" I asked. "Grab the other end of the stretcher there."

By the time I had said that, the two policemen grabbed me, spun me around, and slammed me into the wall of the truck. They pulled my arms up behind me and cuffed me. "Did you hear what he just told you?" one of the officers asked. "He said to get out of the truck."

"I will," I said. "But I'm taking the dolphin with me."

Joe Roberts yelled like an Army sergeant. "This is trespassing, Mister. And you will *pay* for that."

"Joe, you bastard!" I said. "You betrayed me."

The policemen, who must have thought I was getting uppity, grabbed me and threw me out of the truck onto the ground. I struggled to my feet and they both led me—still in my wet suit—to the squad car.

They drove me to a precinct police station, where I was questioned, then chained as if I were a dangerous animal. My feet and hands were both chained and both of those chains were connected to a third chain around my waist. Then I was thrown into a paddy wagon that was heading downtown, with stops along the way to pick up a variety of drunks and dope addicts who were throwing up and groveling in self-pity. I looked around. Nine of us, and I was the only one in a wet suit, the only one in chains, and probably the only one who had to go to the bathroom.

When the formal charge of trespassing was finally filed against me the next day, I had to dig up $500 in bail to get out of jail. Jay Temple, outraged by the way I had been treated, put up the money for me. Six months later, just before the trial date, the charges against me were dropped and I returned the bail money to Jay.

12

ROOMS WITH A DOLPHIN VIEW

We're here because we're not all there.

—Key West saying

WHEN DR. BETTY GOLDENTYRE of APHIS failed to come up with violations against Sugarloaf, NMFS sent down its most rigorous white-glove team of federal inspectors. They were led by Dr. Joseph P. Geraci, a Canadian and professor of veterinary medicine at Guelph University in Ontario. Tall, dark, and handsome in the style of a 1950s movie star, Geraci was known to us in the dolphin welfare community as "Oil Can Joe," a moniker he earned for his dolphin experiments at DRC in the 1980s. Using grant money, Geraci built a tower of about fifty feet at DRC so that he could film dolphins from on high and see exactly what happened when he dumped fuel oil in the pens with them. Dolphin activists have often wondered who would pay him to find out the answer to that little mystery, unless it was a petroleum company. Geraci is credited with probably knowing more about dolphins under stress than anyone else in the world.

The day he and his team of inspectors arrived at Sugarloaf, Lloyd was involved in another problem. Sugar was not eating again, this time for eleven days. Dr. Cruz had ordered tube feeding twice a day, but up till now Lloyd argued that it would be too traumatic. Perhaps he was actually thinking he might have a problem getting volunteers to help. At one time, volunteers were readily available, but after months of almost daily attacks in the media, Lloyd had a difficult time getting people to help.

A day or two earlier Lloyd was playing out a death-bed scene with Sugar. Slumping down in the front seat of his truck with Sharman, he frowned as he watched his beloved pet floating listlessly in her lagoon. He grumbled that he had done everything he could for her. "If she wants to die," he told Sharman bitterly, "she can just die." But at the last moment, he called on all the volunteers he could find, and now he prepared to feed her by force.

I was in Key West filling out my formal complaint against Trout at the State Attorney's office when Geraci and his team arrived. They watched the feeding and busied themselves by going over the logs and medical records.

For some time I felt sure that NMFS would never permit us to release the dolphins. They had authority over transporting dolphins, not releasing them. And since Sugarloaf Bay had a very limited fish population (and no dolphins), it was obvious that Buck and Luther could never be successfully released there. We would need NMFS's approval to transport them to some place where there were lots of fish. The Navy dolphins were originally captured in the Gulf of Mexico off Mississippi, and that's where we needed to move them. We thought that if we could find a pen site in that area, we could petition NMFS for a permit to move the dolphins there, a special permit like the one they issued for moving Bogie and Bacall. Once there, if the fence happened to be destroyed by vandals or by an act of God, as had happened even here—presto!—the dolphins will have escaped to their own freedom.

That would be ideal, but since nothing had been ideal up till now, I gave it little chance of happening. We could diddle around with this bureaucratic double bind forever, or we could do what had to be done. The dolphins are ready to go, I told Lloyd, so let's take them somewhere off Key West and release them—without a permit. Ultimately, Lloyd and his father did not agree. It was against the law.

Lloyd and I clashed continuously about his theory of whale sociology, that these dolphins were a pod or a family and should be released gradually as a group—the "soft release," as he called it.

I called it nonsense. This idea might work as a Disney fantasy, I told him, the dolphins swimming off into the sunset together, but these actual dolphins were not like that. "The social dynamics of these dolphins is that Molly has become their leader," I said. "Where she goes, they will follow. And she will always lead them back to be fed. She will go up to boats to be fed, and so will the others. And when they do that, they will be caught by Trout. The first thing we must do," I said, "is get them away from Molly." But Lloyd had already fallen in love with his own idea.

News broke that both Bogie and Bacall were five months pregnant. Blame fell on Lloyd, who argued in the November 1, 1995, *Keynoter* that "Keeping the dolphins separated from each other was unnatural. It was creating a lot of stress among them. . . . " In the same article Dr. Baker, the vet who had resigned from Sugarloaf's board after a falling-out with Lloyd, said he suspected Lloyd allowed Bogie and Bacall's pregnancies in an "attempt to sabotage the dolphins' release into the wild."

o   o   o

When Geraci's Sugarloaf report was issued, nobody was surprised. If he was unsympathetic with Sugarloaf's mission, why would he be sympathetic with anything we did at Sugarloaf? He questioned why, for instance, we couldn't get the dolphins to cooperate in "presenting themselves" for drawing blood and other fluids, why we needed so many volunteers to capture them in the first place. He recommended that the dolphins be taken away from Sugarloaf—all of them—because of inadequate veterinary care.

Geraci failed to mention that four other dolphin facilities he had passed on his way to Sugarloaf also relied on part-time veterinarians: DRC, Dolphins-Plus, Theater of the Sea, and Hawk's Cay.

Reporter Becky Squires wrote in the October 11, 1995, *Keynoter* that Geraci recommended that Sugarloaf needed "a major overhaul of its philosophy, program and resources. If not, the government could consider relocating the dolphins to one or more facilities with strong established health care facilities."

When the report was published, Lloyd explained: "Every policy decision we make at Sugarloaf Dolphin Sanctuary is made from a standpoint of the absence of control. Basically we do nothing with our dolphins and it drives scientists mad and dolphin trainers utterly cuckoo."

In the November 22, 1995, *Islamorada Free Press,* Dr. Rene Cruz of Cruz Animal Hospital on Ramrod Key said, "One of the problems occurs in the taking of periodic blood samples. Earlier, they would offer their fluke for blood samples. But as they were prepared for their release to be more and more independent, they became less and less cooperative about giving blood." Cruz then admitted that he did not "fully understand why dolphins being prepared for release, as opposed to performing in some commercial display, require such stringent regulatory enforcement."

Morast read Geraci's report and published it on the Internet. About the same time, Sugarloaf's request to NMFS that its license be changed from public display to research was denied.

Ann Terbush of NMFS sent Lloyd a letter saying we should apply for any permits we needed to go forward, and Lloyd worked on his version of an open-water permit application.

o   o   o

Ben White had warned me first. "Get out of there, man," he said. "They're coming." Then an APHIS veterinarian warned us. Grandy tipped off Mr. Good, who passed word of an impending raid on to me. An acquaintance of mine at DRC and a source at NMFS also reported the same thing. Despite all these warnings, Lloyd continued what he was doing. I think he was engrossed in trying to prove that his "soft release" would work.

Kathleen and I, who made up two-thirds of the sanctuary's board of directors, could feel them closing in on us. We were alarmed, too, about Lloyd's behavior, believing that it posed a threat to the dolphins. But what could we do? When Lloyd banned Kathleen from Sugarloaf, she went home and cried all day, believing that her life with dolphins was at an end.

Lloyd, realizing that he might have driven her into an alliance with me, tried to make up by offering to take her back if she resigned her board position. She could work on his "soft-release" proposal, he told her, and sell T-shirts.

Kathleen was insulted. It was one thing to be treated rudely, another to be treated as if she could be bought. She rejected what Lloyd proposed the moment it was out of his mouth. She and some of the other staff members and volunteers got together and wrote down a list of their grievances. Then she called me on the phone. She wanted me to sign it. We met in a café south of Sugarloaf. She presented the document, a list of about twenty-five complaints. I read it, approved, and signed with a flourish. Only Caren, Lloyd's sister, at the last moment refused to sign.

This was mutiny, yes, and it sealed the breach between Lloyd as director of Sugarloaf and two-thirds of his board of directors. The document was delivered to Lloyd, with copies going to his father, Dr. Cruz, and the media.

The next step was so natural we hardly even talked about it. Kathleen and I called a noon board meeting at her cottage, and invited Lloyd by phone. At noon, Lloyd had not shown up, and since Kathleen and I were a quorum and had the votes to determine the future of Sugarloaf Dolphin Sanctuary, the meeting was called to order. I proposed that Buck and Luther be transferred to Dolphin Project, Inc., the motion was seconded, the vote was duly held and the motion carried. We also voted to fire Lloyd. About thirty minutes later, Lloyd arrived, snarling like a wounded bear. He didn't like having to meet at our convenience, he didn't like our voting to take the Navy dolphins away from him, and he was furious about being fired. He stormed out, grumbling that the whole thing was illegal.

But apparently it was legal. Or at least it met Mr. Good's test because he wanted the dolphins out, and this was a way to do it. He said we could have the Navy dolphins but we must remove them at once.

And yet, we were not allowed on the property, and the dolphins couldn't be moved without a permit. If we could get a permit to move them out of Sugarloaf to a temporary pen, the next step would be to build a pen off the coast of Mississippi, take them there, and release them.

We called Ann D. Terbush, chief of the permits division of NMFS and told her about our plan and asked for special permission to do that for the good of the dolphins. It couldn't be done, she said, citing chapter and verse. In a follow-up letter, she wrote, "During our telephone conversation I recommended that you submit a scientific research permit application and receive a permit before moving the dolphins to Mississippi since it is your sole intention to prepare the dolphins for an experimental, scientific release to the wild. The only other mechanism provided by the MMPA is to transport the dolphins to a facility that meets all public display requirements. APHIS is responsible for licensing facilities under the Animal Welfare Act. All public display facilities have to meet the following three criteria under Section 104 (C) (2) (A) of the MMPA. . . . " And then she listed them.

"If it is not your intention to move the dolphins to a public display facility, you will have to obtain a scientific research permit in order to maintain the dolphins in captivity prior to a release program. The review process for scientific research permit applications generally takes a minimum of ninety days. Therefore, I encourage you to submit an application as soon as possible."

Ninety days? We needed it in ninety minutes!

We called Dr. Watkins at APHIS and Dr. Schwindman, who said the USDA would expedite approval of a license application for the new facility.

Kathleen, Jack, and Vanessa fanned out all over the lower Keys in search of a new site for the dolphins.

Meanwhile, another emergency occured. I was summoned by Cruzada Por La Vida, an environmental group in Lima, Peru, about a shocking practice going on in Peru. Fishermen were catching dolphins, cutting off a part of their dorsal fins and dumping them back in the sea to die.

Catching dolphins is illegal in Peru, but fishermen were doing it anyway, then selling the small part they had cut off at the base of their dorsal fin on the black market as "muchame" (*chancho marino* or "sea pig"), which sold for three dollars a kilo (2.2 pounds). It is an Italian delicacy. I flew down, tried to go underground and stop it, but didn't get to first base. So I used my position as Flipper's former trainer to launch a public awareness campaign to educate the public about this awful practice and hopefully put an end to it.

o   o   o

When I returned from Peru, I found that Lloyd had banned practically every-body from working with the dolphins, including Caren, his sister, who now worked only in the restaurant. We needed volunteers to help Helene, who was now working in the fish house. I enlisted the aid of an old buddy, Fred Neil, cofounder of the Dolphin Project.

By now, Lloyd's thinking was set in concrete. The dolphins were not to be returned to the wild, they were to be part of his "soft release." For him it made perfect sense, particularly since the federal government had never disapproved. In fact, Lloyd must have thought the government would go along because it didn't involve transporting the dolphins anywhere.

But Lloyd's "soft release" theory was flawed, and I told him so. "As long as you keep feeding the dolphins, they'll keep coming back," I told him. "They have to. There's not enough fish out there." I was pointing out to the bay from one end to the other. "You know that as well as I do. These dolphins are not at the sanctuary anymore, they're at the Tiki Bar." In fact, when I drove up I had noticed that the marquee in front of the lodge had changed. It now said, "Rooms with a Dolphin View". Right next to it were the usual signs: "World's Best Key Lime Pie" and "Margaritas".

"Get it through your head," I told him, "as long as you've got these dol-phins, you've got me, too. And somehow, some way, they're going to be free."

o   o   o

Then one night Jake was mauled by Luther. Jake was bleeding from his mouth and had bad rake marks on his side and face. We feared that he might have internal injuries, and Kathleen called a veterinarian, who refused to come because he felt I had insulted him publicly. I told Kathleen that I would apologize, but nothing came of it. We tried to find several other vets, but they all refused because they said they agreed with the doc-tor I'd called first.

By now we were all banned from the sanctuary, so Kathleen and I held a meeting in Key West, declaring an emergency due to Jake's injuries. On a radio talk show, Becky Barron said a tourist had reported to her that Jake "looked dead."

Despite the ban, Kathleen and I went to Sugarloaf and confronted Lloyd about Jake. I videotaped the dolphin. Kathleen told Lloyd, "I don't know you anymore."

He replied, "You *never* knew me."

Kathleen and I informed Mr. Good that since Lloyd wouldn't allow us on the grounds, he (Mr. Good) would be held responsible for what happened to the dolphins.

Dr. Cruz visited Jake and tried to talk to Lloyd about the dolphin's condition, but Lloyd said, "No. The pod is harmonizing."

By this time, Lloyd was letting the dolphins out in the canal. I couldn't control Lloyd. He was definitely on his own. Up till now Lloyd and I had presented a unified front, but enough was enough. I called the *Miami Herald* and was quoted the next day in their April 25, 1996, issue saying, "[Lloyd] Good is out of control. He is sabotaging our efforts. When I left yesterday, Jake was in the marina dodging outboard motor boats. This is so irresponsible."

Patricia A. Montanio, acting director of the office of protected resources in NMFS, wrote to Lloyd about "alarming reports" that dolphins at Sugarloaf were leaving their pens and swimming in open waters. She expressed concern over what would happen to the dolphins and wanted assurance that they would not be released without a permit.

"This is unlawful," she wrote, "unless the release is authorized by way of a scientific research permit issued by NMFS. . . . On the permit to Sugarloaf Dolphin Sanctuary allowing custody of the Navy dolphins, it clearly states that:

> No marine mammal obtained under this permit may be released into the wild unless such a release has been authorized under a separate scientific research permit that has been issued for that purpose.
>
> If you fail to respond, we will assume that you intend to release these captive animals in violation of the terms of your permit. Be

advised that we have alerted our Office of Enforcement and the Department of Justice to these new developments. In the event adequate assurances are not provided, we will act accordingly."

Seeking distance from Lloyd, I wrote to NMFS: "Our attempts to resolve the existing problems through board actions are ignored and have been futile. Therefore, we must rely on enforcement of the regulations of the Animal Welfare Act and the Marine Mammal Protection Act."

Then, virtually pleading with them, I added, "We would still like to be able to move at least Buck and Luther to the interim facility as soon as possible. We would appreciate the courtesy of a reply to inform us as to how you are actually empowered to respond to these recent violations. As we wait, the dolphins are in jeopardy."

They never replied.

Jack, Vanessa, Kathleen, and Caren complained to Mr. Good about Lloyd not feeding some of the dolphins. Mr. Good's response: "Then *you* feed them."

The fish house was locked, so they broke in. Lloyd saw them and called police. Mr. Good vouched for them, admitting he had told them to feed the dolphins, but had not authorized them to break in. The police let them go, and the next day Lloyd and I made a deal that we could come on the property to feed Buck and Luther.

We finally found a vet to run tests on Buck and Luther. Dr. Forrest D. Hayes of Gainesville, Florida, charged standard rates of $1,000 a day plus expenses to draw blood and have it analyzed. When he arrived, we couldn't catch the dolphins, that's how wild they already were. Dr. Hayes returned home and the next day we called in additional volunteers. Dr. Hayes came back, costing us another $1,000 plus expenses, and we caught the dolphins. Blood analysis showed that Buck and Luther were free from any sort of contagious disease.

A suitable spot for the interim facility was found at Caribbean Village on the Gulf side of Big Coppitt Key, a little south of Sugarloaf. On this little island, Kathleen and I held board meetings at Bobalu's Southern Café.

o   o   o

Suddenly, on May 16 everything changed. Bogie and Bacall were freed. In the dark of night, someone had cut the fence. Suspicion fell on me, of course, which I denied. An NMFS team began searching the Indian River Lagoon for Bogie and Bacall. That team had been assembled to confiscate Buck and Luther, but when Bogie and Bacall were released, they were switched to Melbourne. HSUS posted a $5,000 reward for information leading to the arrest and conviction of whoever cut the fence. Trout and Joe Roberts were scouring the waters off Melbourne. Several sightings of Bogie and Bacall were reported and the search expanded.

I called Dr. Schwindman of APHIS, seeking special permission to move the Navy dolphins to Caribbean Village, a permit like the one we got for Bogie and Bacall. At first he said he would help. We collected more than $20,000 from friends in Europe and started getting a place ready for the dolphins. Then Dr. Schwindman changed his mind.

I had tried to go by the book, but the book was closed. NMFS had gathered a formidable force of captive-dolphin power to hunt down Bogie and Bacall, and I knew that we were next.

I sent out word to everyone I knew, including Michael Lang, my longtime friend of Woodstock fame, Lincoln and his friends, Captain Ron Canning and his friends, even grizzled Bubba Jones, who explained his presence in Key West style: "We're here because we're not all there." There were twenty or more of us—make it thirty if you count photographers, including a French film crew. And even Lloyd, defying his father, joined us, offering his twenty-two-foot outboard Mexican workboat.

Lloyd had constructed a plywood shelter on his boat to protect the dolphins from the sun. While cameras recorded the scene, we tossed half a dozen live finger mullet in with the Navy dolphins, who snapped them up. They were excited. They knew something big was about to happen. We had so many people helping, it was easy to capture them. We put the dolphins aboard Lloyd's boat on sponge mattresses, we held a brief, mock ceremony involving passports issued by the Conch Republic to all dolphins, the gates were lowered and we motored out to a spot about twelve miles northwest of Key West where we could see wild dolphins all around. In the boat were

Lloyd and I, Lincoln, and Michael Lang. Most of the others followed in a fishing boat, video cameras rolling. And finally, amid prayers and singing, we set them free. Luther was first. He circled the boat, we freed Buck, they teamed up and took off together toward the northwest.

I felt terrific, like a great weight had been lifted from me. I knew for an absolute certainty that these two dolphins were ready to live again. They were in mint condition, and if given half a chance they would absolutely make it in the wild. On the other hand, I knew I was taking a chance with my own life. It would appear that I was flouting the law. I didn't have a permit because they wouldn't give me one. And I could have abandoned this project at any time up to the final moment. A merely prudent man would have. But didn't these dolphins deserve a chance to live again? I knew that nothing I could do or say would change the minds of those in power. In weighing one against the other, I had no choice.

When the dolphins swam out of sight, I was elated, yes. They were free of us, and I was free of a never-ending nightmare. At the same time, I knew that it wasn't over yet. Above us, circling, was a single-engine airplane someone had chartered to follow the dolphins. And before we had returned to port, a swift Florida Marine Patrol boat chased after us till Lloyd reached the flats where their boat couldn't go.

Before it was over, officials from about ten government agencies would move in for the kill.

13

NO WAY OUT

You will be damned if you do—
and you will be damned if you don't.

—Lorenzo Dow, 1777–1834

THOUGH BOATS AND TRUCKS and carloads of men had been sent to Melbourne in search of Bogie and Bacall, finding them in the waters off Melbourne would be tough because they had never been freeze-branded, and by now, having blended in with the resident dolphins, they were practically invisible. When Buck and Luther were released off Key West, the trucks and capture crew in Melbourne turned and headed south toward Sugarloaf.

We were sitting ducks. Our release of those two dolphins was the target of almost as much strategic planning as Reagan's invasion of Grenada. Sugarloaf Key was swarming with law enforcement agents and the military, including the U.S. Coast Guard, U.S. Navy, Florida Marine Patrol, APHIS and NMFS, and the Monroe County Sheriff's Office.

NMFS Enforcement Agent Mac Fuss, who had arrived by helicopter, was waiting for us at the Tiki Bar when we docked. When the fishing boat with the French film crew pulled in and tied up, Agent Fuss walked over to them, flashed his badge, and said, "Give me the video."

The French crew was flustered. Most people don't have a clear idea of their rights, especially in a foreign country, so I intervened, asking Agent Fuss if he had authority to take these things.

He turned to me. "You're O'Barry, aren't you?"

I identified myself and said that I was in charge. "What about the search warrant?"

He ignored my question. "Where are the dolphins?" he asked.

"I released them. We've been working on this for a long time, now they're free. Are you going to arrest us?"

"I want to ask you some questions." He turned to Lloyd. "Were you in on this?"

"You will have to talk to my lawyer," Lloyd said.

I stepped forward. "He wasn't involved," I said. "I released the dolphins and I take full responsibility. If you're not going to arrest us, I'm going back to my room to pack."

I took Helene's arm and the two of us walked deliberately toward the lodge. Agent Fuss watched for a moment, then turned to the film crew, his hand out. "The video tapes."

They gave him two videos, and within a minute and a half, Helene and I had piled everything we had in the car and were heading north on US 1. For about twenty miles, we drove in silence, my eye on the rear-view mirror. Suddenly I realized that I was practically on the lam. Though Agent Fuss had said he would give me a citation, he never did. I wasn't officially running from authorities, but I could feel their hot breath on my neck. I had no idea what was coming next. I had proclaimed loud and clear that I wanted my day in court, that I would turn the court into a bully pulpit to tell the world what was really going on here.

But then what? I glanced at Helene. She was staring straight down the highway. Did I have the right to drag her into this?

"If you want to leave me now, Helene, I'll understand."

She looked at me. She has the most innocent blue eyes in the world. "*What?*"

"I may be in some trouble, and I don't want to get you involved."

"Trouble? What trouble? We're in this together anyway." She touched my hand. "Don't you know me by this time?"

We had crossed the Seven-Mile Bridge and were driving down the highway through Marathon. "I don't mean it like that," I said. "I know what kind of person you are, and, well, maybe you *should* leave me. That's what I'm saying. Look, Helene, I may be in big trouble. I might even be on the lam right now. I don't know."

"You might be on the *what?*"

"On the lam . . . the lam. It's slang. It means, well, I might be running from the law. I don't know."

"Look at me, Richard. Do I look worried about this lam of yours?" She smiled.

"I don't want to drag you into it."

"And I don't care about that."

"For your own good—"

"My good is your good."

My God, I thought, this is it. I said, "You know something, Helene? I truly love you."

"And I love you too."

o   o   o

Becky Barron, director of the Wildlife Rescue of the Florida Keys, had been the first to spot us gathering at Sugarloaf early that morning. She noticed us while driving past the sanctuary on her way to work. From her office, she alerted Trout by phone that there was a large gathering of people in swimsuits around the dolphin lagoon. Trout in turn alerted NMFS and HSUS.

Becky and her assistant, Denise Jackson, arranged to get the airplane we had seen circling above us. They spotted Lloyd's workboat and two other vessels near the Northwest Channel, also a pod of wild dolphins in the area where Buck and Luther were released.

"A part of me says they're going to be fine," she told the *Key West Citizen* of May 24, 1996. "But how do you know?"

I didn't have a chance to reply directly to her, but if I had, I would have said that I knew, that the dolphins would have done just great in the wild, and they were healthy, strong, and vigorous. Did they also have a few trace behaviors learned in captivity? Of course. But these were fading day by day. These behaviors are like memories. Use them or lose them. Most memories we forget in time. They all fade if they're not reinforced, but a few, for whatever reason, you never completely forget. The dolphins needed a little time to adjust. This shouldn't be too difficult. After all, their natural world is in what we call "the wild," and once they open up and became part of it again, it would all come rushing back. When? A few days, probably, or at most a week.

But no, Trout and his minions were lusting for them. The DRC with its nets was eager for the hunt, and several government agencies had sprung into action, their orders based upon rules and regulations laid down by bureaucrats working with the captivity industry.

Buck and Luther had no idea what they were up against, nevertheless they did the right thing in the circumstances: they split up. Luther was spotted first near the Blue Lagoon Motel at Key West in a foot and a half of water, causing some to fear that he might strand himself. Later he went out into deeper water and reportedly chased a personal water craft. Somebody said they saw Buck miles away near Trumbo Point, Navy property.

Helene's visa was up, so I drove her to the airport in Miami. Lincoln called, said the dolphins had appeared in a marina on the Gulf of Mexico side of Key West and that Trout was trying to lure them into his net with dead fish. Trout was pictured doing this on page 1 of the *Key West Citizen*. Jack and Vanessa Martini were depicted on US 1 with placards that said "Honk If You Love Dolphins" and "Let the Dolphins Alone!"

Helene returned to Denmark, so I drove back to Key West. The battle now was for headlines. Journalists for the *New York Times* and the *Miami Herald* were locked solid in NMFS's camp, telling the government's story, not mine. A June 1, 1996, *New York Times* article reported that I had "kidnapped" Buck and Luther from Sugarloaf. Kidnapped? How could I kidnap my own dolphins? This was blatantly wrong and I had to hire a lawyer to make them retract it, which they did on June 27, 1996.

Nancy Klingener of the *Miami Herald* wrote on May 24, 1996:

Luther and Buck, two dolphins retired from service in the U.S. Navy, were taken from Sugarloaf Dolphin Sanctuary by Ric O'Barry, a dolphin freedom zealot so committed to his cause that he once clung to an ocean buoy in a military weapons range to halt tests of explosives that might harm the mammals.

When I saw that word—"zealot"—I almost went postal. I'm not a zealot, not even about dolphins. It's true that for a whole day I clung to that buoy with a 2,000–pound bomb hanging below it, but I had been in the Navy and I was sure they wouldn't blow it up with me or anyone else on it. Later when thunderstorms came through and might have touched it off, I let them rescue me. If I were a zealot, I would have wanted lightning to strike, to die for a cause. A zealot would say that all captive dolphins must be freed, and then proceed to try to free them. But I don't say that. I say only that all captive dolphins are *candidates* for freedom. There's a big difference.

Nancy called later and apologized about her choice of words. No problem, I said. And the newspaper gave me space on its op-ed page to correct the record.

More serious misstatements in the media were never corrected, however, biased accounts by people like Trout, Rector, and Trevor Spradlin, an NMFS marine biologist. They were spinning events into so many stories I couldn't keep up.

Neither could the dolphins. Luther, who was at Stock Island Marina near Key West, reportedly had a "gash" on his back.

Jack Martini checked it out. "A gash?" he said with amazement. "You call that a gash? That's not a gash. At most it's a rake mark. Nothing's wrong with that animal." Spradlin also noted that Luther had a drooping dorsal fin, which he claimed was a sign of dehydration. Jack and Vanessa explained that Luther always had a drooping dorsal fin, at least from the time he came to Sugarloaf. "We've got photos of it," they said.

Jack summed it up in the May 28, 1996, *Miami Herald* like this: "A Navy dolphin . . . who served seven years in the military and was honorably discharged is being reincarcerated on trumped-up charges. It's a farce! What's wrong with this animal being free?"

At Sunset Marina, a large inlet where the waters teemed with fish, a slew of wild dolphins, including Luther, were seen feeding. NMFS officials asked Ed Gartenmayer, who owned the marina, for permission to use nets to capture him. He refused.

"[Luther's] just as healthy as can be," he said in the same *Miami Herald* article. "I'm not a dolphin expert, but I've been around the sea all my life. If he showed any signs of distress, being sick, I would be in favor of [capturing him]. He's catching his own food. I've seen him. I know a healthy dolphin."

Things were looking up at this point, and I told newspaper reporters, "I feel very good about how it's going so far, except for these people harassing him [Luther]."

Spradlin was concerned about genetic mixing. Luther and Buck were captured off the Mississippi coast, and he said, "We don't know what effect the introduction of different genes might have."

Was he kidding? Where does he think these dolphins are from? They're all from the Gulf of Mexico. They mix all the time. That's definitely not a problem. If he had been talking about dolphins that came from the Gulf mixing with *Pacific* dolphins, that might be different. I cited the Navy's own records showing that several of their dolphins had escaped like that, and none of them occasioned the recapture efforts or concern shown here.

At Stock Island, Trout was reportedly feeding Luther from a bucket. In fact, the *Key West Citizen* ran a photo on May 28, 1996, of Trout doing just that. Jack Martini was watching when Luther was lured with dead fish within range of a capture boat, but when they lowered the net into the water to trap him, it spooked Luther and he fled.

Then for three days there were no sightings. I held my breath as Trout and his crew scoured the waters off Key West. They searched the Lower Keys and were expanding outward. Maybe it was wishful thinking on my part, but I thought it was over, that if the dolphins could hold out just a little more, they would be really free. I was too tired to cheer. This whole experience had been too messy. I thought I might learn a good deal from what had gone wrong here.

○   ○   ○

For about a year I had been planning to attend a dolphin and whale conference hosted by SOS Grand Bleu in the south of France. In fact, I was the guest of honor. I had the plane ticket, and I wanted to get as far away from Sugarloaf as I could. So I left, leaving Lincoln in charge and planning to be back in a few days to start tracking Buck and Luther. I wanted to keep tabs on them and make sure they were okay.

While I was in France, Lincoln called and said that Trout and the others were about to recapture Buck and Luther. So I flew back again.

Luther thought he had found a haven in a submarine pit at Boca Chica Naval Air Station, a long, deep canal or lagoon. But the capture team found him there and ran a net across the entrance. He was trapped. In the *Miami Herald* on June 1, 1996, Luther was pictured leaping into the air on command, and Spradlin told the newspaper that, "The fact that this animal is still doing commands he supposedly hasn't seen in three years is very telling. It says that this is still a highly conditioned animal, and is therefore entirely dependent on people for his food, his health and his well being."

On June 4, Buck was sighted and then caught at Vaca Cut near Marathon. "There was no drama at all," Spradlin told the *Miami Herald* on June 5, 1996. "This animal came right up to the boat. . . . No nets, no drama, no nothing." He left out the main point, that Buck was responding to the Navy's recall pinger, which produces a sound (12,000 vibrations a second) that Navy dolphins are trained to come to. With the pinger and a trail of dead fish, Buck was lured directly into the holding pens at DRC. Even now I don't know how that particular behavior—responding to the recall pinger—can be extinguished, except by the healing of many years.

The *Miami Herald* asked for my reaction and I told them, "I'm just infuriated at this. They don't have a legal right to do this."

Spradlin, who represented NMFS and the captivity interests, told the newspaper that our releasing Buck and Luther was " . . . a complete in-your-face violation of the Marine Mammal Protection Act. This is a precedent-setting case here."

It was not a small thing they were talking about. The charge was "unauthorized transport of the dolphins," which carried possible fines and penalties of up to $10,000 for each violation.

In the *Miami Herald* I was quoted as saying, "We did this openly. There was nothing sneaky about it. We followed very strict protocol. We have a legal right to do it. These people make my skin crawl. They're disgusting. And they're not going to get away with this."

Ed Gartenmayer told the *Key West Citizen* of June 5, 1996, that he saw Buck swimming with four other dolphins. "At first I thought it was just another pod of dolphins," he said, and went on to comment that he didn't understand why the government was harassing the dolphins.

Two days later, NMFS officials and their capture team from DRC, Sea World, the U.S. Navy, and the Chicago Zoological Society descended upon Sugarloaf and captured Jake, loaded him onto a truck and with a police escort drove ten miles down the road to the Naval Air Station on Boca Chica Key where Luther was.

Charges of transporting and releasing the dolphins without a permit were filed later against both Lloyd and me by NMFS.

In a *Miami Herald* article on June 7, 1996, Spradlin claimed that both Buck and Luther were severely underweight. "[Buck's] emaciated," he said. "He weighs under 300 pounds. A male bottlenose dolphin of this age and length should weigh over 400 pounds."

Spradlin's comment about Buck's weight was important to me because now, instead of opinion, we were talking facts. I have the Navy records on all three of our Navy dolphins, and it shows that Buck's weight varied from 291 pounds to 329. The fact is that dolphins in captivity are usually *over*weight. They get free food for very little activity. Almost all dolphins in captivity are obese, chubby little clowns, the result of eating oily fish like herring and not exercising enough. That's what Spradlin and others in the captivity industry are used to seeing. Dolphins in the wild are trim. Also when Shaney Frey of Boynton Beach, a writer and Kathleen Brooks's mother, heard that Buck was "emaciated," she checked him out at DRC and reported that Buck looked the way he always did.

I publicly labeled what the NMFS and their allies had done to us an act of sabotage. "Luther and Buck never had a chance," I said, "and it's absolutely disgusting what they did. These are vile, evil people."

Several things happened almost at once. NMFS suspended the dolphin display license at Sugarloaf. Jake and Luther were flown back to San Diego. And Buck and Molly were given to DRC as a reward.

The *Key West Citizen* of June 23, 1996, reported that before Molly was moved, Trout donned a wet suit and swam into Sugarloaf and up to Molly. He was arrested for trespassing " . . . three hours after he was spotted in the water near Molly, trying to give her a towel and a fin, two of her favorite toys." Trout told the newspaper that Molly was depressed because her companion Jake had been removed from their pen." He said that his arrest was " . . . tantamount to telling a parent you can't go see your sick kid and give him a teddy bear."

o   o   o

Here's the "official" version of what happened from the NMFS MMPA Bulletin of Sept./Oct. 1996:

> Buck and Luther . . . were illegally transported and released to the wild off Key West, Florida, in May 1996. In a related action, NMFS, in cooperation with the Animal and Plant Health Inspection Service (APHIS), seized the dolphin Jake from the Sugarloaf Dolphin Sanctuary . . . in June 1996. Both efforts were conducted under the authority of the MMPA and at the direction of on-site NMFS personnel from the Office of Protected Resources and the Office of Enforcement. NMFS and APHIS had been in the process of planning and obtaining a warrant for the seizure of all three dolphins when the unauthorized release of Buck and Luther occurred. The team organized by NMFS to assess the health of Buck and Luther was comprised of personnel from the Dolphin Research Center (DRC), the U.S. Navy's marine

mammal research program, Florida Keys Wildlife Rescue, the Marine Mammal Conservancy, and the Florida Keys National Marine Sanctuary. Additional logistical assistance was provided by the U.S. Naval Air Station in Key West, the Florida Marine Patrol, and the U.S. Coast Guard.

Immediately after the release of Luther on May 23, he appeared in Key West marinas and public waterways alone, visibly underweight and with three deep lacerations on his right side below the dorsal fin . . . begging for food. . . . On May 30, the NMFS reserve team was able to safely secure him in a lagoon at the U.S. Naval Air Base on Boca Chica Key. . . .

On June 4, Buck was found in Vaca Cut near Marathon Key in considerably worse body condition than Luther. Buck was emaciated and had . . . three deep gashes on his head . . . a deep puncture wound on his right side below the dorsal fin, and four long horizontal lacerations on the left side. Members of the public . . . reported that he, similar to Luther, had been approaching people begging for food. . . .

o   o   o

Talk about spin. I guess it depends on your viewpoint. When Helene returned from Denmark, she and I spent a lot of time at my place in Coconut Grove, most of it doing damage control, trying to correct the record. I tried to find a pro-bono lawyer, one who would work for free just to establish the truth of things. Failing that, I hired a lawyer for a couple of thousand dollars merely to be told that filing a lawsuit against federal agencies was a waste of time and money, and that I could never recover the dolphins.

I kept expecting Agent Fuss to show up at the door any minute with a citation or to call me on the phone. I wasn't running from anybody. I was in the phone book and I've had the same post office box for more than thirty years. But he never called or wrote, and I thought that with all the really important problems in the world, mine must have slipped through the cracks.

Then one day two years later, there was a knock on the door. I looked out the peephole and saw what I thought was a FedEx guy with a packet. I unlocked the door and opened it. And there was Agent Fuss. "Remember me?" he asked. Then he handed me my citation. "See you in court."

o   o   o

Life was passing us by, but I didn't mind because Helene and I were happy. The trial was a long way off and we were adjusting to another kind of life. On one of those lazy, hazy days, Helene and I were washing Yoko out in the back yard when I heard the fax turn on. I dried my hands with a towel, went in, and got it. I came back and Helene asked who it was from. I told her it was from Mark Berman.

"Mark Berman? Didn't he vote against you when he was on the board?"

"He sure did," I said.

Yoko was jumping around shaking water, frisky as a pup.

Helene dried her hands and sat down on the grass, her hands clasped around her knees. "That wasn't right, what he did," she said.

I shrugged. "I know. But we're cool." Yoko brought me the coconut and I tossed it. She ran and got it, then squatted in the grass to chew on it.

"I don't get it," Helene said, tossing her head. "He didn't help you when he had the chance. What kind of friend is that?"

"You're right," I said. "It was not his proudest moment." I shook my head, thinking back on Sugarloaf, a million miles away. "But he was under enormous pressure. I found out later that he could have lost his job if he had voted with me. Is that an excuse? I don't know. But we all made mistakes." She looked at me and nodded. Suddenly it swept over me that this was the woman for me, that Helene, beautiful and true, was also a real person and someone I wanted to live with forever.

Mark Berman needed no forgiveness from me. His track record includes almost single-handedly, in 1992, outlawing not only the capture of dolphins in the waters off South Carolina but also displaying them, the first and still the only state with a law like that.

I mentioned it to Helene, she smiled and said, "Still friends, then?"

"The best," I said. I held the fax up, smiling. "He's heard about a dolphin that needs help."

"Is it Cheryl?"

"No, I wish it was Cheryl. It's a new one, Menique. Mark says he's being moved from Peru back home to Cuba and the government wants to set him free. But I doubt that they know how to do it. Anyway, maybe this means I'm back in business."

She smiled. "You know something?" I said, taking her in my arms. "I love you when you smile like that." Her chin fits almost perfectly on my shoulders.

"Does that mean you're on the dolphin trail again? To Cuba?"

"Me? No. Not me," I said. "*Us*. Don't you remember? We're in this together."

14

DOWN TO EARTH (SUMMER 1997)

Tear down the walls,
listen to freedom singing out . . .
  —"Tear Down the Walls," Fred Neil

FULL TO THE RAFTERS with about fifty passengers, the small plane, a rickety, old, recycled Russian Antov 24, took off for Havana from Nassau, about two hundred miles away. Because of the embargo, this is how people in South Florida must visit Cuba and the relatives they left behind. As we were taking off, engines straining their guts, one of the passengers, a beefy man in a fancy white guayabera with a pencil-thin mustachio above his full upper lip, waved vigorously to the stewardess in the front of the plane and said that water from the air-conditioner was dripping on his wife, who was seated next to him. A small, corpulent woman, she had shrunk away from the drip, but it was still hitting her, and she held up a small, delicate hand to show what was happening.

"Por favor," her husband said, holding his hands out plaintively. The stewardess, trained in emergency procedures, rushed to the front of the plane where the pilots were sitting behind a curtain, reached in and reappeared a moment later with a large Styrofoam cup. This she held under the drip for a moment, then gave it to the man, who caught the water meant for his wife. A few minutes later, when the plane struggled higher into the air and leveled off in flight, the dripping water moved forward to the next seat, and the man in the guayabera passed his cup to the passenger ahead of him.

In Havana it had just rained. Puddles here and there. Steamy hot. The plane taxied over to the passenger terminal and the engines stopped, the hatch popped open and we walked down single file, then over to the fence. I had a bag, which had been checked earlier, and my backpack. We lined up at the passport control desk, and I unslung my backpack. Helene, wearing a cotton summer dress, sandals, and a perky straw hat with a wide, black silk band, looked like she had just stepped out of a Renoir painting. She carried some things in a straw basket, including a portable computer. She was doing a story for a Danish publication.

We lined up at the passport control desk, and I unslung my backpack. At some point, I knew, they would want to check it again. A young man in an olive-drab uniform asked for my passport. As I handed it to him, I said, "But please don't stamp it." The passport control officer wasn't sure what I had said. So I said the same thing in gestures, my balled-up right hand coming down as if holding a stamp, then waving it off while shaking my head. He nodded. Most people who go through this circuitous business of getting to Cuba from the United States don't want their passports stamped. Not that they're necessarily doing anything illegal, but who knows what the policy will be tomorrow? And as for the Cubans, they're happy to oblige. To them we're "blockade runners" and they think it might mean that we're on their side. The officer didn't use his stamp, but I think he made a tiny bookkeeping mark in my passport.

We were pointed to the next checkpoint, customs and immigration, where an officer looked through our baggage, probably to keep weapons out. Most passengers to Havana are Cubans living in South Florida, and, of course, there is no language barrier. But for the rest of us, the customs and immigration officials tried to make themselves understood by using a form of English made up mainly of nouns. The officer checking my bag was tall and thin, and he was asking about the purpose of my visit. How strange, I thought, for this was the very question I was asking myself. I was composing an answer that would not involve the tragicomic disaster at Sugarloaf, when he asked, "*Turista?*" (Tourist?)

I nodded. Then, mouthing each syllable as if to someone hard of hearing, I said, "But also, I intend to help in the release of Menique, a captive Cuban dolphin."

The clerk shook his head. "*No comprendo*" (I don't understand).

"Sorry."

"You," he said in English, pointing at me with a long, bony index finger. "Hotel?"

"Sí. We're at the Ambos Mundos."

He nodded and wrote that down in a ledger next to my name.

"That's where Hemingway stayed, you know."

He was rifling through my backpack, unimpressed by my reference to Hemingway. Suddenly he came up with something very strange to him, a foot-and-a-half-long bronze rod with a wooden handle. He held it up, puzzled. "*Que es eso?*" (What's this thing?) I explained with a few words in Spanish and sign language that this was a freeze brand for the dolphin. He shrugged, so I began moving my hands up and down like a dolphin swimming through the water. Then, as if holding the freeze brand solidly to the dolphin's dorsal fin, I pressed it firmly in, held it for a moment, and suddenly released it, giving a satisfied grunt. I smiled at him. "Amigo, you comprendo?" I asked, nodding my head and grinning.

He had backed off a step and was frowning. He shook his head. "No comprendo," he said as if it didn't matter. He gazed at the end of the dark brown bar curiously, then at me.

"Peace," I said in English. Then I corrected myself, "I mean *pace*." There on the business end of the rod was the peace symbol from the 1960s. But wait a minute. The word for "peace" is *paz*, not *pace*. And what had I said to him? I had no idea. I shrugged, the clerk shrugged back. He'd heard enough. He put the rod back in place and poked around among the other things in the bag. Nothing there. He sniffed and closed it up again. Originally I had ordered that freeze brand for Jake. Now, it seemed to me, letting Cubans use it on their own captive dolphin would be appropriate somehow in the ironic clash of symbols.

The customs official said something in Spanish and tossed his head, indicating that we were cleared and could go. We grabbed our things and headed for the taxis outside.

The story I heard was that Menique had been captured in Cuban waters and sold with another dolphin to an amusement park in Chile. The other dolphin died, the amusement business folded, and Menique was returned to Cuba, where officials decided to free him. Why? I have no idea. Capturing and selling dolphins on the international market is a cottage industry in Cuba. For the article Helene was writing, she and I talked to some people who said they knew what was going on around the waterfront. According to them, Cuba was capturing about fifteen dolphins every year and selling them "green" for about $40,000 each. A trained dolphin would be worth about $130,000.

In charge of Menique's release was Señor Guillermo Garcia Montero, director of El Acuario Nacional de Cuba. This aquarium was supposedly a tourist attraction, but it was so dilapidated that few tourists came. School children came by the busload, though. I was with Señor Garcia several times and would have asked him about capturing dolphins and selling them on the international market, but the right moment never happened. Language problem. He and the other officials I talked to spoke some English, but haltingly, as if by committee. They finally understood what I was doing there—or trying to do, I think—but they never really trusted me. I wanted them to use my protocol for the release of captive dolphins and the freeze brand too. It would prove, at least to some extent, that my system works.

I was not applying for a job. No way would I have worked for Castro's government. But as a consultant? Yes, they could have listed me like that. I had been told that this was their first release, and I expected that they would welcome my help. But no, they had released dolphins before, they said. Later when I showed them the freeze brand, they had no idea what it was for. I handed Señor Garcia the bronze freeze brand and he stared at me for a long

moment. Then he said gravely, "With your reputation, Mr. O'Barry, I'm surprised you would subject dolphins to such pain."

"Pain? What pain?" I said. "You've got it wrong." Suddenly I realized
what they were thinking. "I get it. You think this brand gets hot? No. Just the
reverse. It gets cold. It's a *freeze* brand. I don't know the Spanish word for it.
Is it *frio?* Anyway, we put the freeze brand in liquid nitrogen. That's 320
degrees below zero. We leave it in there . . . maybe ten minutes . . . then, when
the brand gets that cold, we press it firmly on the dolphin's dorsal fin for
twenty-three seconds. He feels nothing. We put him back in the water, then
in about ten days, the mark turns white. It doesn't hurt him." Then it dawned
on me that if they had no way of marking the dolphins, they had not monitored their previous releases. I shook my head. "No," I said. "I wouldn't
do it if it hurt the dolphin. But we must mark the dolphin so that we can tell
him from the others, then monitor him until we know that he's made it in
the wild. You know what I mean? Okay?"

"Okay," Señor Gomez said, nodding his head and smiling broadly.

At our first brief meeting I left the material and some videotapes that
show me doing what I do. The second meeting, which occurred the next day,
lasted four hours. Señor Garcia and Señora Maida Montolio Fernandez, cura-
tor, showed us around the aquarium. I asked to see Menique, but he was in
quarantine, they said. Señor Garcia said they had studied the material I left
with them and liked it. Then I tried to explain my own frustration with several agencies of the U.S. government, that I was on the outs with them just as
they were, that I had something to prove, and that it would be fitting, I thought,
if we could team up on behalf of Menique. I'm not sure that they appreciated
the subtleties of all this, because somehow I knew that Señor Garcia was
merely telling me what he had been told to say, that no outsiders were to be
involved in the release. My heart sank. Then with a smile he said that
because of my unique background, I might be the exception.

I was elated. This was all I wanted—a foot in the door. I told them I was
ready to help. Helene and I shook hands all around like we were all the best
of friends and left, then got the plane back home, where I waited for some
word from them. Three weeks went by, no word. I thought about calling, but

because of the language problem, that wouldn't do. Money was tight, so I flew back alone. Señor Garcia told me that he hoped I understood his position, that the Cuban government was at that moment in delicate negotiations with U.S. officials, trying to ease the embargo, and he could do nothing that might affect those efforts.

"And so?" I said.

"And so," he said, "it has been decided that there would be no outsiders at all, including you."

I had a feeling this would happen. I thought I was braced for it, but it sickened me anyway. For a long moment I just sat there.

"However," he said, "if you wish, you could be . . . " He stopped, searching for the right words. "What do they call it?"

"Consultant?" I suggested.

He shook his head. "No, that's not the word."

"Advisor? That's a good word."

"No," he said. "No. It must be unofficial."

"Unofficial? You mean like unofficial consultant?"

He thought about it, then shook his head slowly.

I shrugged. "Then I have no idea what it could be."

His face brightened suddenly. "What about unofficial advisor."

I looked at him to see if he was joking. "Unofficial advisor? What's that?"

He shrugged. "It means—" he hesitated, looking for the right word. "It means you are welcome to come by. We'll show you what we're doing. You can see our data . . . medical reports . . . anything you want."

"And?"

"And if you have suggestions—"

"Yes?"

"—we'll listen to them."

Was this guy kidding? Unofficial advisor? That's not even a real title. I stood up slowly, thanked him with a little smile, and said I would be back to look in on the release from time to time. Then I shook hands all around and left.

15

TO FREE OR NOT TO FREE

This is not about freeing Stephania,
it's about doing the right thing.
  —Helene Hesselager

FALLING IN LOVE WONDERFULLY expands the mind; priorities and problems magically fall into place—or so it seems. I saw clearly that, above all, I must restore my good name, and the key to that was to document my method of untraining and freeing captive dolphins. It worked with Joe and Rosie, it worked with Flipper in Brazil, and with all the others. It would have worked at Sugarloaf too, if our efforts hadn't been sabotaged.

It would also have worked with Menique in Cuba if only the Cuban government had been capable of a little trust. Menique was never freed, however, dying later of a liver ailment.

Living with Helene, I yearned for a normal life, a 9-to-5 job, children, watching TV, and whatever else normal people do. Surely by now, I thought, I had paid my karmic debt, and perhaps I'd gone as far as I could in redeeming captive dolphins.

I enjoyed the life I lived. I was my own boss, I could do what I wanted to do, and work when I wanted to work. The bad part is that it's only an illusion. When people called about a dolphin in trouble,

I felt that I had to go. There was no regular paycheck, no paid vacation, no insurance. And at the end of the trail, there would also be no pension or gold watch, maybe not even a pat on the back.

Was it right to drag Helene into this kind of world? I put out a few feelers to some old friends, letting them know that I was considering a change of life. And hanging over everything like a dark cloud was the lawsuit Agent Fuss had delivered. But these things drag on, sometimes for years, and there was nothing I could do about it now. Both Lloyd and I had been cited for certain alleged violations of NMFS's regulations—civil charges, not criminal. Lloyd called from time to time and said that he had legal representation. I told him I couldn't afford a lawyer, that I had myself as a client with two possible strategies. Plan A was to use the court as a bully pulpit and expose the conflict of interest at the heart of NMFS. Plan B, which I was leaning toward more and more, was to plead "no contest" and throw myself on the mercy of the court.

Jean-Michel Cousteau, son of Jacques Cousteau, came through town and took me to lunch at Monty's in Coconut Grove, posing the question: "Can you think of anything that hasn't been done in a film about dolphins? Something we could collaborate on?" He had grown up on the Calypso, his father's famous research ship, and though he loved the sea he was not following in his father's footsteps. He founded his own film company, Jean-Michel Cousteau Productions, and was looking for a film to do about dolphins. I told him I would think about it and get back to him.

Helene and I met a Scandinavian couple, Einar and Anna Gruner-Hegge, and became friends. He's from Norway, she's from Sweden. They moved to Coconut Grove and purchased the Dolphin Cruise Line, five ships operating in the Caribbean. We talked about my joining their staff and giving lectures about the sea, showing videos and holding seminars about dolphins and the sea for guests. I would also dive under the ship in interesting places with closed-circuit underwater video and show guests in their rooms what was in the water beneath them. Jean-Michel was doing the same thing for another cruise line based in Miami.

These projects and others were percolating when, from out of the blue, I received a fax from Tele Images Nature, Paris, asking if I would like to collaborate on a dolphin documentary to be produced by Frederic LePage. I hadn't met him, but I knew he had a good pedigree: author, television producer, entrepreneur, and a jolly good fellow.

When he said the word "dolphin," all the business prospects I had been nurturing, wonderful as they might have been, were suddenly forgotten. "Yes, yes," I said to myself. "*This* is what I was meant to do." I called the number on the fax and said I was very interested. We met later in the luxurious Delano Hotel on Ocean Drive in Miami Beach, where Frederic was staying. I met him and two of his business associates for lunch, and while we ate he asked if I was available to help rehab and free a captive dolphin for a television series about the Caribbean Sea. The series would be called *The Blue Beyond,* a documentary blend of *The Big Blue, The Abyss,* and *Free Willy.*

"We have the crew," he said in a light, pleasantly accented voice. "We have the story line, the location, and the star—Umberto Pelizzari. You know of him, don't you?"

"I certainly do," I said, nodding emphatically. "I've never met him, but I certainly know who he is. He's the Italian free diver—430 feet deep! He broke the records held by Jacques Mayol, a good friend of mine."

Frederic smiled. He had a brown flattop, wire-frame glasses, and a light-hearted grin. "The series is about freeing a dolphin," he said, "and that means we'll need a dolphin. Are you interested?"

"Absolutely," I said, jumping at the chance. "But let me say up front that getting a dolphin seems simple, as if it's a matter of just buying one, like anything else. But it's not that simple, really, because if we bought a dolphin from an amusement park, in most cases they would simply go out and capture another one. My feeling is that we must make sure that any dolphin we get will *not* be replaced."

Frederic flashed a smile. "Ah, yes," he said. "I hadn't thought of that. Excuse me," he said, turning to his companions. There was a rapid-fire conversation in French, then he turned back to me. "That's a very good point. Yes, and it's not a problem, Ric."

"One other thing," I said. "Preparing a captive dolphin to live in the wild is not an exact science."

"Of course."

"To free a dolphin, one must be almost positive that they will make it in the wild. If not," I said, shrugging, "we cannot do it."

He nodded and shrugged. "No problem. We're building a location in the Bahamas, a place near Georgetown in the Exumas. It's beautiful . . . three houses there . . . crystal clear lagoon." He turned to the others with a wave of his hand and said, "It's perfect, hey?" They nodded agreement.

It was a great plan, but it never had a chance. I believe that when those in the captivity industry got wind of Frederic's plan to produce an anti-captivity film, they must have lobbied members of the Bahamian government. The plans were rejected.

When he told me about this, I said, "Welcome to the world I live in. These are the people I've been fighting all my life. When I say that there's a war going on, some people think I'm exaggerating. But I'm not. The first rule of anything I do is secrecy. The moment they learn what we're doing, they'll do everything they can to sabotage it."

Frederic didn't give up, and Helene and I began searching for available captive dolphins that would not be replaced. This is not done by hopping on a plane, running here and there to check out dolphin shows. I have an updated computer list of all dolphins in captivity in the world, and it's not hard to tell which of them we might purchase without replacement. But I also knew that no dolphin show in the world would sell *me* a dolphin, not at any price. Concealing my own part in the search, Helene and I made a list of the possible dolphins in Europe and set out to buy one. At the same time, Frederic and his production manager, Guillaume Bernard, checked similar dolphin prospects in Central and South America.

Helene and I concentrated on Switzerland and Italy. The Adriatic beaches of Italy are littered with small, roadside dolphin shows. For several months we searched, but found nothing that fit the bill. We even scouted the Caribbean for Cheryl, finally locating her as one of two performing dolphins in a Colombian traveling dolphin show called *Waterland,* owned by what were rumored to be drug interests in Cali, Colombia. Like a traveling carnival, the dolphin show would blow into town with a parade down main street. Workers would dig a hole in the ground, spread a liner, and fill the hole with water to make a pool, then they'd pitch a tent and sell tickets and have Cheryl jump through hoops. Helene and I tracked her through Jamaica and three locations in Venezuela, finally catching up with her on the island of Margarita, Venezuela. But Cheryl had just died and the dolphin show packed up and returned to Colombia.

Having run out of options, Helene and I returned home. I checked the fax machine, there was a message from a former dolphin trainer who lived in Switzerland. Veronica Duport, who worked in a drug store, asked if the Dolphin Project could save the life of the dolphin she had trained in Santa Marta, Colombia. The dolphin's name: Stephania. I called Veronica on the phone and asked exactly what Stephania's problem was.

Stephania was dying, she said, starving to death at a dirty dolphin park on a small Colombian island in the Caribbean, San Andres. It's a tourist resort with a population of 85,000, nearly 500 miles north of the Colombian mainland, 100 miles east of Nicaragua. With a tear in her voice, Veronica said, "My dolphin Stephie is in a filthy little tank at the Seaquarium with a blind sea lion named André. They hardly ever feed her, and she's wasting away. I trained her about a year, and we trainers had to spend our own money for fish to feed them. I couldn't stand it anymore," she said, almost sobbing, "so I left. Now I'm doing everything I can to help get her out of there. Can you help?"

I called Frederic, told him about Veronica and the dolphin, he called her, then flew down with Dr. Cyril Hue, a marine mammal veterinarian, and checked out the dolphin. Assured that Stephania would not be replaced, Frederic bought her and called me. Helene and I flew down, and when we saw the dolphin they had bought, we were shocked. Stephania had the dreaded peanut head, her body having wasted away, except for the head, which had the shape of a peanut. She weighed a mere 218 pounds, about 140 pounds below normal. We could count her ribs. She looked limp, her eyes unfocused. Obviously she had given up. Floating on top of the water like she was, in this hot tropic sun, that in itself is a death knell. An active dolphin, in and out of the water, is not harmed by the sun. But when she always floats, half in the water and half out, she gets sunburned—even blistered—and that means one thing: She doesn't care.

Dolphins, smiling and leaping out of the water almost as if with wings, are used in advertisements to represent the zest for life. There was no zest in Stephania. When I gazed down at her in this miserable tank, I wondered how such an ebullient creature could be brought so low. It's more than just being captive. That's terrible enough, but she was also isolated, which is like being ostracized.

When Stephania lost interest in the barren world around her, she stopped eating. Then her serious problems began. The dolphins' only source of water is in the fish they eat, and when they stop eating, that leads quickly to dehydration and a multitude of physical and mental repercussions.

o   o   o

Stephania had originally been captured about a dozen years before off the coast of Colombia near the Rosario Islands, site of a beautiful national park. Ideally, we should take her back there, her home. But that was nearly 500 miles south of San Andres, and she probably wouldn't survive the trip. As Helene and I stood there looking down on this wretched creature, Frederic and Dr. Hue came up to us, and Frederic asked, "What do you think?"

Staring down at the dolphin, I shook my head and said softly, "I don't know about this. I don't know if she'll make it or not."

Frederic turned to Dr. Hue. "And what do you think?"

Dr. Hue, whose specialty was working with stranded marine mammals, said, "I've seen healthier stranded dolphins than this one."

Earlier on I had briefly considered what my enemies would say if I got involved trying to free a dolphin and it died. But that didn't matter now. I said, "The important thing is that we get her out of here immediately."

Dr. Hue's tests showed that Stephania was okay physically except for a stomach fungus. He prescribed medication, and I told Frederic that getting her back to normal would take more than just medicine and good food. "She needs TLC, and a lot of it. I think Veronica, her trainer, could help." Frederic agreed and sent for Veronica, a young woman in her late twenties, with sandy hair down to her shoulders, and an outgoing, affectionate personality.

Almost the moment she arrived, she got in the shallow tank with Stephania and began hugging and kissing her. I watched for a while, and it was clearly a tonic for Stephania. But it went on and on, and I noticed Stephania popping her jaws at Veronica. This is how dolphins warn others to back off, that she wanted to be alone. Veronica didn't know about this, though, and I realized that freeing Stephania was going to be more complicated than we first thought.

o   o   o

Working closely with officials in Colombia, Frederic had acquired the use of a small island about twenty-six miles south of San Andres, a double-island called Albuquerque. One of the twin islands was used by fishermen, the other, where we would be, was for a squad of soldiers.

"What's the island like?" I asked.

Frederic, a master at painting word pictures, said, "Remember when you were a kid and fantasized about an island in the Caribbean, a small island with coconut trees, white sand beaches, and beautiful water all around?"

"Yes," I said, "I had that dream."

"Well, this is that island."

The island itself was just the way Frederic described it, maybe better. It was about 700 feet long, 425 feet wide, and without a single mosquito, sand flea, or sandspur. It did have falling coconuts, though. You could hear them fall day and night. You could be walking down a path and suddenly hear them crash in the spot you had just left. So Helene and I pitched our tent near the beach. Conch shells, another problem, were everywhere, big ones and little ones with sharp pieces sticking up in the sand. We were always cutting our feet and having to bandage them up.

At low tide I could walk around the little island in 958 paces, Helene in 1007. For exercise, we snorkled around the island in thirty minutes. It was protected by a heart-shaped barrier reef all around about three miles out. There were fish and sharks inside the reef, but no dolphins. The dolphins were beyond the reef. They were transients, dolphins that swim long distances at sea, much larger and stronger than so-called shallow-water resident dolphins like Stephania and "common" dolphins half Stephania's size. This was not a problem in the beginning because our only goal then was nursing Stephania back to health. It would become a larger problem later, though, when Stephania was ready to be released, because there were no dolphins like her to connect with.

When we first arrived with Stephania, we put her in the pen that Frederic's production crew built for her. It was large enough—about 100 feet square—but too shallow, only five feet. The fencing material itself wasn't right, either. It was a rather tightly woven nylon mesh, which would foul easily with seaweed.

When we got to the little island and put Stephania in the pen, a brown four- or five-foot nurse shark got in with her. Nurse sharks look like large catfish and feed on the bottom, eating crustaceans like lobster. They're not aggressive toward swimmers if swimmers keep out of their way.

Back in my *Flipper* days we worked with sharks all the time, so this was nothing to me. I got a rope and was going to loop it around her tail and drag her out. For nearly an hour I chased that little shark all over the pen. Cameramen were shooting this, and I began to feel a little foolish, being outwitted this way, so I gave up the rope and simply grabbed the shark by her tail. She was twisting around, snapping her teeth viciously at me, and I dragged her up on the beach so that I could get her out of the pen, then down in the water again where I could let her go.

This is not to say that in the right circumstances nurse sharks are not sometimes dangerous. One day Helene took the bucket of fish and was going to feed Stephania from outside the pen. Fish blood was dripping down into the water, as it always does, and suddenly I heard Helene screaming with terror at the top of her lungs. I was in my hammock. I spun out of it and saw that she was being harassed by three sharks, including a five-foot nurse shark, all of them trying to get the fish in her bucket. She dropped the bucket and they scrambled to get the fish, still brawling and splashing around Helene, so I dashed out into the water, picked her up, and carried her onto the beach. We did a quick check for damage and found that they had only bruised her left thigh.

The soldiers, an ever-present reminder of the rest of the world, were quite young—just kids. They lived in barracks amid the coconut trees, Helene and I lived in a four-person tent near the leeward beach, and on the other side of the island were Veronica and the cook, Patricia, both in their own tents. The soldiers, barefoot and wearing olive-drab shorts and T-shirts, usually had their rifles slung on their shoulders. They patrolled and kept a watchful eye over us. Their duty included picking up palm fronds and keeping the conch-lined paths that crossed the island clear. Their main function, however, was to maintain a military presence because the Nicaraguans (only about 100 miles away) felt like this island chain ought to be theirs. And except for one dark night when "mysterious" lights appeared offshore and the soldiers, fully armed, charged down to the beach to repel an "enemy invasion," they kept to themselves and their routines. The lights, incidentally, were actually a convoy of ships far at sea heading south toward the Panama Canal.

I was told that an important part of their job was to recruit more soldiers—not on Albuquerque or San Andres, of course, but on the mainland. As in so many South American countries, they drove through the streets in trucks and other vehicles. Then, spotting a possible recruit, they hopped out with their rifles at the ready, demanding to see his papers. If the papers were not in perfect order, they told him to get in the truck, that he was in the army now.

Colombia's notorious drug culture did not affect us except perhaps in providing a boat for the twenty-six-mile trip back and forth to San Andres. We chartered the boat from Larry Zogby of the Amigos Foundation, whose mission was to rescue seamen in trouble. Larry was tall with dark hair, a well-organized young man from a prominent San Andres family.

In good weather, we could make the trip to San Andres in an hour. Most of the time, though, the sea was violent, with strong Caribbean currents and winds of twenty knots producing ten-foot waves that crashed on the reefs. We could hear it all the time, an endless raging. When the weather was like that, the trip to San Andres might take as much as four hours if we weren't forced to turn back. Inside the reef the water averaged about twenty feet deep, clear as gin when the weather was nice. On the other side of the reef, it was several thousand feet. During our five months on the island, half a dozen fishermen were lost in storms at sea, a few of them turning up much later in Nicaragua.

We called them fishermen because they fished, but many of them were not fishermen until they arrived in San Andres. They had come to escape the lawlessness of mainland Colombia, becoming fishermen for the first time because it was the best thing they could find to do.

°   °   °

Veronica, a typical trainer, was the center of a typical problem I have in using trainers to help untrain a captive dolphin. At first she was helpful in comforting a traumatized Stephania. She was in the water a lot with the dolphin, hugging and kissing her, holding on to her dorsal fin and riding around in the pen. She referred to Stephania as "my dolphin Stephie." This was all very well at first, while we were coping with immediate health problems. It boosted Stephania's sagging ego.

Then it began to pose problems. Early on while the camera crew was recording, I told Veronica that we all appreciated her help in getting Stephania to eat and start to gain weight, but now the idea was to break the bonds between the dolphin and her life in captivity. And that included her, I said. This was the same kind of instruction I had given Trout and the other trainers at Sugarloaf, and I saw the same kind of resistance in Veronica.

"My dolphin Stephie and I," she said, "are very close."

Here we go again, I thought. "Look," I said. "She's not your dolphin. You can't *own* a dolphin. *Nobody* owns a dolphin. And her name is not Stephie. Please don't keep calling her that. We're trying to get her to take control of her own life. And treating her like a baby is not helping."

We were standing on the beach not far from Stephania and I put my hands on both of her shoulders, bent down, and looked her straight in the eyes. In a soft, deliberate voice, I said, "Veronica, please try to imagine what she was like *before* her capture." I paused, giving her a chance to lock on, then I said, "Hold that thought, and try to see her like that from now on."

"Okay," she said, nodding. "I understand."

After my debacle at Sugarloaf, I was careful about my dealings with others. And I suspected that nothing I had just told Veronica made even the slightest impression. I smiled with resignation and said, "Good."

The next thing I noticed was Veronica snorkeling out by the pen. I called her in. "Look, Veronica," I said. "You remember our little talk awhile back about not bonding with Stephania?"

"Yes, of course," she said. "I remember."

"Well, that's what I'm talking about."

"You mean snorkeling, too?"

"Yes," I said. "Everything. She sees you, she wants to be with you. That's bonding. You walk by on the beach, she follows you. That's bonding. You've seen her, haven't you? The way she keeps watching you? That's bonding. And that's not good. That reminds her of the past, and we're trying to get rid of the past and give her a new beginning. Veronica, you've got to leave her alone. Remember, this is about preparing her for life alone in the wild. Know what I mean? That means *without you*."

"Okay," she said softly. "I get it. From now on, I'll leave her alone."

The very next day, though, Helene and I were up on the beach working on the palm-frond blind, a place where we could watch Stephania without her seeing us. Suddenly up to the shore next to the pen came a Zodiac, a ten-foot inflatable dinghy, the motor roaring, with Veronica, Guillaume, and one of the soldiers. Guillaume stepped out, and then Veronica hopped out gaily with a bucket of fish and proceeded to toss them one by one to Stephania.

It makes a pretty picture, a young, attractive woman in a colorful swimsuit leaping out of a boat to feed a dolphin who adores her. But I was appalled. Now, I don't ordinarily give orders to people, I give them responsibilities and I expect them to do the best they can to get the job done. I run a rather loose ship, in other words, because it's more fun for everyone that way.

The soldier sped off in the Zodiac and I walked down to Guillaume on the beach. "You see what I'm talking about?" I said, my hands sweeping around to indicate what had just happened here. "I've told her not to do that."

Guillaume looked at me quizzically. "Oh?"

"I've told her not even to come around the dolphin. And now this! You see?"

Guillaume nodded his head gravely. "I'm sensing some tension here, is that right, Ric?"

There was a fish hawk on the island and we used to watch it hunt. It was flying high in the sky and we both watched as it circled, then swooped down to the water and scooped up a small fish in its claws. It wheeled over the island and was gone. We turned to each other and I said, "Yes, Guillaume. You are definitely sensing tension. I'm glad you were here to see what just happened with Veronica. I told her not to do this kind of thing. This is bonding. You know how I'm trying to get rid of that."

"I know, yes. And you told her not to do this?"

"Over and over, yes. Stephania cannot be Veronica's pet and a wild dolphin at the same time. It's impossible. I even asked her to stay on the other side of the island, totally away from Stephania."

"You explained to her why she must break this bond she has?"

"Yes, till I'm blue in the face."

"Do you think it's possible that there's a language problem?"

I shrugged in the French way. "That's always possible," I said. "Maybe if you spoke to her in French—that's her native tongue—maybe then she would get it." I shook my head in exasperation. "Here's the problem I'm facing, Guillaume. They want me to prepare Stephania for the final scene, Stephania taking off on her own—free at last. We all want this. I want it for the film, I want it for Stephania. That's what it's all about. But it will never happen with Veronica always around the dolphin. It's impossible." I looked him in the eye. "Veronica is a nice person. I don't dislike her. But there is tension here, maybe a lot of tension." I glanced down at the beach. "Look there," I said, pointing. "That's what I'm talking about." Veronica was walking along the beach and past the dolphin, Stephania following her in the pen along the shore. "You see?"

I was not the only one telling Veronica to back off. Stephania occasionally gave her the same message by snapping at her, and on at least one occasion Veronica burst into tears because of it. But moments later, all was forgotten and Veronica was back again, trying to be close to the dolphin—too close.

o   o   o

Early on in the first month it became obvious that our pen was on the wrong side of the island. It was on the east or windward side, and simply wouldn't hold up against the sometimes fierce weather. I called Lincoln in Miami to order some of the material we would need to build a proper pen. He arrived with it and we quickly erected the new pen on the west or leeward side. It was a little bigger than the first one, about 145 feet square, and much deeper, twenty-three feet at the deep end.

Then the big day arrived, moving Stephania into her new home, perhaps her final home in captivity. This was a chance, also, to take cultures, blood samples, and to weigh her. We hung a scale in a nearby banyan tree, then, all of us working together, we trapped Stephania, got her in her special canvas sling, and hoisted her up on the scale. When we first got her, she weighed 218 pounds (99 kilos). Now she weighed 277 pounds (126 kilos). She still had a distinctive peanut head and was 55 pounds (25 kilos) under her optimum weight, but she was making great progress. We were confident that at least she would live, and we celebrated, yipping it up and slapping each other on the back.

Frederic flew in for a quick visit. He put on a swimsuit and snorkeled to the deep end of the pen on the outside with Helene. I was in a small dinghy next to them, tossing live fish into the pen for Stephania, and we all watched as she caught them. For about thirty minutes Stephania put on the show of her life. She was almost like any wild dolphin in the world, flashing through the water, leaping into the air and catching fish. Frederic beamed with delight, all of us swept up in the camaraderie. We were on schedule for Stephania's final scene.

Frederic walked up the beach to our hut and sat down in the sand, leaning against the trunk of a coconut tree. A simple structure, the hut was between two coconut trees, and was made of driftwood bamboo and palm fronds. Between the coconut trees we had strung our colorful Colombian hammocks side by side, mine blue, Helene's red. We were lying in them when Frederic called Veronica to join us. She sat down in the sand across from Frederic, and he told her, in his deft style of cutting quickly to the meat in the coconut, that things must change. He told her it was a shame that it had come to this, that he recognized the beautiful relationship she had with Stephania, that she was a valued member of the troupe and would continue to be, but her relationship with Stephania had become a problem.

"I am going to solve that problem," he said. "Imagine a line going down the middle of the island." He made a cutting motion with the edge of his hand. "The pen is on one side, your camp is on the other. From now on, that's how it must be. Do you understand?"

She nodded sadly. I thought she was about to cry, but she didn't.

"In fact, Veronica, you have plenty to do in San Andres, getting supplies for those on the island. Plan to spend three days a week in San Andres from now on." He turned to me. "Does that about do it, Ric?"

I had complained to Guillaume about Veronica, but I had said nothing to Frederic, so I assume that Guillaume told him. Veronica and I got on better after that, perhaps because of our understanding. Whether she understood what we were really trying to do or not, I still don't know, but she accepted her new role in good grace.

∘   ∘   ∘

There were times on the little island when it was a Caribbean paradise, beautiful in every way. Stars at night were like a million fireflies. It was warm and soothing—romantic, too—and I could feel the healing going on through every fiber of my being. There were also times when the wind howled, rain came down in almost horizontal sheets, thunder rolled back and forth above us, and the whole sky was spectacularly alight with fire.

One night I popped awake—a sharp noise from the pen. It was Stephania slapping her tail on the surface of the water. Dolphins do this as a warning. I grabbed a flashlight, ran down into the surf, shining the flashlight here and there. I saw Stephania, floating as she often did during the day. Nothing else. I walked slowly back out of the water, sat down on the beach, and watched for a while, listening, hoping she would slap the water again so that I could find out what it was all about. But nothing happened. I watched for a while longer, thinking that if it wasn't a shark, it could have been a dream, a vagrant fear, anything.

Though the real work had begun and we had made enormous strides in just saving her life and getting her back on track, we were still not working with a healthy dolphin. Sometimes you can treat patients as if they are well and suddenly, for whatever reason, they get well or at least improve. Sometimes these are not specific problems with specific remedies, they're general problems, and sometimes anything you do can help. When we moved to the large pen, Helene and I approached the job as if we were starting out anew and this was just another dolphin. And in a sense she was. She was in a larger pen, and a more interesting one too, because of the reef in the middle of it, a working reef alive with fish of all kinds.

"Do you think she'll like the new pen?" Helene asked with a smile.

"She'll love it," I said.

Helene tilted her head and archly asked, "And how do you know she'll love it?"

"Because if I were a dolphin, I would love this place."

We laughed.

But Stephania wasn't me. She was afraid of the new pen. She was also afraid of the old one. She was afraid of everything. Most of the time she hung around in one little part of the new pen, not knowing what to do, and when she swam, it was clockwise circles, as if she were back in her old tank at San Andres.

Some problems solve themselves. I was hoping this was one of them. So we waited, watching Stephania's every move. When she wasn't swimming in endless clockwise circles, she floated in that same little corner of the pen.

Watching this from our blind, Helene shook her head slowly. "This is not good, Richard. She seems melancholy."

"I know," I said. "Depressed."

"To be always smiling, and behind it all, so sad—it's heartbreaking. What can we do?"

"I'm not really sure," I said with a shrug. "How do you get anybody to be happy? She has her moments, I think. They're rare, yes, but in those moments when she's like a wild dolphin—those are the moments we must build on. Exactly how do we do that? I don't know. We can try to encourage it. We can set things up for her . . . a good place to live . . . plenty of fish. Then we get out of her way and let it happen. That's all I know to do. And when those moments of happiness come, they've got to be their own reward. She's got to want to feel good." I gave Helene my optimistic look: big smile, eyes brightly open. Then I said, "And I think it's happening. I sense more vitality. Don't you? I get the feeling that she's almost over the hump."

Helene tried to match my optimism but couldn't quite. "Maybe," she said, glancing down the beach at Stephania. The dolphin was floating in the shallow water, the tip of her beak against the fence. "But too often, Richard, I see an unhappy dolphin."

And she was right.

During the move to the new pen, we had included four twenty-five-pound female hawksbill turtles with beautiful jewel-like shells that had been with Stephania at the Seaquarium in San Andres. Later, when a Colombian Coast Guard boat struck the pen and knocked down one corner of it, the turtles got out. Stephania could have escaped at the same time, and I wish she had, but she didn't.

We built a wooden fish pen, three foot square, five deep. We caught live fish and put them in the fish pen. We would feed them to Stephania, usually dunking them in ice for a few minutes to slow them down and give Stephania a chance to catch them. And she did catch them—even at night. Her sonar was perfect. She enjoyed catching fish when we released them for her. But the fish was secondary. What she enjoyed even more than the fish was her interaction with us.

Basically, she was still a pet and seemingly had no interest in interacting as a dolphin in a dolphin world.

Ironically, though Stephania's problems stemmed from her isolation, in order to set her free we had to isolate her from us. Our first priority, I thought, should be to eliminate her obsessive clockwise swimming, a remnant of her confinement in the tank at San Andres. I wanted her to use the whole pen we had built for her, especially the deep end of it, and then it would come naturally, perhaps, for her to chase her own fish. There were plenty of fish in the pen, all kinds, but she wouldn't leave that one little spot, much less chase down the fish and eat them.

The only way she would chase live fish was if we caught them for her first, chilled them in ice and released them for her. So we all spent a lot of time fishing. This was easy and fun in good weather, Helene once netting an incredible thirty-four yellow jacks in a single cast, but when the weather was bad, as it often was, we depended on Veronica to buy them in San Andres. That was her job now, getting supplies to us on the island. Our tent was destroyed in a storm once and we had to get another one. The generator broke down, we sent it back with Veronica to San Andres and they spent eight weeks fixing it. For Stephania we needed lots of fresh fish and crushed ice to keep them fresh. We kept in touch with Larry Zogby by radio, chartering his boat and, on occasion, his airplane for emergency air drops. He helped Veronica find the stuff we needed, traveling the back roads of San Andres to fish camps and buying fish and crushed ice, loading it into large coolers and making the run to our island. The ice lasted only a couple of days, then we needed more, so they were going back and forth all the time.

o   o   o

In trying to get Stephania into the deep water, I went to the deepest part of the pen and down about twenty feet, where I cut a flap in the pen, a flap I could close with an elastic cord. Stephania, curious and wanting to interact, would follow me down on her side. I took the fish out of the bag, thrust my whole arm through the flap while Stephania hovered there. When I released the fish, she would chase them down and eat them. I thought she was beginning to enjoy chasing the fish as much as eating them.

When Umberto Pelizzari came to the island, he and I liked to feed Stephania at the deep end of the pen. He was doing different film sequences with whales, rays, turtles, and other sea life in various parts of the Caribbean, but he would return to Albuquerque to check on Stephania's progress. We talked a lot about diving and exchanged stories of the sea. When we fed Stephania, we wore belts of fifteen-pound weights and went straight to the bottom like a rock. Umberto can hold his breath an amazing seven minutes; I hold mine about two.

I had tied a diving tank with a regulator to the bottom of the pen and we both used it, sometimes passing the regulator back and forth between us, buddy breathing. We would go down to the flap with a bag of live fish, open it up, and push the fish into the pen where Stephania, always eagerly watching, would chase after them and snap them up if she could. But we noticed that many of the fish, when they saw Stephania, bolted back through the mesh and to freedom. After that, we fed Stephania at the surface, throwing the fish deep into the pen where she had more of a chance to catch them.

When everybody had finally left the island, Helene and I wrestled with the problem of getting Stephania back into the real world of wild dolphins, and it began, we thought, with getting her spirits up and keeping them up. We could always get her to interact with us. What we wanted, though, was for her to interact with her new world. When we weren't with her and making her the center of things, she slipped back into her melancholy ways, circling or floating sadly in a small part of the pen.

o   o   o

I asked Helene to go down and spend some time with her, just to perk her up. During the long hot days in the sun, Stephania was again beginning to get sunburned, so we made a heavy cream of zinc oxide, lanolin, and fish oil, and smeared it on her for protection. When Stephania began to bond with Helene, I got Patricia the cook to go down and be with her. And I went down myself sometimes, all of this to get her swimming normally, in and out of the water so that she wouldn't get sunburned.

Stephania's problem was the kind she had to solve herself. We could lead her to the world of wild dolphins, but we couldn't make her become one. She had to *want* to be a wild dolphin, like all the other dolphins I had freed— Joe and Rosie, Flipper, and the Navy dolphins. They had wanted to be free. But not Stephania. She was afraid, unsure of herself. She was like Molly in having adapted too well to the world of captivity. If there had been other dolphins inside the reef, it might have been different. Before I started this project, they told me that dolphins come to the island all the time. During the entire five months we were there, we never saw a single one inside the reef.

I was looking for the slightest sign of improvement in Stephania. Helene was helping with the cooking one day and I went down to the water to be with Stephania. This was the breakthrough day, I thought. Or I hoped it was. I was looking for patterns of improvement, a sign of some kind. Regaining health is complex—for dolphins as well as humans. Today is not always better than yesterday. You may gain something today, but you may also lose a little of something that you gained the day before. Back and forth, sometimes several days at a time, and then, if all goes well, you reach a kind of plateau, a base line that is, for now, normal.

Independence was the long-range goal, but more immediately we simply wanted to break the negative cycle she was trapped in, her cycle of weakness, fear, and despair that fed on itself.

We closely watched whatever Stephania ate, whatever she looked at, or wherever she swam. If she noticed anything besides us, that was something to build on. If she swam over to anything outside her little circle, this was marvelous. Even better if she were to chase a fish on her own—but never once did I see that.

◦   ◦   ◦

Living on an island like Albuquerque, you tend to lose track of time in the soothing ebb and flow of tides. But it's there anyway. The expectations of Frederic and the film crew provided a relentless reminder of why we were there.

As hurricane season approached, a particularly strong storm struck the island one night and blew down our tent. Helene and I were clutching each other at the base of the banyan tree just to survive. As the wind shrieked and howled, I wondered how Stephania was taking it. When the storm finally went through, at first light the next morning I dashed down to the pen, secretly hoping she might have escaped. Half of the pen was down. But there was Stephania, circling as usual.

We fed her, then I went out with snorkeling gear to check the fence under water. Half the posts were uprooted, and the fence, which normally stuck a foot or so above the water, was mostly down. Repairing it would take several people, and we had nothing to fix it with. As I went from one post to the next along the bottom, I glanced up at Stephania, who was looking at me, I thought, with an amused expression. And in this moment, I knew that if we had "freed" her, she would do circles in the water until she died. And even if she didn't mope around or do circles, she wouldn't survive because of sharks. In the wild, dolphins are with other dolphins and they're almost invulnerable to shark attacks because they look out for one another. But Stephania was all alone, and time was running out.

I walked back to the beach, sat down on the sand, my knees drawn up, my arms around them. My head bent down to my knees and I was rocking back and forth, sort of an upright fetal position. It's one thing to know something, quite another to be *filled* with it, and suddenly, rocking back and forth, like an avalanche I was filled with the realization that there's no way Stephania could be freed at this time. Not here. I was breathing very fast, very shallow. I wanted to free her. Though I would never release her if she wasn't ready, I wanted to make the film's deadline—and it was impossible.

Helene came up. "Richard," she said, alarmed. "What's the matter?" She sank down on the sand with me. "Richard." She pushed my head back. "Tears? What's the matter?"

"Stephania," I said, looking into her face. "She cannot be freed. She's not ready. And she'll *never* be ready in this place." I looked up at her. "Don't you see? It's the wrong place."

Helene was holding my head and saying soft things. "That's okay," she said. "It's okay. This is not about freeing Stephania, it's about doing the right thing."

o   o   o

I was summoned to Paris, where I met with Frederic, Guillaume, and several others, including Laurent Frapat, the director. It was about lunch time so we all went down to eat, and Frederic, sitting across from me and in a jolly mood, asked me when Stephania would be ready for her freedom in the final scene. I reached in my backpack, got a stack of photographs and put them on the table. They passed them around.

"She *is* free," I said. "See the fence? It's down. There's nothing keeping her in captivity except her own fears. But you're talking about the final scene, when she *really* swims to freedom. And she's not ready for that. It's too much, too soon. This project must be done in two phases. She's done phase one. That's the one about saving her life. The second phase should be about taking her back to her home waters and reconnecting her with her own kind."

Frederic, no longer jolly, nodded his head. "I understand," he said. "But this is *also* about finishing a film."

"Right. The scene you want, the scene of Stephania swimming out of the pen and becoming a wild dolphin, that cannot be done now, nor can it *ever* be done at that place."

There was a moment of rather stressful silence, then Frederic, at his diplomatic best, said, "If we can't actually free her now, could you do this, Ric? Could you have her swim out of the pen on camera? We're not going to lie about it. We won't say she's free, but we can say that she left the pen, that she's better off than she was before, and that this shows progress." He was smiling. "We'll still have a happy ending for our film."

"No problem," I said. "And there's no danger of her leaving. Don't worry about that. She'll swim out and then she'll swim back, back to the pen."

I returned to Albuquerque, my spirits soaring. My mission now was merely to get her to swim out of the pen, then back—a simple piece of business.

o   o   o

A week later, they all came down for the final scene, a crew of about fifteen. Not Frederic, though. Guillaume, speaking for Frederic, said that they had changed their minds. They wanted her free for the film, and they expected *me* to get the job done. Their thinking was that they had a story line with a dolphin being freed and it's been five months and they *still* don't have the dolphin ready to be freed.

Guillaume and I were both very calm. I reminded him that I took on this project without even seeing Stephania. When you talk about freeing a captive dolphin, I told him, it's assumed you mean a healthy dolphin, not one on the verge of death.

Guillaume and Laurent Frapat presented what they thought was a compromise, that we lead Stephania out of the pen with a boat, feeding her on the way, then the boat takes off while we film her. And she's free!

That was so unrealistic I just shook my head. Guillaume suggested that since most of the pen was down now anyway, why not take it all down? He smiled as if he had just solved a problem in a very clever way. "And that will be her freedom," he said. "Do we have your cooperation on that?"

I shook my head. "No way," I said. "When you release a dolphin, you leave the pen up for at least six weeks. That's in case of emergency. The dolphin might come back to be fed." I shook my head again. "Take the pen down? That's unacceptable, and there's no way I can be associated with that."

Guillaume, wearing a patient smile, said softly, "Ric, I sympathize. But we've got a job to do. And we've got to get it done. This is the French way."

I was shaking my head slowly. "Guillaume, leaving her alone out here like that is banishment. Do you know what Stephania would do if we abandoned her at sea? Just what she's doing now. She has no place to go. No dolphins of her own kind. There are no dolphins of *her* kind in any of these islands, and no dolphins of *any* kind inside the reef. Helene and I have checked it out. We've been to all these islands, and we've talked to the people who live there. Stephania needs dolphins like herself to connect with."

This was not a vote or an encounter session, we were simply exploring options. But Frederic had authored his own report that began:

"The time has come to put an end to the readaptation process of Stefania [sic]. This is a general opinion shared by everyone."

Not me, though. When I stubbornly held to my own standards, first Dr. Hue sided with me, and then so did Laurent Frapat.

Earlier, before the camera crew arrived, I had swum with Stephania out of the pen to see what would happen. She went out for a while, looked around, then returned to the pen. She didn't like it out there.

We did it again for the final scene. With cameras rolling, I pretended to cut the four-foot door in part of the fence, then rolled it back and coaxed Stephania out. She went out with me and explored a little with her sonar, then made a beeline back to the pen.

o   o   o

Suddenly it was over, the movie crew gone. I couldn't even get in touch with them anymore. Veronica was still bringing supplies, but my paycheck had been cut off and the job now was to find a proper place for Stephania. There was only one option: the *Oceanario* on Rosario Island near Cartagena, Colombia, her native waters.

With Dr. Hue, Larry, and Veronica's help, we flew her down and put her into a large sea pen with a beautiful reef and lots of edible fish. Also it had what she needed most, dolphins of her own kind all around. Officially, Frederic still "owned" Stephania, but she had served his purposes and he was now editing his documentary to give the impression that we had freed Stephania. Everybody who watches *The Blue Beyond* on TV would think Stephania was free, but she wasn't. She was *still* in captivity.

Helene and I were sitting on the seawall looking down at Stephania. "Look how happy she is," Helene said. "She's perked up. No more circles."

Rafael E. Vieira, who owned the *Oceanario,* sat down next to me. He had curly brown hair and was wearing a swimsuit. "Yes," he said, "Sephania is very happy here." He looked at me with a big smile. "You can tell."

Helene and I smiled at each other.

"You two," he said, "are very happy, too."

"Very happy," I said. "Yes, we're heading to Denmark to plan our future."

"No wonder you're happy," Rafael said with a laugh.

"Right," I said, kissing Helene. "But we'll be back. This job is not done, and Helene and I will be on the dolphin trail together from now on." I took Helene's hand and spoke softly to her: "You're sure about this?"

"About getting married? I'm positive."

"No, I mean the trail."

"The dolphin trail? Of course."

"It's not all fun and games, you know."

She pretended to take umbrage. "Richard," she said. "After Sugarloaf and Albuquerque, do you think I don't know what it's all about?"

Suddenly I wondered what it was all about, why I was locked into this endless, sometimes thankless task of freeing dolphins. I don't know why. It's a mystery to me. But nothing compared with the mystery of why some people capture dolphins only to destroy them. Why would they do that? Why would they desecrate the marvel of a dolphin swimming free?

I felt silly questioning whether Helene knew what it was all about. She probably knew it better than I. "I know that there's more to life," I said, "than the dolphin trail. But you know I'm committed to the trail."

"Richard, I *love* the trail. And I love you too."

"You know I'm facing federal charges, that I might end up broke and broken."

"And then you'll know I didn't marry you for your money."

Had I found the perfect woman for me? Finally, yes. I had no doubts.

"I love you, Helene," I said. We kissed. "Next summer, we'll be back for Stephania."

"Yes," she said. "Together."

16

JUSTICE IN AMERICA

Some days you're the pigeon,
some days the statue.
　　　—Lloyd Good III

IN A TRIAL, WHERE time stops dead in its tracks, you go back and dig up all the contending versions of what happened and you go over and over it until, in some mysterious way, you understand what actually happened.

After five days of testimony, I was thinking that if we could have held the trial earlier, back when the problems at Sugarloaf began, or if we could have just talked to each other and really listened, we might have avoided the final catastrophe. It was obvious that we had all been wrapped up in our own self-interests. The bureaucrats in Washington, who were in ultimate control, had the impossible task of administering a law that didn't cover the subject. Forced to improvise, yet knowing nothing about dolphins, it's no wonder they gave us bad advice. The captive-dolphin industry, for which the laws had been written, saw me and what I was doing as the ultimate threat to their own survival. Former Sugarloaf employees who joined the other side against us, well, they must make their own peace. Lloyd, who had fallen in love with his own theory about freeing dolphins, nevertheless did himself proud, I thought, shooting well-placed zingers at the high and mighty. And yes, I was absorbed in my own self-interests, too, but it was singularly different from that of the others, I thought, in being the same as the dolphins'— their freedom.

In a trial with so many loose cannons, something wild and crazy was bound to happen, and, sure enough, it did that first day—during a break when I went to the men's room and, coming out, encountered Trout going in. As we passed he said something sarcastic.

I brushed by him without a word, but when court resumed, I stood up and told the judge, "Your honor, before we proceed, I would like to be excused just long enough to get a restraining order against Mr. Trout until this trial is over. Or in the interest of time, perhaps I could have a marshal or the court clerk follow me to the bathroom so I could be alone and be away from him. I'm being provoked. I'm being harassed. I am being verbally abused. It's hard enough defending myself as a lawyer without being stalked while this is going on."

Judge Fitzpatrick sat bolt upright. "And you are saying that someone in this courtroom is doing that?"

"Rick Trout," I said. "I would like to get a restraining order just like his girlfriend has one against him right now." Lynne was in the courtroom, sitting on the far side, away from Trout.

JUDGE: Mr. Trout?

TROUT: Yes, sir.

JUDGE: Please come forward.

Trout stood up, trudged forward, and stopped before the bench.

JUDGE: I'm not passing judgment on anything that has been said or anything that is being done, but I do want you to be aware that this a sensitive matter.

TROUT: Yes, sir.

JUDGE: That passions fly high in this particular area. But you must be very careful, and I don't want you to have any contact with Mr. O'Barry whatsoever.

Trout protested that he was innocent, but agreed, and from then on when I went to the bathroom everybody in it cleared out.

o   o   o

Dressed alike the whole trial through, Lloyd and I conferred not even once on strategy. And yet, because we're such different people, it worked okay, my strong points, experience, and passion, meshing with Lloyd's doggedness and messianic flare for the abstract.

When I stood up to deliver my extemporaneous opening statement, I understood what Lloyd had once said about pigeons and statutes as a metaphor for life, because for a moment I was the statue with a very large pigeon on my head. Now, though, I had to play the lawyer, and I made a typical lawyer's gesture, a little flourish with my hands, ending with the palms up in a pleading posture.

"We are talking about a discotheque," I said, "with dolphins jumping through hoops. . . . " I paused, glanced around. "No problem there. They [NMFS] give you a permit. They will help you. But if you want to get a permit to *release* them, well, [they say] we are *worried* about the dolphins. They have issued permits to kill between seven and ten million dolphins by the tuna industry." I stopped momentarily as if in silent prayer, then I said, like a gong ringing, "*Big business.* No problem there." I let a little smile play on my lips as I said, "But they are worried about the two dolphins we want to help." I stopped dead and said softly, "There's something strange and bizarre about that."

I gazed around to let those words, "strange and bizarre," sink in. Though Judge Fitzpatrick paid close attention to everything, I found myself speaking not to him but to the court reporter who was taking down every word.

"There's something strange and bizarre about using dolphins as advanced biological weapon systems," I said. "And we do our best to try to create a way out, a revolving door for [the dolphins] in a responsible way."

I tossed my hands up in the air and shook my head, allowing the unfinished sentence to hang in the air where the irony of it might come to rest even among my critics.

"It's true [about this business of untraining a captive dolphin], it is a healing art. It's not science. And it has been done successfully. I have good documentation by the National Geographic Society showing the last dolphin I released in Brazil—named Flipper, incidentally. That dolphin has been seen and documented on television a year and a day later and twenty-two months later, absolutely irrefutable—I mean, it was absolutely successful. And they will tell you it was a failure, it doesn't work. That's because it's [the dolphin slave trade] a billion-dollar industry. And many of the scientists have prostituted themselves to this industry. That's where the money is. There is no money in what we do. I don't get paid to do this work. And I have been doing this work since Earth Day 1970, trying to expose the National Marine Fisheries Service.

"I don't have much more to say except that Lloyd shouldn't be held responsible, because the record will show that he turned the dolphins over to me and the Dolphin Project to set them free. We were having conflicts, Lloyd and I. . . . We are not partners. I was trying to responsibly release them into the wild because—was it the right thing to do? It was the *only* thing to do. . . . The problem was when we released them there were so many people wanting to sabotage this thing." I gestured vaguely to the audience where Trout was sitting. "Sea World was there," I said. "The Dolphin Riding Center was there." I pointed to Randy Wells in the audience and said, "We had his group from the Chicago Zoological Society there. We had the Navy, the Coast Guard. And they were like—it was like a film I once saw in England, where the people in red jackets on the horses are chasing one fox. There were hundreds of them going after this one fox."

I felt suddenly like I was about to choke. What was it about that desperate fox that went through me like an electric jolt? I don't know. I cleared my throat and went on.

"They harassed [the dolphins]. They called them into harm's way using this recall pinger. And although I extinguished all of their trained behaviors in that nineteen months, I didn't give them a lobotomy. They still remembered to come to that pinger. And [the dolphin capture team] had it, and they used it the day the dolphins were released.

"That would have been a successful release," I said as forcefully as I could, "had they not interfered with the period of adjustment. But you see, it's hard [to get cooperation] in this country, especially in Florida. From Orlando to Key West alone, it's a billion-dollar industry. And they are fighting to keep these dolphins in captivity. And that's what this is all about."

I sat down, limp. That was my defense, my explanation of what happened.

Lloyd, who had some help at home from his lawyer-father, had three main arguments: the Agency had acted without authority (jurisdiction) in confiscating the dolphins; the Agency had acted in bad faith; and when Lloyd finally helped free the dolphins, it was an act of "civil disobedience." Civil disobedience is deliberately breaking a law to bring attention to the fact that it's a bad law and there's no other way to correct it.

The government called several witnesses that week, mostly paid employees of either NMFS or APHIS, to verify their version of what happened. They included Ann Terbush of NMFS, Naomi Rose, Mary Lycan, Mac Fuss, Trevor Spradlin, Gregory Bossart, and Randall Wells.

Naomi Rose of HSUS had perhaps the most central and curious role in the Sugarloaf disaster, and yet she remained unscathed. Though she was crucially involved in everything that happened, officially she was only the "facilitator-advisor," and as such was technically free from responsibility for actions taken after her advice. In my opinion, she had twisted our original idea of freeing dolphins in our custody into manufacturing a cookbook for freeing captive dolphins in general. In answer to an Agency lawyer's question, Naomi Rose testified that she wasn't interested in releasing dolphins as such, she was interested in the "precedent-setting aspect" of releasing them, and in "releasing them in such a way that the public display industry could find no fault with it."

Though she got Joe Roberts to hire Mary Lycan to write the protocol, Naomi testified that she would never let anyone who had no experience freeing captive dolphins write the protocol for it. Was Mary Lycan supposed merely to assist me in preparing Bogie and Bacall for release and writing the protocol? Mary thought not, according to the transcript of the trial. Indeed, her job description indicated that she was in charge. So who had actually written that job description? We had always thought it came from Naomi Rose, but she testified that to the best of her recollection Rick Spill wrote it—Rick Spill who had not been heard from since he was accused of being a mole for the captivity industry. To suggest that Spill wrote letters of scientific description for Naomi is hard to swallow, because Spill was not a scientist and the job description that was produced read like the way Naomi Rose spoke.

In a marvelous exchange, Lloyd questioned Naomi Rose about her role at Sugarloaf:

LLOYD: When you insisted that Mr. O'Barry was part of the project during the involvement phase, the beginning of your involvement with the sanctuary, you were aware that Ric is not a scientist?

NAOMI: Yes, that's correct.

Q: So why then later in your testimony did you say that Ric was being held accountable for things of a scientific nature with the scientific research permits?

A: He was the only one that I was aware of who had the expertise and background and experience of having rehabilitated and released dolphins in the past. So clearly he had the knowledge in his head. And what we wanted from him . . . was just what did you do to get them prepared. And the scientific expertise of turning it into a permit application would obviously—you know, that would not be his responsibility. That would be the responsibility with somebody with that background.

Q: He did give you his methodology?

A: He did.

Q: But you didn't like it?

A: As I said in my testimony, if it's without words, I can't turn it into words.

Q: Well, I mean, is science actually a process; or is science more a way of documenting something?

A: I would say it's both.

Q: So the science itself is the process?

A: In this particular regard, what we were looking for was a sort of a cookbook or step-by-step sort of recipe that anybody could repeat. And you know, that's all—it wasn't, you know, the methodology section of any scientific project. So that's all it is. It's just a description of what the researcher did and would do again to repeat the results. And so all we wanted from Mr. O'Barry wasn't anything that, you know, is some magical language of science or anything. It was just what did you do to prepare these animals for release.

Q: Well, he told you?

A: But if I can't reproduce it in any kind of step-by-step words, that makes it unrepeatable. That is, part of the scientific process is you have to be able to repeat it.

Q: What if there is no process, what then?

A: I don't know. If there's no process, then it's not—. That leaves me without a response. I don't know.

(If there's no process, then it's not—*what?* Not a *science?* Is that what she was going to say? I think so. And isn't that what I kept telling her? That this is not science? If science is about repeatable things, why try to apply it to the untraining of captive dolphins, no two of which are alike?)

Agency lawyer Robert J. Hogan asked Naomi: Was it ever envisioned to your knowledge that when Mary Lycan was hired that she was going to supplant Mr. O'Barry's position as director of the readaptation and release of Bogie and Bacall?

A: She had never released a dolphin in her life. Nobody there had except for Mr. O'Barry. There was no interest whatsoever in ursurping or supplanting him, certainly not with Ms. Lycan.

When Mary Lycan took the stand, Mr. Hogan asked her: Can you tell me what you were hired to do at Sugarloaf Dolphin Sanctuary?

MARY LYCAN: My job title was behaviorist. And the job duties mainly included collecting baseline data on the activity budgets and the association patterns of the female dolphins. I also was to develop and implement a protocol for reintroduction.

In seeming contradiction to Naomi's testimony, Mary did not say that she was hired to assist me or even to work with me.

Under cross-examination, when Lloyd asked Mary Lycan if she thought her testimony against him and me might be affected by her having filed a $15,000 lawsuit against him (Lloyd) when he fired her, she said no.

One thrust of my argument in the trial was to expose NMFS's "selective enforcement," capriciously allowing horrors with dolphins on the one hand, and preventing efforts like ours to help them on the other. The agency has no problem with dolphins in swim-with-the-dolphins programs, where dolphins pull tourists through the water, tourists of all sizes, at $100 a pop. Nor do they apparently mind if dolphins are permitted to go from DRC to a disco in Switzerland, where the music is so loud it could be nothing but torture to a sonic creature like a dolphin. And yet they hit the panic button when we free two dolphins that had been prepared for more than a year and half, dolphins that I feel would definitely have made it in the wild if they hadn't been hounded almost to death.

They cracked down on us because we didn't have the permit, and we didn't have the permit because they wouldn't give us one. They knew we were going to free the dolphins and that this was the point of everything we were doing. We spent a few hundred thousand dollars at Sugarloaf, scraping for pennies, begging, hawking T-shirts, and staging small benefits. And isn't it the very definition of cynicism to allow us to get the wrong kind of permit, a display permit instead of a scientific one? When we discovered what was wrong and tried to get the right kind of permit, they refused, demanding we answer a host of questions that couldn't possibly be answered.

This was the heart of Lloyd's "bad faith" argument, which the judge in his wisdom acknowledged, finding in his decree that we had been given "official misadvice."

A government that misleads its citizens—what could be worse? If I had been the judge, I would have thrown the case out at that point. But Judge Fitzpatrick was more tolerant than I.

Besides myself, the only other person who has properly released dolphins is Randy Wells, having freed Misha and Echo off Sarasota, Florida. Did he provide NMFS with a "cookbook" as I was required to do?

Not yet.

Of such arbitrary policies is the seed of paranoia fed. Yes, I feel like they targeted me. And I proved it to my own satisfaction during my cross-examination of Naomi Rose, the facilitator. Referring her to the time just after she and Rick Spill came to Sugarloaf, then Rick Spill and I and Cathy Kinsman had gone to my room where he got down with me, *mano a mano,* to see if a protocol could be written, I asked Naomi about the luncheon meeting she and Rick Spill had with Ann Terbush, permitting specialist of NMFS.

Q: Do you remember when you called me back after the luncheon meeting and said that NMFS basically wants me out of the picture and . . . for me to step aside because the NMFS is not going to permit us as long as I'm there, and I agreed to step aside?

A: My recollection was [that] I made it clear to you, based on my conversation with her [Ann Terbush], that your name associated with this project was not a plus to their office . . . and that my counsel to you—and again, I had absolutely no authority to order you to do anything—but my counsel to you was to allow your name, not your person but your name to be disassociated with the project on the permit application while we put somebody who had credentials as a representative for the project.

Q: I thought about that all night that night, and I remember calling you back the next day, and I changed my mind [about stepping aside] because this was discrimination. They were—they had a vendetta against me. I asked if your organization would file a lawsuit against them for this.

A: I remember you calling me back and being very upset. Yes, I do.

Even now I can hardly believe what was happening then. They wanted me to get the job done, but without letting officials in Washington know that I was doing it. Deception aside, isn't that at least discrimination against me? And aren't we sort of opposed to that these days?

o   o   o

Our almost fanatical dedication and work on behalf of dolphins means nothing to the law. Our lives, our hopes, and inspirations were reduced to nothing as Judge Fitzpatrick, a fair but tough man, applied the law and found us wanting. He also found the agency wanting, dismissing one of their seven charges against both Lloyd and me and two others against me.

I wanted very much to win because it would have meant vindication. When the trial was over and we were awaiting the verdict, I thought I had won. I celebrated. I sent a thousand volts of positive energy, joy, and happiness in the judge's direction. But no. The judgment against us, "jointly and severally," was $40,000, and an additional $19,500 against Lloyd.

The judge proved not to be much of a fan of civil disobedience. When he spoke of Lloyd's saying that he had acted in civil disobedience, the judge declared, "This blatant disregard of the law will not be tolerated."

Though I believe with all my heart in civil disobedience, I didn't plead that because my position was that there was no law, and if there was no law, how could I deliberately break it? I also argued that if there was a law, it was so vague that nobody could understand it. In fact, just after Buck and Luther's release the Marine Mammal Protection Act was amended to include more specific language about the requirement of a scientific research permit to release a dolphin.

Most of my argument was about "selective enforcement," but I might as well have saved my breath. According to the judge, agency decisions are not subject to judicial review. As Judge Fitzpatrick said, the agency has "absolute discretion."

Lloyd called no witnesses; I called only one, Shaney Frey, mother of Kathleen Brooks. She had taken meticulous notes about what happened at Sugarloaf and was able to refute some of the exaggerated claims made by government witnesses.

In hindsight, I was right about this trial. I knew that I had no chance. Being poor, I had no lawyer, and without a lawyer, I had no chance. Or more succinctly: being poor, I had no chance.

o   o   o

My thoughts keep turning back in dismay to the lost opportunity at Sugarloaf. This could have been a textbook case in environmental activism, a grassroots movement getting officials of the government to do the right thing. We could have set a precedent for the successful release of captive dolphins all over the world. We had the dolphins, we knew what to do, the world was watching—and we still blew it. What happened? We were facing archaic governmental regulations and primitive egos, yes, but we're always facing those problems. Why did we botch it this time?

I think the seeds for the fiasco at Sugarloaf were planted long ago. Back in 1972 we got the Marine Mammal Protection Act passed by Congress, but then Congress gave the job of actually protecting marine mammals to the wrong people. They gave it to the Department of Commerce, whose NMFS understood only how to regulate fish for the fishermen. And suddenly a law for the protection of marine mammals became a law for the protection of those in the captive-dolphin industry.

Many other things more directly combined to cause us to fail at Sugarloaf. Our detractors were a constant thorn in our side, so was the captivity industry, looming over us and feeding our tendency to self-destruct, and the media, snapping at our heels in pursuit of a hearty meal. Even as shaky as we were, we could have withstood all that, I think. Until you toss in a few pearls of poisoned advice from agents of the government and others we trusted. That was the final straw.

In the aftermath, some of the dolphins fared well, others not so well. Luther and Jake, two of the Navy dolphins, were returned to solitary confinement at San Diego Naval Base. Jake died there soon after. Buck and Molly were awarded to DRC, and Shaney Frey, who went by to see them, said they were painting abstract pictures. Buck and Molly swim up on a platform, she said, trainers put paint brushes already dipped in paint into their mouths, then they hold T-shirts so that the paint on the brushes is smeared on the T-shirts, and tourists buy them as dolphin paintings.

Then Buck died. Poor Buck, who had been picked on so much by Luther.

After thirty years as the Good family's pet, Sugar finally died, her lagoon now lovingly marked by a bronze plaque.

Helene and I returned to Columbia, researching the possibility of freeing Stephania, and met a brick wall in Rafael of the Oceanario where Stephania was. He strongly opposed releasing Stephania there. It would be "irresponsible," he said, because of what happened a year earlier when Naomi Rose of HSUS attempted to free two semi-captive dolphins. One of the dolphins, Dano, was found dead in a fishing net ten days later. The other, Kika, was never seen again. The main danger is that 200 fisherman are now using long gill nets for fishing in these waters. So Helene and I began looking for another solution. Meanwhile, WSPA has picked up Stephania's bill for food and other expenses.

Trout filed a lawsuit against DRC, not for using dolphins in another tourist scam, but for custody of Molly, and he lost, in part because Lloyd testified on DRC's behalf. Joel La Bissonniere, the Agency's lead attorney against Lloyd and me, attended the trial and commented, "Lawsuits make strange bedfellows."

Lincoln went to New York City to pursue his acting career. Helene and I moved to Paris to work on Europe's first halfway house for captive dolphins, and we talked to Frederic LePage several times about acquiring custody of Stephania. He offered to sell us Stephania for one French franc (about twenty cents), but the contract included some tricky language that we objected to. We think about her every day, though, and we're making plans with Andrew Dickson and WSPA to see what can be done for Stephania.

When I first met Frederic and agreed to take part in the documentary with Umberto Pelizzari, Umberto's most sensational free-diving record was 430 feet. It's more of a slide than a dive, because he gets on a sled attached to a cable, takes a deep breath, and down he goes. When he gets to the right depth he lets go of the sled, inflates a balloon, and up he comes. Competition is so fierce that he was forced to keep setting new records until October 1999 when he hit 492 feet. Then that record was broken in January 2000 by Francisco "Pipin" Ferreras, a thirty-eight-year-old Cuban-born Miamian, who rode the sled down to 531 feet off Cozumel, Mexico.

I separated myself and the Dolphin Project from Lloyd and his Dolphin Sanctuary, then I paid the fine levied by NMFS with the proceeds of a benefit organized by Fred Neil and gypsy songman Jerry Jeff Walker ("Mr. Bojangles") of Austin, Texas, which was broadcast live on Jimmy Buffet's "Margaritaville" radio station on the Internet.

Helene and I were wed at sea among the dolphins off Key West on Captain Ron Canning's boat, the *Patty C.*

o   o   o

Though a lot of things we tried to do didn't work, our main objective did. In the Welcome Home Project we set out to get Bogie and Bacall away from ORC and to free them, and that's what happened. Someone in the dark of night sneaked in the old-fashioned way and cut the fence. But Bogie and Bacall are still free. They were sighted several times swimming peacefully in pods. And after that—nothing! Which means, I'm sure, that they made it.

Was it worth all the turmoil, the expense, and the time to free two dolphins? To me, yes. Free is free. And without the Welcome Home Project, Bogie and Bacall would still be doing tricks at ORC. A thousand times I regretted getting involved at Sugarloaf Dolphin Sanctuary, and if I could have gotten out of it without endangering the dolphins, I would have. But I couldn't, and now I'm glad I stuck, because the captivity industry must never get the idea, not even for a moment, that we might give up. And yes, I'll keep working to free captive dolphins within the law. But not like Sugarloaf. No, never again like that.

About the Authors

Richard O'Barry is the founder and director of the Dolphin Project, Inc. O'Barry graduated from the Diver's Training Academy as a commercial deep-sea diver and scuba instructor. He served in the U.S. Navy where he received a commendation for his underwater work. As a diver and dolphin trainer at the Miami Seaquarium he became the head trainer for the original *Flipper* television series. Since then he has received international acclaim for his pioneering work in the rehabilitation and release of captive dolphins. In 1991 he was the recipient of the Environmental Achievement Award by the United Nations Environmental Program (UNEP) for his efforts "to safeguard the environmental destiny of the Earth and all of its inhabitants." He resides in Coconut Grove, Florida.

Keith Coulbourn is a graduate of the University of Miami at Coral Gables. He has worked as a newspaperman on the *Orlando Sentinel-Star, Shreveport Times, Atlanta Journal and Constitution* mazagine, *Tampa Tribune,* and *Lakeland Ledger.* He resides in Miami, Florida.

O'Barry and Coulbourn have also authored *Behind the Dolphin Smile* (Renaissance Books).

YOUR SUPPORT IS APPRECIATED:

Dolphin Project
P.O. Box 224
Coconut Grove, FL 33233
USA

PHONE/FAX: (305) 668-1619

E-MAIL: ricobarry@cs.com
Visit our Web site at www.dolphinproject.org